The MAILBOX®
The Idea Magazine For Teachers®
PRESCHOOL

1996–1997

YEARBOOK

Jayne M. Gammons, *The Mailbox*® **Preschool Editor**
Angie Kutzer, *The Mailbox*® **Preschool Yearbook Editor**

The Education Center, Inc.
Greensboro, North Carolina

The Mailbox® 1996–1997 Preschool Yearbook

Editor In Chief: Margaret Michel
Magazine Director: Karen P. Shelton
Editorial Administrative Director: Stephen Levy
Senior Editor: Jayne M. Gammons
Contributing Editors: Ada Goren, Marie Iannetti, Angie Kutzer, Mackie Rhodes
Copy Editors: Lynn Bemer Coble, Jennifer Rudisill, Debbie Shoffner, Gina Sutphin
Cover Artist: Lois Axeman
Contributing Artist: Lucia Kemp Henry
Staff Artists: Jennifer T. Bennett, Cathy Spangler Bruce, Pam Crane, Teresa Davidson, Clevell Harris, Susan Hodnett, Sheila Krill, Mary Lester, Rob Mayworth, Rebecca Saunders, Barry Slate, Donna K. Teal
Editorial Assistants: Elizabeth A. Findley, Mickey Hjelt, Wendy Svartz

ISBN 1-56234-164-2
ISSN 1088-5536

The Education Center, Inc.
P.O. Box 9753
Greensboro, NC 27429-0753

Look for *The Mailbox*® 1997–1998 Preschool Yearbook in the summer of 1998. The Education Center, Inc., is the publisher of *The Mailbox*®, *Teacher's Helper*®, *The MAILBOX*® *Bookbag*™, and *Learning*® magazines, as well as other fine products and clubs. Look for these wherever quality teacher materials are sold, or call 1-800-714-7991 to request a free catalog.

Contents

THEMATIC UNITS

Teddy Bears Go To School

Give a warm-and-fuzzy welcome to your preschool pals. With this collection of activities, your classroom will soon be filled with teddy bear friends, teddy bear hugs, and teddy bear learning fun!

ideas by Pamela K. Priest

A Warm-And-Fuzzy Welcome

Any feelings of uncertainty about the first day of school will "bearly" be visible if you invite your little ones to bring along a familiar friend—a teddy bear. Several weeks before the first day of school, prepare an invitation to send to each child. Duplicate the invitation on page 11 onto colorful paper so that the illustration is on the top half of the paper. Fold the pages so that the invitations resemble cards. On each card write a different child's name and the name of your own teddy bear. Ask a friend to take a picture of you holding a teddy bear. Once you have the negative of the picture, order a class supply of duplicates. Mount a picture inside each child's card; then sign the card, "Your teacher and teddy bear friend, [your name] and [your teddy's name]." After you have addressed the envelopes, send the cards on their way and wait patiently for that special first day!

Making Memories

Keep a camera handy during the first teddy bear days. You'll want to capture the fun on film to complete the "Teddy Bear Annual" described on page 10.

Teddy Bear Talk

Prior to the first day of school, prepare matching nametags for each child and her bear. From tan construction paper, cut a bear shape for each child and a miniature bear shape for each child's bear. Personalize each child's nametag; then punch a hole near the top of each student and bear nametag. Pair a bear's nametag with each personalized nametag; then divide them into four groups. Using a different color of ribbon for each group, thread a ribbon through each nametag.

As youngsters arrive at your door on the first day, greet them with a hug from your own teddy bear. (Use the same bear shown in the photo included in your invitation.) Tie each child's nametag and place it around her neck. On a bear nametag with the same color of ribbon, write the name of the child's bear. Tie it around the bear's neck.

When every child has arrived, gather them together at your group area. Talk about the color of ribbon on each bear's nametag. Then encourage your little ones to find other teddy bears with the same color of ribbon. Ask the children to help the matching teddies say, "Hello." Who says teddy bears can't talk?

Dear ___Ben___,

Welcome to preschool! We're going to have tons of teddy bear fun. Please bring a teddy bear to preschool with you on your first day. Don't forget to name your bear.

Open this card to see a picture of me with my bear, ___Bobo___.

Your teacher and teddy bear friend, Ms. Priest and Bobo

Teddy Bear, Teddy Bear

Everyone loves to chant—even teddy bears! Teach your little ones the following rhyme to help them learn their new preschool pals' names. Seat the children—and their teddy bears—in a group on the floor. Ask a volunteer to stand up with his teddy bear. Chant the rhyme with the rest of the class, using the child's and his teddy bear's names. Continue until each child has had an opportunity to stand.

As students gain knowledge of their new friends' names, try this variation. Seat the children in a circle on the floor. Ask a volunteer to stand in the middle of the circle with his teddy bear. As a class chant the first line of the rhyme while the child in the center walks around the circle. Direct the child in the center to select another child from the group and to say the second line of the rhyme, filling in the selected child and his bear's name.

Teddy Bear, Teddy Bear, whom do you see?
I see [child's name] and [bear's name] looking at me!

Teddy Bear Tour

While you have your preschoolers and their teddies lined up, why not take a stroll around your school so everyone can get their bearings? Lead a teddy bear tour to the important locations in your school such as the director's office and the cafeteria. Using a Polaroid® camera, take pictures of the school personnel you meet along the way. Later, during a group time, discuss the people in the pictures. Give your preschoolers practice learning these new names and faces by saying the "Teddy Bear, Teddy Bear" chant above as you show each picture.

Let's Go, Teddies!

Leaving home to go to preschool each morning is no big deal when you have a teddy to take with you. This get-acquainted movement song will help youngsters get excited about getting up and getting ready. Seat the class in a row on the floor. Place each child's teddy bear in a row facing the children. Ask the children to pretend it's time to get ready to go to school and remind them that they should take their teddies with them. Sing the following song, inserting a child's name where appropriate. Ask that child to jump up, hold his teddy by the arm, and join you in line by holding your hand. Continue to sing the song until every child has had an opportunity to get his bear and join the line by holding the paw of the child's bear whose name was previously sung. When the children and bears are all in the line, lead them in skipping around the room. Ready, Teddy? Let's go!

Going To Preschool
(sung to the tune of "Down By The Station")

Going to preschool, early in the morning.
See all the teddy bears sitting in a row.
See [child's name] grab [his/her] little teddy.
Jump up, skip, skip. [Child's name], let's go!

Mrs. Desimone
Cook

7

How To Get
Your "Bear" Share

Teddy bears know how to be the "beary" best of friends. After learning this action rhyme, your little ones will, too! Assure the children that even though they will share their bears during this activity, every bear will be returned to its original owner when the fun is over.

Teddy Bear Hugs

Teddy bear hugs	*Hug bear.*
Are eyes that see,	*Point to bear's eyes.*
Ears that listen	*Point to bear's ears.*
To you and me.	*Point to another and self.*
Teddy bear hugs	*Hug bear.*
Are hands that share,	*Point to bear's paws.*
Arms for helping	*Hold out bear's arms.*
To show you care.	*Smile at bear.*
Teddy bear hugs	*Hug bear.*
Are from the heart.	*Point to bear's chest.*
So be like a teddy—	*Put nose on bear's nose.*
A friend from the start.	*Share bear with a friend and repeat rhyme.*

fuzzy
gentle
quiet
warm
kind

The Beary Best Bears

Teddy Bear Time

When a child is bearing more resemblance to a grizzly bear than a teddy bear, use this positive approach to help her get back on the right track. During a group time, assist youngsters in describing the lovable characteristics of a teddy bear using words such as *fuzzy, gentle, quiet, warm,* and *kind.* Write the youngsters' descriptive words and phrases on a large bear shape cut from bulletin-board paper. Discuss with your little ones ways they can be more like a teddy bear. Post the chart in a small area of your room that has been designated as a "time-out"-only place. Place several teddy bears and other bear paraphernalia in the area as well. Then, when a child needs to be reminded to act more like a teddy, ask her to visit that area. After the appropriate amount of time, visit the child and use the bears to discuss the situation. When the teddy bear time is over, be sure to give the child a great big teddy bear hug!

8

Grin And Share It!

Grin and bear your show-and-tell time with this idea related to a favorite bear story—*A Pocket For Corduroy* by Don Freeman (Puffin Books). To prepare for show-and-tell, dress a tan teddy in overalls. If the overalls do not have a pocket, cut a felt pocket and glue it on. Cut a class supply plus one more of cards that will fit inside the pocket. Label one of the cards "CORDUROY" and place it in the bear's pocket. Label each of the remaining cards with a different child's name.

During a storytime, point out the card in the bear's pocket; then read aloud *A Pocket For Corduroy*. At the conclusion of the story, take the card from the bear's pocket and read the word *Corduroy*.

As often as you would like to have show-and-tell, place a child's card in the pocket. Give positive, descriptive clues about that child. When the children guess the child's name written on the card, take the card out of the pocket and give the bear to that child. Ask him to take the bear home and to put something special in the pocket. The next day, when the child returns the bear, encourage him to lead a guessing game about the object he brought to share.

Teddy Bear Takes A Pose

Youngsters who participate in "What To Wear, Teddy Bear?" will want to visit your painting center to paint school portraits of their teddy bears. Create a background for the portraits by placing school props such as crayons and scissors on a shelf near the area. Encourage each child to set her dressed bear on the shelf and to arrange the provided materials around the bear as desired. At a nearby easel (yet far enough away to avoid getting paint on the posed teddy), have her paint a portrait of her well-schooled bear. Write the name of the child's bear on the paper. When every child has had an opportunity to paint a masterpiece, bind the paintings between covers. Title the collection "Teddy Bears Go To School." Share the book during a group time; then display it in the art center for other aspiring artists. Ready, Teddy? Smile!

What To Wear, Teddy Bear?

Give youngsters extra paws-on practice in going through a morning routine in order to get ready for school. In advance collect props such as a toothbrush, a comb, a washcloth, and other items that a child might use when getting ready for school in the morning. Also collect a wide variety of multiseasonal baby or doll clothes.

Ask your little ones and their bears to join you for a teddy bear circle time. Display the props and clothing, and ask youngsters to share with you their morning routines. Describe different types of weather and ask youngsters to help you select the clothing that might be appropriate for a teddy to wear to school on each different type of day. Then place the props and clothing in a dramatic play area. Encourage youngsters who visit the center to pretend to assist their bears in getting ready for school. As each child dresses his bear in the provided clothing, encourage him to visit your painting center for the activity described in "Teddy Bear Takes A Pose."

This is Freddy.

Amy

Teddy Bear Graduation

When the children are feeling comfortable in their new learning environment, celebrate by having a teddy bear graduation. Duplicate the teddy bear diploma on page 11 for each bear. Program each diploma with the appropriate information; then, on the back of each diploma, write the name of the child who will receive it. Roll each diploma so that the name is visible; then tie it with a length of yarn. To make a graduation cap for each bear, cut a five-inch square from black construction paper. Tie a knot at one end of a seven-inch piece of yarn. Tie the other end of the yarn to a brad; then insert the brad into the center of the paper square. To the underside of the cap, tape a rubber band for securing the cap on the bear's head.

On graduation day, present each child's bear with a diploma and secure the cap on its head. Take a picture of each graduating teddy and its owner to include in the "Teddy Bear Annual" (below). Serve teddy-bear-shaped crackers as a special treat. Explain to the children that since the teddy bears have officially graduated from preschool, they can begin staying at home. Wish the teddies good luck and congratulate the preschoolers on a terrific start!

Teddy Bear Annual

A teddy bear annual is the perfect way to introduce each child's family to the other children and teddies in the class. Compile the pictures taken during the activities of the first days of preschool into a scrapbook. Label each picture with the names of the children and teddies shown in the picture. Also include a brief description of the activity captured on film. Send the annual home with a different child every few nights. What a class!

The Bear Necessities

There are tons of teddy bear books available for reading aloud! These favorite titles are all about teddy bears and school.

Where Is The Bear At School?
Written by Bonnie Larkin Nims
Illustrated by Madelaine Gill
Published by Albert Whitman & Company

One Bear In The Picture
Written & Illustrated by Caroline Bucknall
Published by Puffin Books

My Brown Bear Barney
Written by Dorothy Butler
Illustrated by Elizabeth Fuller
Published by Greenwillow Books

Eddie And Teddy
Written & Illustrated by Gus Clarke
Published by William Morrow & Company

Our teddies say, "Hello!"

We have new teddy bear friends.

We hold paws when we walk.

Maddie and Brown Bear on graduation day.

Dear _____,

Welcome to preschool! We're going to have tons of teddy bear fun. Please bring a teddy bear to preschool with you on your first day. Don't forget to name your bear.

Open this card to see a picture of me with my bear, _____.
name of bear

©The Education Center, Inc. • THE MAILBOX® • Preschool • Aug/Sept 1996

Teddy Bear Diploma
Use with "Teddy Bear Graduation" on page 10.

Teddy Bear Diploma

This certifies that _____ has "beary"
bear's name

successfully completed teddy bear preschool.

Graduation congratulations to _____!
child's name

_____
teacher

_____
school

_____
date

©The Education Center, Inc. • THE MAILBOX® • Preschool • Aug/Sept 1996

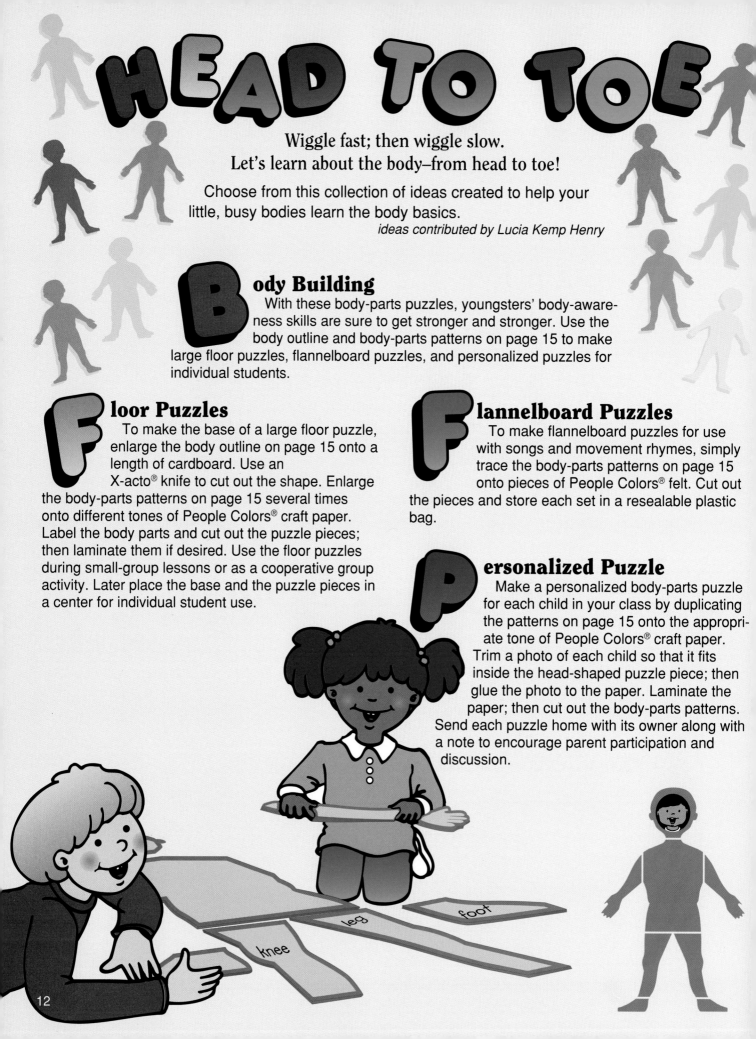

HEAD TO TOE

Wiggle fast; then wiggle slow.
Let's learn about the body–from head to toe!

Choose from this collection of ideas created to help your little, busy bodies learn the body basics.

ideas contributed by Lucia Kemp Henry

Body Building

With these body-parts puzzles, youngsters' body-awareness skills are sure to get stronger and stronger. Use the body outline and body-parts patterns on page 15 to make large floor puzzles, flannelboard puzzles, and personalized puzzles for individual students.

Floor Puzzles

To make the base of a large floor puzzle, enlarge the body outline on page 15 onto a length of cardboard. Use an X-acto® knife to cut out the shape. Enlarge the body-parts patterns on page 15 several times onto different tones of People Colors® craft paper. Label the body parts and cut out the puzzle pieces; then laminate them if desired. Use the floor puzzles during small-group lessons or as a cooperative group activity. Later place the base and the puzzle pieces in a center for individual student use.

Flannelboard Puzzles

To make flannelboard puzzles for use with songs and movement rhymes, simply trace the body-parts patterns on page 15 onto pieces of People Colors® felt. Cut out the pieces and store each set in a resealable plastic bag.

Personalized Puzzle

Make a personalized body-parts puzzle for each child in your class by duplicating the patterns on page 15 onto the appropriate tone of People Colors® craft paper. Trim a photo of each child so that it fits inside the head-shaped puzzle piece; then glue the photo to the paper. Laminate the paper; then cut out the body-parts patterns. Send each puzzle home with its owner along with a note to encourage parent participation and discussion.

knee   leg   foot

Some*body* Special

Need somebody special to help your little ones identify the parts of the body? If so, have them work cooperatively to make a class body buddy. Ask a child volunteer to lie down on a lengthy sheet of white bulletin-board paper. Trace the outline shape of the child's body; then cut along the resulting outline. (Or enlarge the body outline on page 15 onto the paper; then cut out the shape.) Using a selected tone of People Colors® tempera paint, have the group paint the body shape. When the paint is dry, encourage the group to cooperatively add facial features, yarn or paper hair, and construction-paper or wallpaper clothing. Provide direction and assistance as needed during your group's cooperative efforts. When the body buddy is complete, ask the group to give him or her a name. Display the buddy on a wall; then label the buddy as the group identifies the body parts.

Tammy Bruhn—Pre-K
Temperance, MI

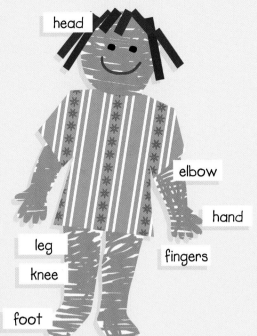

head

elbow

hand

leg

fingers

knee

foot

My Body, Your Body

Bodies come in all shapes and sizes. Introduce youngsters to *We Are All Alike...We Are All Different* (Scholastic Inc.) by reading aloud the first sections of the book. Lead a circle-time discussion about the similarities and differences in youngsters' bodies. Encourage pairs of students to stand in front of a full-length mirror. Assist them in identifying likenesses and differences in their appearances. At the mirror, have each child individually explore the various poses he can create with his body. Then take a full-length photo of each child in the creative pose of his choice. Embellish the background paper of a bulletin board with youngsters' handprints; then mount the paper on the board. Display the developed photos on the board along with the title "Our Bodies Are Alike...Our Bodies Are Different."

We Are All Alike

Help your little ones learn that even though we are all alike, we are different, too and can classify ourselves by hair, eye, and skin color. Ask each child in a small group to identify the color of his eyes and of his hair. When you read the following poem, have youngsters stand as you describe their eye color in verse one and sit as you describe their hair color in verse two. Have everyone stand again as you read verse three.

We are all alike. We all have eyes.
But we are different, too.
Some have brown eyes,
Some have green,
Some have hazel or blue.

We are alike. We all have hair
That grows upon our heads.
But some have black hair,
Some have brown,
Some have blond or red.

We are alike. We all have skin
That covers us outside.
Our skin looks different,
But we know
We're all the same inside.

13

What A Pair!

Hey! These hands really are handy. And these feet? Well, they just can't be beat! Sing this song to the tune of "Bingo" and youngsters will soon recognize their terrific body-part twosomes. Encourage the group to name additional body-part pairs; then create new verses by adding a variety of movements. As a literature link, read aloud *My Feet* and *My Hands,* both by Aliki (HarperCollins Children's Books).

Oh, I have arms. I need my arms.
I use my arms all day, oh!
Arms, arms—swing those arms.
Arms, arms—swing those arms.
Arms, arms—swing those arms.
I use my arms all day, oh!

Hands, hands—clap those hands.

Legs, legs—wiggle those legs.

Feet, feet—stomp those feet.

The Eyes Have It

You'll see an opportunity to enhance visual-discrimination skills when you take a look at this fascinating book. Focus youngsters' attention on facial features by reading aloud *Two Eyes, A Nose, And A Mouth: A Book Of Many Faces, Many Races* by Roberta Grobel Intrater (Scholastic Inc.). Observe the book's photos with a small group of children. Then make a class book that youngsters won't be able to take their eyes off of.

To make a class book, cut one tagboard rectangle that is slightly larger than a child's face. Cut a smaller rectangle from the tagboard so that when a child holds the rectangle in front of his face, only his eyes are revealed. Then take two pictures of each child—one with and one without the child holding the tagboard in front of his face. When the film has been developed, mount each picture on a sheet of construction paper. Label the pages as shown. Sequence the pages and bind them between covers. Title the book "The Eyes Have It!" Lead the class in a guessing game as you look through the book together. Then place it in your reading center or send it home for parents to enjoy.

Jodi Sykes—Pre-K
Barton Elementary
Lake Worth, FL

Whose eyes?

Michael's eyes!

Literature Links

Get your hands on these additional body-awareness titles:

Here Are My Hands
Written by Bill Martin, Jr., & John Archambault
Illustrated by Ted Rand
Published by Henry Holt And Company
(Turn to page 110 for a story extension activity.)

My Hands Can
Written by Jean Holzenthaler
Illustrated by Nancy Tafuri
Published by Dutton Children's Books

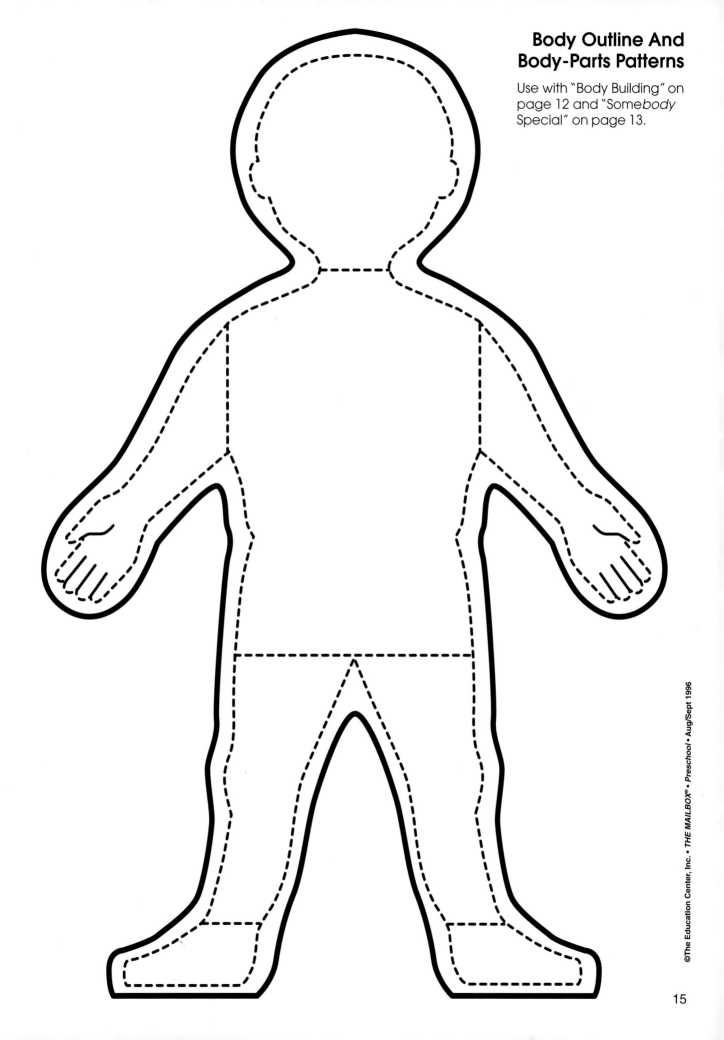

Body Outline And Body-Parts Patterns

Use with "Body Building" on page 12 and "Some*body* Special" on page 13.

Happy Birthday!

Birthdays are so much fun, isn't it a shame they only last a day? Stretch a special day into a special week by adding festive touches to your classroom centers. The learning opportunities are sure to be cause for celebration!

ideas by Dayle Timmons

It's A Party And Everyone's Invited!

Turn your dramatic play area into party central. Purchase or have the children help you decorate a birthday banner. Suspend the banner over the area along with streamers and balloons. (Make sure that the balloons are out of little hands' reach.) Stock the center with birthday plates, cups, napkins, paper and crayons, gift-wrapped boxes, hats, and horns.

To make a permanent birthday cake for the center, spread plaster of Paris over the top and sides of a cake-shaped piece of Styrofoam®. Before the plaster sets, insert birthday candles or candleholders. Add decorative details to the cake with plaster that has been tinted with food coloring, or decorate the top of the cake with colored glue once the plaster is dry. If desired hot-glue fabric trims or beads to the base of the cake.

As children visit the center, seize the opportunity to reinforce math skills and language development as youngsters prepare invitations, set the birthday table, and more. What a celebration station!

Birthday Royalty

Everyone celebrating a birthday deserves to feel like a king or queen. If you're having a weeklong party, that includes everyone! Set up a birthday crown-making station at your art center for your birthday royalty. Cut crown shapes from wrapping paper or construction paper; then mount the shapes onto colorful sentence strips. Provide a variety of art supplies such as wrapping-paper scraps, metallic paper, sequins, jewels, glitter, colored glue, and scissors for decorating the crowns. Happy birthday, Your Majesty!

Creative Collages

Take a breath and make a birthday wish for the creation of creative collages. Stock an art center with geometric shapes cut from birthday-style wrapping paper. Also provide die-cut, birthday-related, construction-paper shapes; curling ribbon; birthday-related stickers; used birthday cards; large sheets of colorful construction paper; scissors; and glue. As students visit the art center, encourage them to use their choice of the provided materials to make a collage. Top each collage with a bow and personalized gift tag; then display it near the center.

Pam Crane

Play-Dough Party Place

Join the fun at the play-dough party place where birthday cakes are the focus of the fun. Collect disposable tart pans, potpie tins, and muffin pans. Place the pans in a center along with play dough, birthday candles or cut straws, craft sticks or plastic knives, and festive paper plates. Let's make a cake!

Birthday-Bash Splash

Adding candles to your water table will really take the cake! Ask parents to donate used candles in a variety of shapes, colors, and sizes. Next cut cake shapes from Styrofoam® meat trays. Using a permanent marker, label each cutout with a different numeral from one to five. As children visit the water table, encourage them to describe and compare the different types of candles. Ask them to predict whether the candles will sink or float. Then allow the students to enjoy free water play with the candles. Challenge youngsters to float a labeled cake cutout in the water and to place the corresponding number of candles on the cutout. How many candles will float on a cutout before it sinks or tips over? Does the size of the candle make a difference? This center is sure to be a birthday blowout!

Celebrate With Sand

As a variation to the "Play-Dough Party Place" (above), encourage youngsters to visit your sand table to "bake" a cake. Excluding the play dough, include all of the items previously suggested. In addition place mixing bowls and big spoons in the center. Also place a spray bottle filled with water in the center to keep the sand damp. Solicit sequential cake-baking directions from your little bakers. Ask, "How many scoops of sand are needed to make a cake? How many scoops are needed for a cupcake? Why does a sand cake need water?" At this birthday center, each discovery is sure to be a special event.

Make A Wish

If you'd like to add math opportunities to your birthday bonanza, then your wish has come true. Place a set of pegboards and pegs in a manipulative center. As a youngster places the pegs in the pegboard, encourage her to pretend she is putting candles on a cake. Have her "blow out" the candles; then sing the birthday song together. Challenge a youngster to put a specific number of peg candles on the pegboard cake or to put only candles that are a requested color. Assist the child in sorting the candles and in creating patterns.

Count On Fine-Motor Fun

Purchase colorful note pads in birthday-related shapes. Or cut out construction-paper birthday cake or cupcake shapes. Mount the shapes on tagboard; then laminate them for durability. To make counting games, label each cutout with a different numeral. Direct students to place the appropriate number of jumbo-sized birthday candles on each cutout.

To make lacing cards, trim around the shape of the laminated cutouts. Using a hole puncher, punch holes around the perimeter of the shape. Tie a knot at one end of a shoelace; then encourage a child to thread the lace through the shape.

The Icing On The Cake

For youngsters, making birthday cupcakes will be the icing on the cake of your birthday celebration. Divide the class into several small groups. Invite each group to visit your classroom cooking center to assist you in preparing cake batter. (Use any boxed cake mix or follow your favorite cake recipe. If desired add sprinkles to the batter.) Have each child spoon some batter into a personalized cupcake liner. When the cupcakes have been baked and are cool, provide each child with his cupcake, icing, and a craft stick. Have him ice his cupcake, then decorate it using small candies and candy sprinkles. When it's time to eat, give each child a candle to put in his cupcake. Have him make a wish, pretend to blow out the candle, and enjoy his treat. Happy birthday to me!

Happy Birthday To YOU!

Ideas For Making
Each Child's Birthday Special

Birthday Bulletin Board

Spotlight your current birthday boy or girl with a bulletin board that has presence. Mount wrapping paper on a bulletin board; then add the title "Happy Birthday To You!" In advance of each child's birthday, send a note home requesting pictures of the child and other mountable items related to the child's interests. If possible feature each child during the week before or after her birthday. Assign a special week for students who have birthdays during the summer or school holidays. Be sure to provide time for the birthday boy or girl to discuss with the class the pictures and items chosen for display. Don't forget to include yourself during your own special week or feature yourself during Open House to introduce yourself to parents!

A Box Of Birthday Books

On or near each child's special day, request that he choose a book from a gift bag or gift-wrapped box of birthday-related titles. Read aloud his selection to the class. If desired, request that he hold the book as you read or that he assist you in retelling the story if the choice is a familiar one. To fill your box, choose from this collection of birthday favorites:

Happy Birthday, Jesse Bear!
Written by Nancy White Carlstrom
Illustrated by Bruce Degen
Published by Simon & Schuster Children's Books

The Barn Party
Written & Illustrated by Nancy Tafuri
Published by Greenwillow Books

Don't Wake Up Mama! Another Five Little Monkeys Story
Written & Illustrated by Eileen Christelow
Published by Clarion Books

It's My Birthday
Written & Illustrated by Helen Oxenbury
Published by Candlewick Press

Sheep In A Shop
Written by Nancy Shaw
Illustrated by Margot Apple
Published by Houghton Mifflin Company

Mouse's Birthday
Written by Jane Yolen
Illustrated by Bruce Degen
Published by G. P. Putnam's Sons

A Birthday Bundle

A take-home bundle is a bona fide way to thrill every birthday boy or girl. Fill a backpack, bookbag, large birthday gift bag, or decorated, handled plastic box with a collection of birthday goodies. Consider including some of these items:

- a birthday-related picture book (See the list at the right.)
- a videocassette of a birthday-related story
- a stuffed toy dressed in a vest or bandana made from festive fabric
- a recipe for a special birthday treat such as cookies or cupcakes
- birthday-party supplies such as noisemakers, birthday hats, and festive plates
- a goodie bag of small prizes
- crayons and a class birthday book (Bind blank paper between laminated wrapping-paper covers.)
  - a note to caregivers requesting that they assist the child in drawing a picture in the birthday book and record the child's dictated description of his special day

Request that the bundle of materials (excluding the goodie bag and party supplies) be returned after one week.

Time For Bed

It's time for bed, sleepyhead. Tuck your little ones in with this dreamy unit about nighttime, bedtime, lights-out fears, and sleepy animals.

ideas by Lucia Kemp Henry

Night And Day

Good-bye, sun. Hello, moon. Start your journey to bedtime with a discussion about the difference between night and day. Ask youngsters to list daytime and then nighttime activities (see page 300 for a suggested display of students' ideas). Then follow up your discussion by making night-and-day banners.

To make a banner, have a child use glow-in-the-dark crayons to color a sun on a 12" x 18" sheet of white construction paper and a moon and stars on another 12" x 18" sheet of construction paper. Have him then paint the day scene with thinned, blue tempera paint and the night scene with thinned, black tempera paint. When the paintings are dry, glue or staple the sheets together along the top. Slide a length of yarn between the sheets; then tie the ends before hanging the banner in your classroom. During a nap time, turn off the lights to watch the celestial scenes glow.

Fast Asleep, Wide Awake

From your discussion about night and day, your little ones will probably have concluded that the daytime hours are a time for activity, and that the nighttime hours are a time for sleep. Ask your little ones to give reasons why they think we sleep at night; then reinforce their ideas by explaining that our bodies need to rest so that they can be healthy and grow.

As you sing this song, have youngsters lie down, close their eyes, and pretend to sleep. Repeat the verse until "good night" has been said to every child. Sing the second verse of the song as a signal for each sleepyhead to "wake up."

Now It's Nighttime, Now It's Daytime
(sung to the tune of "Frère Jacques")

Now it's nighttime. Now it's nighttime.
Time to sleep! Time to sleep!
Say, "Good night" to [child's name].
Say, "Good night" to [different child's name].
Go to sleep. Go to sleep.

Now it's daytime. Now it's daytime.
Time to wake! Time to wake!
Say "Hello" to [child's name].
Say, "Hello" to [different child's name].
You're awake. You're awake.

I take a bubbly bath.
I brush my teeth with the green stuff.
I go to sleep.

Bedtime Routines

Starlight, star bright. How do you get ready for bed at night? Ask youngsters to describe their bedtime routines; then encourage volunteers to act out some of their getting-ready-for-bed activities such as brushing teeth, taking a bath, or eating a bedtime snack.

Following your discussion, ask each student to draw a picture of himself getting ready for bed. Write each child's description of his bedtime routine on his paper. Bind the pages together between covers to create the perfect bedtime book. If desired, enhance the illustrations in the book with photographs of students getting ready for bed. Purchase several disposable cameras; then send a camera home with a different child each night. When each child has had an opportunity to have a picture or pictures taken of himself getting ready for bed at home, have the pictures developed. Mount each child's picture(s) on his page in the class book. Good night! Sleep tight.

Can't Sleep? Count Sheep!

What to do when lullabies and "good nights" aren't enough? Count sheep! Or try reading one of these charming stories written especially for little insomniacs!

Zoë's Sheep
Written & Illustrated by Rose Bursik
Published by Henry Holt and Company

Dad! I Can't Sleep
Written & Illustrated by Michael Foreman
Published by Harcourt Brace & Company

Counting Sheep
Written by John Archambault
Illustrated by John Rombola
(This book is out of print. Check your library.)

Three sheep help me sleep.

One Sheep, Two Sheep, Three Sheep, Four!

Jump in the bed and snore, snore, snore! What more could youngsters need to help them fall asleep than this woolly counting booklet? For each child, duplicate the booklet pages (pages 24 and 25) onto light-colored construction paper. Cut the pages apart along the bold lines. Assist each child in counting the number of sheep on each of her pages. Provide her with numeral-shaped stickers, stamps, or sponges to fill in the empty clouds. Or have her write the correct numeral to complete each page. Finally have her glue a cotton ball on each sheep. Sequence the pages; then staple them together along the left side. Encourage each child to share her easy-to-read booklet with a caregiver at bedtime.

Lights Out!

Nightmares and the fearfulness of a dark room can turn bedtime into a scary time. Provide an opportunity for small groups of youngsters to talk about their nighttime fears. Read aloud *Kate's Giants* by Valiska Gregory (Candlewick Press). Talk about Kate's decision to "think out" scary monsters and to "think in" friendly ones. Or share *There's An Alligator Under My Bed* by Mercer Mayer (Dial Books For Young Readers); then discuss the boy's methods for making his fear go away. *Can't You Sleep, Little Bear?* by Martin Waddell (Candlewick Press) is yet another perfect read-aloud selection for little ones facing a fear of the dark.

Just in case positive imagery isn't enough, provide youngsters with magic monster spray to keep handy at bedtime. For each child, fill a trial-size, pump spray bottle with water and a drop or two of vanilla. Ask each child to decorate a construction-paper label; then tape it around his bottle. The selling point for magic monster spray? Its assistance helps little minds make monsters freeze, become friendly, or simply go away.

Animals Sleep, Too!

Your little ones may be surprised to find out that even most animals end their busy days with slumber. Be sure to tuck these charming, animal-related titles into your bedtime unit.

Time For Bed
Written by Mem Fox
Illustrated by Jane Dyer
Published by Harcourt Brace & Company

Little Donkey Close Your Eyes
Written by Margaret Wise Brown
Illustrated by Ashley Wolff
Published by HarperCollins Children's Books

Asleep, Asleep
Written by Mirra Ginsburg
Illustrated by Nancy Tafuri
Published by Greenwillow Books

Sleepy Book
Written by Charlotte Zolotow
Illustrated by Ilse Plume
Published by HarperCollins Children's Books

When I'm Sleepy
Written by Jane Howard
Illustrated by Lynne Cherry
Published by Dutton Children's Books

Sleepy Animals

Follow up a reading aloud of any of the above titles with this song about slumbering animals. As you sing, include the names of the animals listed in your favorite title from above. Or prepare a puppet for each child by duplicating the patterns on page 23 several times onto heavy paper. Color the patterns and cut them out. Then mount each one to a craft stick. Give each child a puppet to hold up when his animal is included in the song.

Sleep, Sleep, Go To Sleep
(sung to the tune of "The Farmer In The Dell")

The [cat] needs to sleep.
The [cat] needs to sleep.
Sleep, sleep, go to sleep.
The [cat] needs to sleep.

Sweet Dreams

These sweet-smelling pillows are sure to bring each of your little ones sweet dreams and restful sleep. Using pinking shears, cut as many pairs of squares from blue flannel or felt as you have children. Sew together three sides of each square. Have each child decorate his squares using white fabric paint and cloud-shaped sponges. When the paint is dry, embellish the pillows with glitter-paint stars, felt star shapes, or decorative star-shaped buttons. Assist each child in stuffing her squares with fiberfill and a dash of potpourri. Sew closed the remaining side to complete the pillow. Cozy!

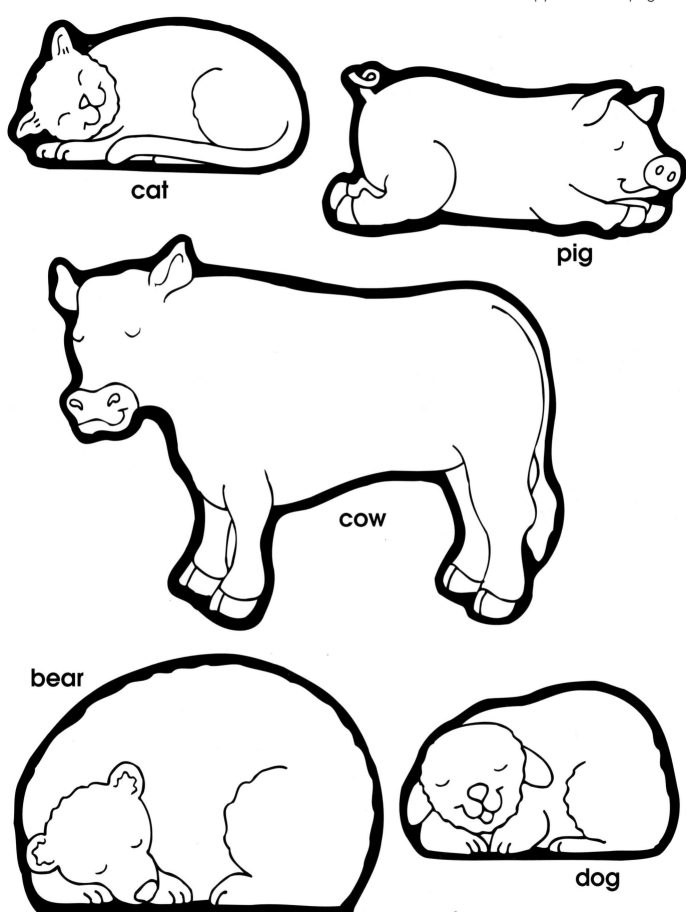

cat

pig

cow

bear

dog

Counting Sheep

Name _____

One sheep
helps me sleep.

Two sheep
help me sleep.

Three sheep
help me sleep.

Four sheep
help me sleep.

Home Is Where The Heart Is

Encourage parent involvement and strengthen the home-school connection with this study of families and home life. After all—learning is a family affair!

ideas by Dayle Timmons

Pictures Of All In The Family

The natural way to begin a unit on families is to ask each child to share a picture of her own family. To ensure that each child has a picture to share with the class—and that the picture is one that the class can keep—purchase several disposable cameras. Send a camera home with a different child each night along with a copy of a family survey similar to the one shown. (Use the information in the surveys for projects throughout your unit.) Request that each family have a group picture taken with the camera and suggest that they discuss the survey together as an adult completes it. When every child has taken a camera home, have the pictures developed. Then prepare a lift-the-flap picture book for the class to enjoy.

For each child, cut a house shape from tagboard. Using an X-acto® knife, cut a window for peeking at the child's family picture. Glue the photo to the back of the cutout so that it is visible through the window. Glue paper hearts to the window if desired. Personalize the cutout; then laminate it. Carefully cut the window open again. Prepare a cover; then bind the pages to create a book that everyone's family will want to take a peek at!

HOME Is Where The Heart Is

Johnson
Family Survey

These are our family members:
Ronnie — Dad
Rachel — Mom
Courtney — sister
Jason — brother
This is what my mommy or daddy does at home:
Daddy wakes me up
When we work together we wash the car

Courtney's Family

Families Come In Different Shapes And Sizes

Help each child learn about the framework of his own family and his classmates' families with this art project. Precut a supply of large and small rectangles from one color of construction paper to represent male family members, and large and small triangles from another color of paper to represent female family members. Based on the information provided on his family survey, assist each child in selecting the appropriate shapes to represent his family members. Direct each child to glue the shapes onto a large, construction-paper house shape. Have him then use markers to draw a head, facial features, and other body parts around each shape. Write as he dictates the names he uses to refer to each family member. When all of the projects are complete, ask small groups of children to compare the shapes of their families.

Jimmy's Foster Family

Ron Sher Jimmy

Tony's Family

Daddy Mama Tony Rachel

Cookie-Cutter Families

Provide youngsters with sets of cookie cutters and play dough, and you'll have an opportunity to discuss family diversity. If possible obtain a Wilton® gingerbread family or nesting teddy bears cookie-cutter set (available from craft stores). Provide students with the cutters, play dough, and large house shapes cut from vinyl placemats. Encourage youngsters to use the materials to make dough representations of their own families, classmates' families, or families in familiar fairy tales and popular stories. Facilitate language development and an understanding of family by asking each child to describe her work.

Who Is In A Family?

Ask youngsters to help you name people who might be included in a family such as fathers, mothers, brothers, sisters, and grandparents. Write each suggestion on a separate sheet of bulletin-board paper. Mount the sheets of paper on a wall or low bulletin board. Then stock your art center with glue, scissors, and a supply of catalogs and magazines that include pictures of people from a variety of ethnic backgrounds. Encourage students to cut out pictures of people, and to decide what membership role each pictured person might have in a family. Then assist students in gluing their pictures to the labeled sheets that correspond with their decisions. Looks like everyone is needed in a family!

You Can Count On Families

Using the cookie-cutter sets described in "Cookie-Cutter Families," trace and cut sets of the large shape from two different colors of construction paper to represent adult male and female family members. Cut similar sets of the smaller shape to represent children. Or use shapes similar to those cut for "Families Come In Different Shapes And Sizes." Have your students create a graph to indicate the number of adults and children in each child's family. (Refer to the information given on the family surveys.) When the graph is complete, ask questions such as, "Which families have boys?", "Which families have girls?", "Who has a family with many members?", "Who has a family with only a few members?"

As a follow-up, graph fairy-tale or popular-story families. "The three pigs have a family like mine—one mommy and some boys!"

Family Graph

The Three Bears	🧍	🧍	🧍		
The Three Pigs	🧍	🧍	🧍	🧍	
Berenstain Bears	🧍	🧍	🧍	🧍	
Little Mermaid	🧍	🧍	🧍	🧍	🧍
Sleeping Beauty	🧍	🧍	🧍		

What Do Mommies And Daddies Do?

Ask your little ones this question, and out of the mouths of babes will come humorous, insightful, and simply delightful answers! Teach youngsters this chant. Then give them an opportunity to share what their daddies (or mommies) do by asking a different child each time to end the chant with his own idea such as "hug," "play ball," or "do the dishes." (If desired, refer to the responses recorded on the family surveys.) Reinforce the steady beat of the rhyme by tapping your hands on your knees.

This is what the daddies do, daddies do, daddies do.
This is what the daddies do. Daddies_____.

Supplement your discussion about the different roles mothers and fathers can have in a family with these titles. Be sure to make these and other family-related titles available for youngsters to check out and take home.

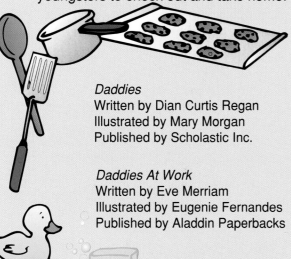

Daddies
Written by Dian Curtis Regan
Illustrated by Mary Morgan
Published by Scholastic Inc.

Mommies
Written by Dian Curtis Regan
Illustrated by Mary Morgan
Published by Scholastic Inc.

Daddies At Work
Written by Eve Merriam
Illustrated by Eugenie Fernandes
Published by Aladdin Paperbacks

Mommies At Work
Written by Eve Merriam
Illustrated by Eugenie Fernandes
Published by Aladdin Paperbacks

Role-Play Day

Now that youngsters have a better understanding of the roles mothers and fathers can have in a family, why not have a role-play day? Ask parents to allow children to wear articles of adult clothing over the children's regular school clothing on the day designated as role-play day. Prior to the day, for each child personalize a bag for the storage of the adult clothing items so that if desired, the children may take off the adult items during the day. During a morning group time, ask volunteers to pantomime some of the jobs that their parents do at home such as feeding a baby, cutting the grass, or cooking dinner. By pretending to do some of the things that moms and dads do for their families, youngsters will gain a better understanding of how families share household responsibilities.

Family Ties

Use these literature links as you discuss the diversity in families and home life. If necessary, paraphrase the text or discuss the illustrations to meet students' interest levels.

Families
Written by Meredith Tax
Illustrated by Marylin Hafner
Published by Little, Brown and Company

All Kinds Of Families
Written by Norma Simon
Illustrated by Joe Lasker
Published by Albert Whitman & Company

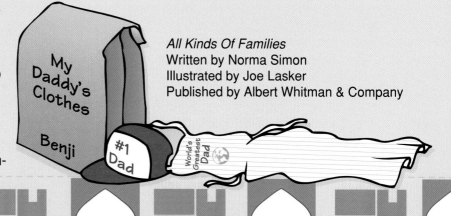

Homespun Family Fun

Fun-filled family projects that every member of the family will enjoy!

Families Work And Play Together

If you'll be sending a family survey home (see "Pictures Of All In The Family"), you might want to ask families to include brief descriptions of how they work and how they play together. Write each child's responses on sentence strips; then mount the statements on a bulletin board. Send an empty envelope home with each child. Request that each family look through catalogs and magazines for pictures of families working or playing together. Ask that they cut the pictures out and return them to school in the envelope. Assist each child in mounting her collected pictures on the board among the children's statements.

Homestyle Homework

Provide each child with a large sheet of art paper, rolled up and ready to take home. Send along a note requesting that each family cut and decorate the paper to resemble their abode—whether it be an apartment building, mobile home, or house. Mount a construction-paper road to a bulletin board along with the title "Home Is Where The Heart Is." Display the returned projects on the board along with pictures of the students' families.

Fine-Feathered Families

This turkey beams with family pride! Mount a large turkey character onto a wall or bulletin board. Send a large, brightly colored, paper feather home with each child along with a note encouraging his family to embellish the feather as desired. When the feathers are returned, display them around the turkey to create a fine-feathered fowl.

Laleña Williams—Special Needs Preschoolers
St. Francis Preschool—LaGrange Site
LaGrangeville, NY

Preschool Pumpkin Patch

Combine a surprise preschool pumpkin patch with a family picnic. Announce the date of a class picnic and pumpkin hunt to parents. Keeping the patch a secret from youngsters, ask parents to donate small pumpkins to your class. Before youngsters arrive at school on the morning of the picnic, arrange the pumpkins in an open area of your school's playground. Enjoy a day of pumpkin picking and picnicking!

adapted from an idea by Linda N. Roth—
  Four- And Five-Year-Olds
First Step Preschool
Black Forest, CO

THERE'S A WHOLE LOT

Shoo-whop, doo-whop! Can you hear the popcorn pop? Shooby-dooby-do! Can you smell it poppin', too? Your youngsters will burst with delight as they crunch and munch their way into learning fun!

ideas contributed by Carrie Lacher

HEY, GOOD LOOKIN'!
WHAT CHA GOT COOKIN'?

Start your sensational popcorn unit with some popping suspense. In advance, prepare a popcorn popper to pop popcorn and place it near an outlet that is out of youngsters' sight. Seat youngsters on the floor; then plug the popper into the outlet. As the youngsters begin to hear and smell the popcorn, encourage them to speculate as to what the secret sensation might be. When the popcorn has stopped popping, ask youngsters to close their eyes and hold out a hand. Give each child some popcorn to feel. Then pop the question, "What's cooking?" Popcorn, of course! Eat and enjoy!

Mary Kathryn Martell, Rochester, NY

OCTOBER IS NATIONAL POPCORN
POPPIN' MONTH!

Adorn your calendar with a blizzard of numbered, popcorn-shaped cutouts. Then pop into calendar skills as you sing this savory song also sung to the tune of "Frère Jacques."

Popping popcorn, popping popcorn.
Every day, every day.
Sunday, Monday, Tuesday, Wednesday, Thursday, Friday,
Saturday—popcorn, yea!

"SENSE-SATIONAL" SINGING

Discuss with youngsters the senses that they used to discover the surprise snack. Then point to the appropriate body parts as you sing each verse of this tasty tune.

WE LOVE POPCORN
(sung to the tune of "Frère Jacques")

We love popcorn. We love popcorn.
Yes, we do. Yes, we do.
Love to see it popping. Love to see it popping.
Pop, pop, pop! Pop, pop, pop!

We love popcorn. We love popcorn.
Yes, we do. Yes, we do.
Love to hear it popping. Love to hear it popping.
Pop, pop, pop! Pop, pop, pop!

We love popcorn. We love popcorn.
Yes, we do. Yes, we do.
Love to smell it popping. Love to smell it popping.
Pop, pop, pop! Pop, pop, pop!

We love popcorn. We love popcorn.
Yes, we do. Yes, we do.
Love to touch the popcorn. Love to touch the popcorn.
Crunch, crunch, crunch! Crunch, crunch, crunch!

We love popcorn. We love popcorn.
Yes, we do. Yes, we do.
Love to taste the popcorn. Love to taste the popcorn.
Munch, munch, munch! Munch, munch, munch!

Dawn Spurck, Westmont Early Education Center, Omaha, NE

OF POPPIN' GOIN' ON!

Popcorn Discoveries

The popcorn is fluffy.
Jack

The kernels shake louder than the popcorn.
Maggie

Two scoops filled the pot.
Sam

POPCORN, PLENTIFUL POPCORN!

Read aloud *Popcorn* by Frank Asch (Putnam Publishing Group). Have your young problem solvers suggest alternate ways that Bear and his friends could have gotten out of their popcorn predicament. Then perk up the learning possibilities at your sensory table by filling it with piles and piles of popcorn! Add scoopers and an assortment of small, lidded containers. Also thread lengths of yarn through large, plastic needles. As little ones play, ask them to describe how the popcorn feels. Encourage them to fill various containers with popcorn, put on the lids, and compare the sounds as they shimmy and shake the filled containers. Promote fine-motor development by encouraging youngsters to sew popcorn strings. Record youngsters' discoveries on a popcorn-shaped chart posted near the center. Be sure to keep a bowl of edible popcorn nearby for snacking!

MOUTHWATERING MEASUREMENT

If you filled your sensory table with popcorn, then you have plenty of the prop needed for this mouthwatering measurement activity. Gather a group of youngsters around your sensory table. Display a small, a medium, and a large paper bag; then ask the group to help you seriate the bags by size. Label the bags accordingly. Ask the group to help you check to see if the bags are labeled correctly by counting as you and volunteer helpers fill each bag with large scoops of popcorn. On each bag, record the number of scoops necessary to fill it with popcorn; then compare the numbers of scoops. To celebrate your findings, fill a small bag of freshly popped popcorn for each child. Nibble, nibble!

A CORNY COMPARISON

"A-maize-ing" discoveries will take place at your science center when you supply students with hand magnifiers and cobs of various types of corn. Encourage youngsters to describe the similarities and differences in the different types of corn. Guide them to compare the corn on the cob to the corn kernels used for popping. Then send youngsters to an art station to create art related to their scientific discoveries (see "Pop Art").

POP ART

Lend an ear to excited youngsters who visit your science center (see "A Corny Comparison"); then invite them to visit your art center to make their own ears of corn using real popcorn. Fill five large, resealable plastic bags with popped popcorn. To each of four of these bags, add a small amount of orange, brown, red, or yellow tempera-paint powder. Shake the bags to coat the popcorn; then pour the colored popcorn in separate containers. To make an ear of corn, have a child use his finger or a paintbrush to smooth a generous amount of glue all over one side of a corncob-shaped piece of tagboard. Depending on the type of corn he would like to make, have him then select a color or colors of popcorn to glue on the tagboard. (For example, he might select the uncolored popcorn to make an ear of white corn, the yellow popcorn for yellow corn, or several colors of popcorn to make an ear of Indian corn. When the glue is dry, staple strips of yellow or green crepe paper to the base and sides of the cob. What a corny and creative craft!

Mary Kathryn Martell
Rochester, NY

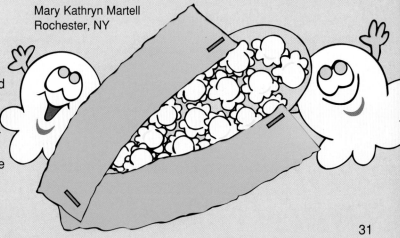

GET POPPIN'!

Due to safety concerns, preschool guys and gals might not have the opportunity to pop their own popcorn. So prepare a popcorn prop box for some hot dramatic play! Decorate a lidded, plastic box or paper-covered box with popcorn-related pictures and labels from popcorn products. Then follow this recipe for filling this box.

1 plastic popcorn container holding several spoonfuls of popcorn kernels (seal its lid with glue)
1 empty, clean cooking-oil bottle
1 empty saltshaker
1 cooking pan
1 clear plastic container (with a lid) containing round Styrofoam® pieces, cotton balls, or plastic popcorn from Christmas garlands

Place the box in your housekeeping center. Imaginations will soon be popping with tasty ideas as your little ones manipulate the props to pop up some fantasy popcorn.

"POP!" GOES THE POPCORN

Youngsters who use the popcorn prop box will enjoy this hip-hop song.

(sung to the tune of "Pop Goes The Weasel")

Put the kernels in the pot.
Don't forget the oil.
Cook it, shake it,
'Til it gets hot.
"Pop!" goes the popcorn!

Dawn Spurck
Westmont Early Education Center, Omaha, NE

PRETTY POPULAR TREATS

These colorful and easy-to-make popcorn balls are perfect harvesttime treats! Just follow the directions to make about 15 three-inch balls.

COLORFUL POPCORN BALLS

12 cups popped popcorn (about 1/2 cup of kernels)
1/4 cup (1/2 stick) margarine
one 10 1/2-ounce bag miniature marshmallows
one 3-ounce package of any flavor of gelatin
cooking spray
waxed paper
colorful plastic wrap
curling ribbon
decorative stickers

Pop the popcorn and pour it into a large bowl. Melt the margarine and the marshmallows in a microwave-safe bowl on high power in a microwave (about two minutes). Add the gelatin; then stir the mixture well. Pour the mixture over the popcorn, stirring until the popcorn is evenly covered. Allow it to cool slightly.

Spray cooking spray on a child's clean hands. Direct him to shape a handful of the mixture into a ball, then set the ball on waxed paper until it cools completely. Wrap the ball in colorful plastic wrap; then tie the ends with curling ribbon. Have each child decorate his ball with stickers.

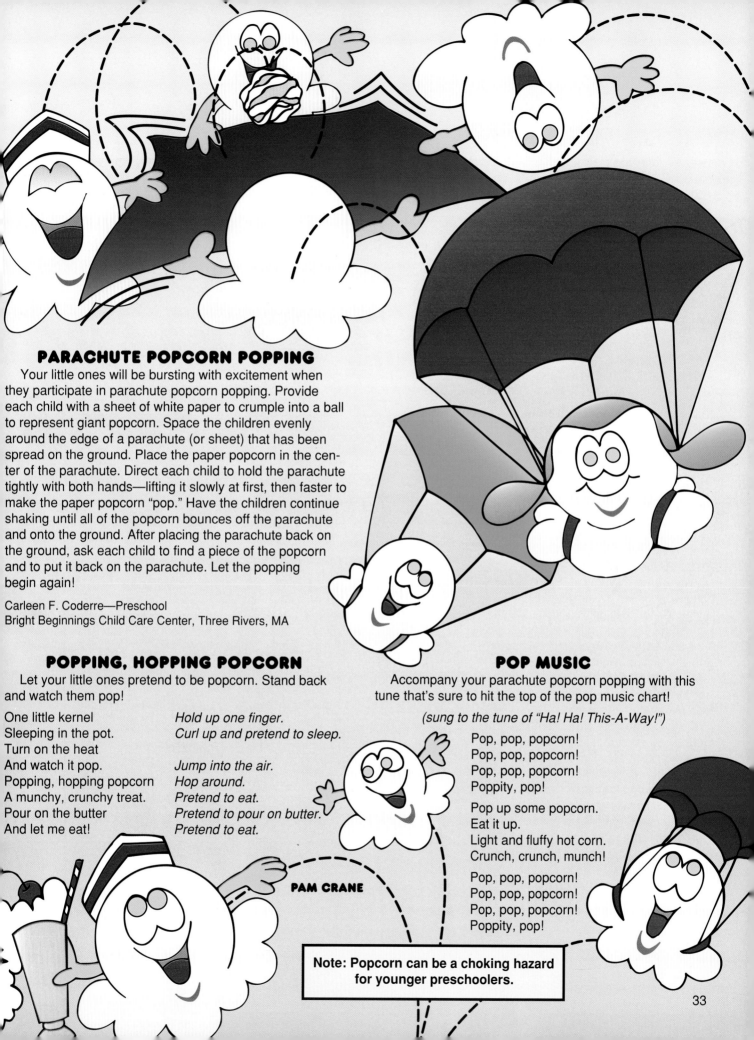

PARACHUTE POPCORN POPPING

Your little ones will be bursting with excitement when they participate in parachute popcorn popping. Provide each child with a sheet of white paper to crumple into a ball to represent giant popcorn. Space the children evenly around the edge of a parachute (or sheet) that has been spread on the ground. Place the paper popcorn in the center of the parachute. Direct each child to hold the parachute tightly with both hands—lifting it slowly at first, then faster to make the paper popcorn "pop." Have the children continue shaking until all of the popcorn bounces off the parachute and onto the ground. After placing the parachute back on the ground, ask each child to find a piece of the popcorn and to put it back on the parachute. Let the popping begin again!

Carleen F. Coderre—Preschool
Bright Beginnings Child Care Center, Three Rivers, MA

POPPING, HOPPING POPCORN

Let your little ones pretend to be popcorn. Stand back and watch them pop!

One little kernel — *Hold up one finger.*
Sleeping in the pot. — *Curl up and pretend to sleep.*
Turn on the heat
And watch it pop. — *Jump into the air.*
Popping, hopping popcorn — *Hop around.*
A munchy, crunchy treat. — *Pretend to eat.*
Pour on the butter — *Pretend to pour on butter.*
And let me eat! — *Pretend to eat.*

PAM CRANE

POP MUSIC

Accompany your parachute popcorn popping with this tune that's sure to hit the top of the pop music chart!

(sung to the tune of "Ha! Ha! This-A-Way!")

Pop, pop, popcorn!
Pop, pop, popcorn!
Pop, pop, popcorn!
Poppity, pop!

Pop up some popcorn.
Eat it up.
Light and fluffy hot corn.
Crunch, crunch, munch!

Pop, pop, popcorn!
Pop, pop, popcorn!
Pop, pop, popcorn!
Poppity, pop!

Note: Popcorn can be a choking hazard for younger preschoolers.

Peanut Butter, Peanut Butter ...Jelly!

First you take the nuts and you crack 'em and you smash 'em. Then you take the grapes and you pick 'em and you squish 'em. Peanut butter and jelly—tasty treats for teeny tummies. Open up this unit and spread out the learning fun!

ideas by Carrie Lacher

"Peanutty" Chanting

Tickle youngsters' taste buds and tummies by reading aloud the popular chant *Peanut Butter And Jelly* as illustrated by Nadine Bernard Westcott (Puffin Books). Once youngsters are familiar with the rhyme, encourage active participation by providing each child with a peanut puppet. To make peanut puppets for each child and yourself, duplicate the peanut pattern on page 39 onto tan construction paper. Cut out the patterns; then glue each peanut to a separate craft stick. Write the letter *P* or the word *peanut* on each stick. Next write the chant on a large, bread-shaped piece of bulletin-board paper; then mount it at students' eye level. As the class chants the rhyme, use your peanut puppet to point to the words. Encourage youngsters to lift their puppets each time they recognize or say the word *peanut*. Get ready—your preschoolers are sure to go "peanutty"!

How Do They Do It?

How do spoonfuls of peanut butter and blobs of jelly wind up in a sandwich? If your little ones would like to know how peanuts turn into butter and grapes into jelly, then share with them the information and photographs in these excellent resources.

Make Me A Peanut Butter Sandwich And A Glass Of Milk
Written & Photographed by Ken Robbins
Published by Scholastic Inc.

My First Book Of How Things Are Made: Crayons, Jeans, Guitars, Peanut Butter, & More
Written & Photographed by George Jones
Published by Scholastic Inc.

From Peanuts To Peanut Butter
Written by Melvin Berger
Published by Newbridge Communications, I
(This big book can be ordered directly from Newbridge at 1-800-867-0307.)

Cooking Up Some PB 'n' J!

Mouthwatering measurement and following delicious directions are two of the tasty skills your little ones will learn when they participate in cooking up some real peanut butter and grape jelly. Since the grape jelly will need to congeal overnight, you might want to make the jelly one day and the peanut butter the next. Be sure to follow up your kitchen capers with the hands-on (or should we say *mouths-on*) math lesson described in "A Mouthful Of Math."

Groovy Grape-Juice Jelly

1 grape per child

2 cups bottled grape juice

one 3-fluid-ounce pouch of Certo® liquid fruit pectin

4 cups sugar

2 tablespoons water

To demonstrate how grape juice is made, give each child an opportunity to press a grape through a sieve. Then ask volunteers to help you measure the sugar and then the bottled grape juice into a large bowl. When each child has had a chance to stir the mixture, set it aside for about ten minutes. Combine the fruit pectin with the water in a small bowl; then pour the mixture into the juice-sugar mixture. Once again have each child stir the mixture, continuing until the sugar is no longer grainy. Pour the liquid into a container, seal it with a lid, and allow it to remain at room temperature overnight. The next day put the jelly in a refrigerator for up to three weeks. (For firmer jelly, store it in the refrigerator for several days before serving.)

Blissful Blender Peanut Butter

one 12-ounce package salted, roasted peanuts in the shell
(or 1–2 cups shelled peanuts)

2 tablespoons vegetable oil

Invite youngsters to a table to help you shell peanuts. Pour the package of peanuts into several small bowls. Designate several empty bowls for the collection of the peanuts only. Encourage youngsters to shell the peanuts. (Keep trash cans nearby!) When the nuts are shelled, pour them into the blender. Add the vegetable oil; then blend the peanuts until smooth. (Use a spatula to scrape the peanut butter from the sides of the blender.) Store the peanut butter in a container in the refrigerator.

A Mouthful Of Math

With a tasty theme like peanut butter, eating the topic is half the fun! To make use of your class-made peanut butter and jelly *and* to introduce the concepts of half and whole, have your little ones make miniature sandwiches. Provide each child with a plastic knife, two slices of cocktail-sized bread, and a paper plate. Encourage each child to independently make a miniature peanut-butter-and-jelly sandwich. When you and each of your students have prepared a sandwich, introduce the word *whole*. Then cut your sandwich in *half* and place both halves atop a child's whole sandwich to demonstrate that two halves equal a whole. Have children cut their own sandwiches in half. Then have them sink their teeth into this early introduction to fractions!

Smoosh And Goosh

Your little ones won't be able to wait to get their hands on these nutty-tasting and sweet-smelling play doughs! Give youngsters plenty of opportunities to describe smells, textures, and colors as they sink their hands into each dough and smoosh and goosh their way into peanut-butter-and-jelly play. By the way, the peanut-butter dough is edible—so little ones with clean hands can be encouraged to eat their creations. The jelly dough smells mighty nice, but is just for hands-on fun.

Power-Packed
Peanut-Butter Play Dough

2 cups creamy peanut butter
2 cups honey
4 1/2 cups powdered milk

Mix the honey and peanut butter together in a large bowl. Slowly add the powdered milk and knead the mixture until the dough is of a thick consistency. Store the dough in a sealed container and refrigerate when not in use.

Jammin' Jelly Play Dough

5 tablespoons cream of tartar
3/4 cup salt
3 cups all-purpose flour

3 cups water
3 tablespoons vegetable oil
blue and red food coloring
.14-ounce package of unsweetened, grape-flavored drink mix

Stir all of the dry ingredients into a large pot. Slowly add the water and oil. Using a large wire whisk, blend the mixture until all of the lumps are gone. Whisk in several drops of blue and red food coloring until the mixture is a medium purple color. (The dough will darken as it cooks.) Cook the mixture over medium heat, stirring constantly with a large spoon until it forms a ball. While the mixture is still warm, knead it on a lightly floured board for several minutes or until the dough has a soft, satiny feel. Store the dough in a sealed container at room temperature for up to a month.

Start Spreading The News!

The smell of these sandwich collages is here to stay! Little ones will get a real feel for sandwich making with this scented, sticky-fingered art exploration. For each child, cut pairs of bread, peanut butter, and jelly shapes (patterns on page 39) from white, brown, and purple tissue paper. To make a collage, remove the backing from a length of clear Con-Tact® covering. Tape the covering to a table with the sticky side up. Have a child arrange and press his pieces onto the covering. Give him purple glitter and a small amount of a powdered, grape-flavored drink mix to sprinkle over the covering. When the child is satisfied with his project, press on a length of plastic wrap. Trim the edges; then display the sandwich collage on a window. Ahh—the sights and smells of a peanut-butter-and-jelly sandwich!

What's For Lunch?

Tempt youngsters to visit this math center by filling lunchboxes with sandwiches made for counting. Using the patterns on page 39, duplicate ten pairs of the bread shape onto white paper, ten peanut-butter shapes onto tan paper, and ten jelly shapes onto purple paper. Label each of the peanut-butter shapes, each of the jelly shapes, and each pair of bread shapes with a different numeral and dot set from one to ten. Laminate the shapes for durability before cutting them out. Place the sandwich fixings in lunchboxes along with ten resealable plastic bags. When visiting the center, a child makes sandwiches by finding the bread slices, peanut butter, and jelly that have corresponding numerals and dot sets. He then places each sandwich set in a plastic bag. Lunchtime!

A Sticky Song

Your little ones are sure to get stuck on this sweet sandwich song!

Peanut Butter 'n' Jelly
(sung to the tune of "Shortnin' Bread")

Chorus:
Peanut butter 'n' jelly,
Jelly, jelly,
Peanut butter 'n' jelly,
Mmm-mmm good.

Verses:
Peanut butter's chewy.
Jelly's nice and sweet.
Put them both together—
Mmm! What a treat!

Fixing up a sandwich.
Gonna make it right.
Get ready, mouth
For a great big bite!

Repeat chorus, singing as if your mouth is full of a great big bite!

Disappearing Sandwiches!

Here's a peanut of a tale that will have youngsters eating out of the palm of your hand. In advance prepare five felt sandwiches to accompany the flannelboard rhyme below. Using the bread pattern on page 39, cut five bread shapes from white felt. Hot-glue each bread shape to a slightly larger piece of purple felt; then cut around the shape. Hot-glue each pair of bread-and-jelly pieces to slightly larger pieces of brown felt; then cut around the shape. Add finishing touches to each sandwich using markers or fabric paint. During a group time, display all five sandwich look-alikes on a flannelboard. As you recite each verse of the rhyme, name a different volunteer to remove a sandwich from the board.

Five Tasty Sandwiches

Five tasty sandwiches of jelly and peanut butter,
[Child's name] took one to share with his brother.

Four tasty sandwiches as chewy as can be,
[Child's name] took one—now there are three.

Three tasty sandwiches, I made them just for you.
[Child's name] took one—now there are two.

Two tasty sandwiches with jelly nice and sweet,
[Child's name] took one for an after-school treat.

How many sandwiches? Uh oh, there's just one.
[Child's name]'s taking it—now there are none.

Peanut-Butter-And-Jelly Jiggling

These simple, gross-motor games are sure to have all
of your little nuts jumping and jiggling for joy.

Peanut Butter, Peanut Butter...Jelly!

Your little ones will quickly catch on to this thematic version of Duck, Duck,
Goose. Seat your students in a circle on the floor. To play, a volunteer leader walks
around the outside of the circle while lightly tapping each seated child on the head
and saying "Peanut butter." When desired, the leader taps a child and announces,
"Jelly!" At that cue, the tapped child jumps up and chases the leader around the
circle. The leader runs to sit in an open spot in the circle or the tapped child catches
him and they both stop. Either way, the tapped child now becomes the leader.
Play continues until each child has a turn as the leader.

Peanut-Butter-And-Jelly Roll

Seat youngsters in a circle on the floor. Give one child a purple ball to
represent a giant grape. To play, the group chants, "Peanut
butter, peanut butter, peanut butter, JELLY!"
On the word "JELLY!" the child holding
the ball names another child in
the circle and rolls the ball to
that child. As a variation,
ask older children to
pass the ball
around the circle
while chanting.
Continue play
until each child
has rolled the
ball.

The jelly slipped out
of my sandwich.

Nathan

That's A Big Sandwich!

A unit as delightfully filling as this one demands an extrabig finish. Capture all the
tasty fun by asking students to help you fill a sandwich big book with their favorite
peanut-butter-and-jelly memories. In advance enlarge the bread pattern on page 39;
then cut a classroom supply of bread shapes from 12" x 18" sheets of white construction paper. Write on each child's bread shape as he dictates his favorite peanut-butter experience; then have him illustrate his page. To prepare covers for your sandwich big book, use the enlarged pattern to trace a bread shape onto two thin pieces
of foam. Cut out the shapes; then add details using fabric paint. Bind the pages between the foam covers using large metal rings. Your little ones will enjoy hearing you
read about their experiences, and afterward the giant book will make a wonderfully
tasteful addition to your classroom library.

Patterns

Use with " 'Peanutty' Chanting" on page 34; "Start Spreading The News!" on page 36; "What's For Lunch?" and "Disappearing Sandwiches!" on page 37; and "That's A Big Sandwich!" on page 38.

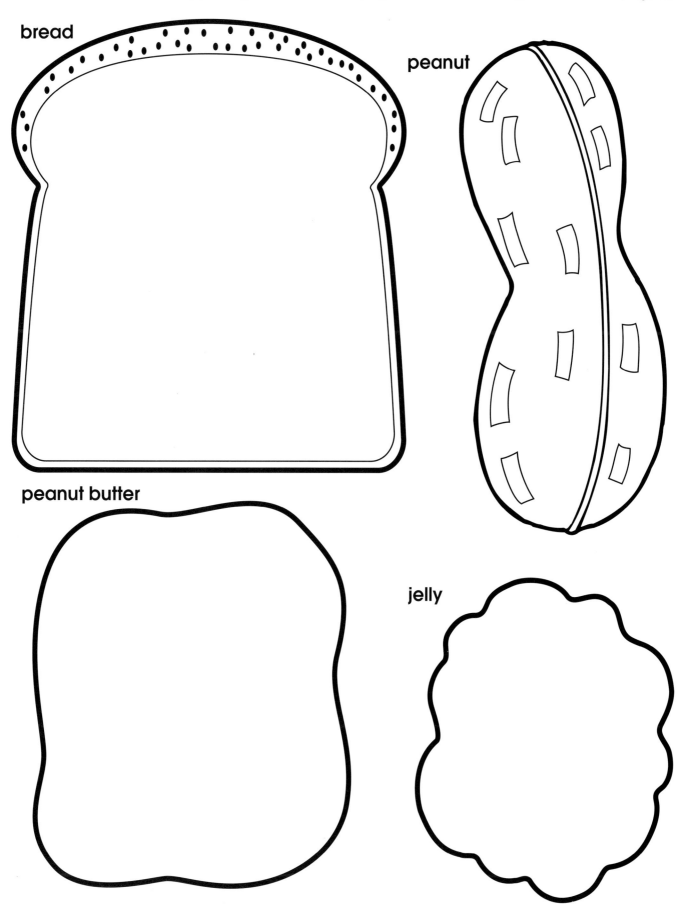

bread

peanut

peanut butter

jelly

Animal Architecture

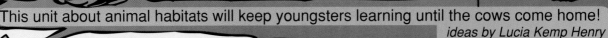

This unit about animal habitats will keep youngsters learning until the cows come home!

ideas by Lucia Kemp Henry

Habitat Happiness

To prepare for your unit, collect books, magazines, and posters that contain photographs of animals and their homes. To introduce the topic of animal homes, explain to your little ones that the place where an animal lives is called its *habitat*. Invite youngsters to describe places where they have already observed animals living such as a nest, a web, or an aquarium. Provide pairs of children with your resource materials and allow adequate time for them to look at and comment on the pictures. Ask your children to consider the reasons that people need homes; then help them understand that animals need homes for similar reasons such as shelter from the weather, protection for their young, food storage, and rest. Then open your animal-house unit with the following action rhyme.

Every Creature Needs A Home

Do you know where animals live—
On the land or in the sea?

Point down. Move hand in waving motion.

Some animals make their homes;
Some live with you and me.

Point to a neighbor, then to self.

Great, big bears live inside caves.
Mice have nests so small.

Open arms wide.
Cup hands together.

Snakes live deep down underground,
Birds in trees so tall.

Wiggle arm downward.
Point up.

Horses live in grassy fields.
Fish live in the sea.

Gallop in place.
Pretend to swim.

Every creature needs a home,
Just like you and me!

Make a shelter over head with arms.
Point to a neighbor, then to self.

Animals Live On Land Or In The Water

Your little ones will feel at home with this crafty classification idea. In advance collect a variety of animal-shaped sponges. Or cut animal shapes from sponges using a die cutter. Prepare your art center by pouring blue and green fingerpaint into separate trays. Then pour several different colors of tempera paint into trays. Direct each child to finger-paint one sheet of fingerpainting paper green, and another sheet blue. When the papers are dry, have each child look carefully at the sponges to decide which animals would live on land and which would live in the water. Using the tempera paint, encourage him to sponge-paint the animals of his choice onto the appropriate fingerpainted papers.

40

Animal Addresses

Just where do animals set up housekeeping? Some live underground, some live on the land, some live in the air, and some live in a body of water such as a pond, a river, or the sea. Have youngsters help you collect and cut out pictures of animals from nature magazines. Then, during a circle time, place the pictures in the center of the group. In turn, ask each child to select a picture. Name the pictured animal and ask youngsters to describe its habitat using broad classifications such as underground, on the land, in the air, etc., or using specific terms such as in a burrow, a cave, or a den. Follow your discussion of each picture by singing the following song, modifying the verse as indicated.

Where Do They Live?
(sung to the tune of "Oh Dear, What Can The Matter Be?")

Where, where, where do the [rabbits] live?
Where, where, where do the [rabbits] live?
Where, where, where do the [rabbits] live?
[Rabbits] live [under the ground].

Housewarming

Your little ones may already know that many wild animals hibernate in their habitats throughout the winter. Many more animals, though they don't hibernate, search out or build warm, safe homes for the winter. Write as your children name animals that need warm winter homes. From your collection of resources, locate pictures of animals' winter homes; then display these near an art center. Using the following suggestions, assist each child in making the wild-animal home of his choice.

Display students' completed projects in a blocks center along with a supply of small toy animals. As youngsters make a house call at the center, encourage them to help the toy animals find homes for the winter.

Bear Cave
To make a cave, fold a paper plate in half. From one side of the plate, cut an opening near the folded edge. Staple the plate closed around the rim. Glue small pebbles (the type used in fishbowls) to the cave.

Beaver Lodge
To make a lodge, fold a paper plate in half. From one side of the plate, cut an opening near a corner. Staple the plate closed around the rim. Glue small twigs (found at a craft store) to the lodge.

Fox Den
To make a den, fold a paper plate in half. From one side of the plate, cut an opening near the folded edge. Staple the plate closed around the rim. Sponge-paint the den brown.

Squirrel Drey
Cut a circular opening in the center of a plate. Staple the plate to another one around the rims. Glue small twigs, craft moss, wood chips, and paper leaf cutouts to both plates.

Places For Pets

Now that your little ones are familiar with the habitats of wild animals, discuss the homes that people provide for domesticated animals. Ask children to describe the homes provided for their own pets or for your classroom pets. What does each type of pet need to make its house a home? If you have pets in your classroom, divide your class into as many groups as you have types of pets. Ask each group to observe a classroom pet's home. Write as the group describes what the animal needs in its home. Share each small group's comments with the class; then display the comments near that pet's home.

If you do not have pets in your classroom, arrange to take a field trip to a local pet store. While visiting the store, take a picture of each different type of animal's home. Later glue each developed picture on a separate sheet of construction paper. Divide the class into as many groups as you have pictures. Ask each group to look carefully at a picture and to describe what the animal needs in its home. Record their comments on the paper. Share each small group's comments with the class; then display the photos near your science center.

Pet Pairs

Help your little ones understand that even though some animals live in our homes as pets, they need their own houses as well. Duplicate, color, and cut out the patterns on pages 43 and 44 of pets and their homes. Attach self-adhesive felt to the back of each pattern. Use the flannelboard patterns to accompany the following song. As you display each pet and its home, modify the verse as indicated.

As a variation, use the patterns with this cooperative activity. Duplicate, color, and cut out the patterns. Then punch a hole near the top of each pattern and thread it onto a length of yarn. Tie the yarn to make a necklace. Give one necklace to each child to wear. Direct each child whose necklace displays a pet to find his partner, the child whose necklace displays the pet's home. As you sing the following song, have the pet partners stand together when their pet and pet home are inserted into the verse.

Did You Know?
(sung to the tune of "The Farmer In The Dell")

A [bird] lives in a [cage].
A [bird] lives in a [cage].
Oh, oh, did you know?
A [bird] lives in a [cage].

bird

cage

Reading About Animal Homes

Enrich your study of animal homes with these books that introduce little ones to animal habitats through simple stories. The Habitats series by María Rius and J. M. Parramón (Barron's) includes the following titles: *Life On The Land, Life In The Sea, Life Underground,* and *Life In The Air.* The My First Visit series by J. M. Parramón and G. Sales, by the same publisher, includes the titles: *My First Visit To The Aquarium, My First Visit To The Aviary, My First Visit To The Farm,* and *My First Visit To The Zoo.* Both series are available in English and Spanish. For ordering information contact Barron's at 1-800-645-3476.

hamster

cage

bird

cage

kitten

basket

Patterns
Use with "Pet Pairs" on page 42.

dog

doghouse

fish

fishbowl

lizard

cage

Let's Celebrate Together

This holiday season you might look about your room of children and observe that they celebrate different holidays. Or you may see a group who have in common the celebration of one special day or week. This year celebrate the holidays *together*. In this unit you'll find ideas for sharing, cooperative activities, and display ideas to help your little ones celebrate together.

> Let's light the menorah
> For the Festival of Lights.
> One candle every evening
> For eight great, joyous nights.
> Latkes, games, and sharing,
> Happiness and cheer.
> Let's light the menorah
> For Hanukkah is here.

Let's Light The Menorah

Students who celebrate Hanukkah will already be familiar with the Jewish tradition of lighting the menorah. Provide instant or disposable cameras and request that each child who celebrates Hanukkah take a picture of his family's menorah to share with the class. Ask a parent who celebrates Hanukkah to visit the class to display and discuss a menorah. Then arrange for the menorah to remain in your classroom for the next eight school days. (If a real menorah is not available, prepare a representation by collecting nine battery-operated candles. Display the candles in a row, elevating the central candle or *shammash*.) On each of the eight consecutive school days or on the school days during the eight days of Hanukkah, read aloud the provided poem. Each day place a candle in the menorah or turn on the battery-operated candles, pretending to use the shammash to light each one.

Let's Make A Menorah

This display will shine ever so bright! To prepare a large menorah for students to decorate, cover pieces of tagboard with aluminum foil as shown. Ask groups of youngsters to paint each tagboard candle. When the paint is dry, tape tissue-paper flames to each candle. Ask each child to choose several objects from a variety of collage items such as dried pasta, juice-can lids, and empty pill bottles. Supervise and assist each child as he spray-paints his selected items silver. When the items are dry, have him glue them to the menorah. Mount the completed group project to a board that has been previously covered with Hanukkah wrapping paper. Encourage youngsters who celebrate Hanukkah to bring seasonal greeting cards to add to the display.

Nancy Barad—Four-Year-Olds
Bet-Yeladim Preschool And Kindergarten
Columbia, MD

Light The Lights! A Story About Celebrating Hanukkah & Christmas
Written & Illustrated by Margaret Moorman
Published by Scholastic Inc.

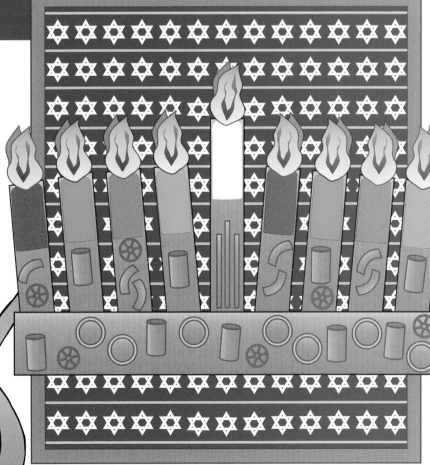

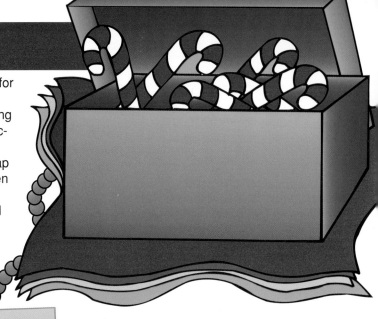

Let's Open A Christmas Present

Christmas is a time for giving gifts and doing kind deeds for others. Ask youngsters to talk about how they feel when someone gives them a gift or when someone does something nice for them. Follow up your discussion with this sharing activity. To prepare, place a classroom supply of a small token—such as stickers or a food item—inside a gift box. Wrap the box with as many layers of gift wrap as you have children in your class. During your group time, give the gift to a child and ask him to share a kind deed that he can do for a friend or family member; then have him carefully unwrap the first layer of wrapping paper. Continue in this manner until each child has had a turn. When the last layer of wrap has been removed, open the box and distribute the gifts.

Let's Celebrate The Advent Season

Many children who celebrate the religious aspects of the Christmas holiday will be able to discuss the meaning of the characters in a nativity set. Ask a parent who owns a nativity set to bring it for the class to discuss and temporarily keep to display. During his visit, encourage the parent to read aloud a book about the first Christmas. As a follow-up, have youngsters make nativity scenes using craft sticks, construction paper, and previously collected Christmas cards that display the nativity scene. To make a scene, have each child choose a card from your collection, then cut the nativity scene from the front of the card. Have her glue her scene to a piece of construction paper, then glue craft sticks around the scene to represent the stable. Display the projects near the nativity set.

One Special Star
Written by Anita McFadzean
Illustrated by Kate Jaspers
Published by Simon & Schuster Books For Young Readers

Christmas In The Manger
Written by Nola Buck
Illustrated by Felicia Bond
Published by HarperCollins Children's Books

Let's Celebrate The Harvest

Some of your little ones may already celebrate Kwanzaa as a time of shared harvest, shared memories, and shared beliefs. Invite a parent to visit and bring for discussion some of the items used to celebrate Kwanzaa such as the unity cup, the mat, and the candleholder. Then give all of your youngsters an opportunity to share in the ideals of Kwanzaa by sharing a harvest of good foods with a family or a group in need. Ask each child to bring food items such as cans of fruits or vegetables from home. Have students place their donations in a decorated box or basket. Later donate the harvest gift to a shelter so that it can be distributed appropriately.

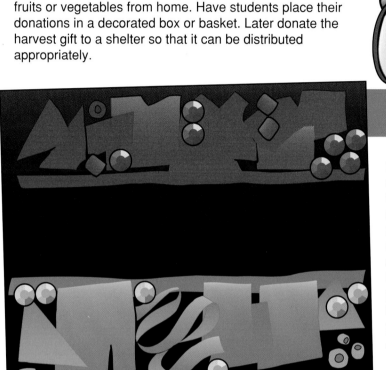

Let's Create A Kwanzaa Collage

The colors of Kwanzaa are red, black, and green to represent struggles, pride, and hope. The colors are also the colors of the *bendera* or flag. Use this idea to make a festive Kwanzaa display. Collect an assortment of red and green art materials such as felt scraps, pieces of gift-wrap ribbon, foil wrapping paper, beads, sequins, etc. Provide each child with a large sheet of black construction paper, scissors, and glue. Encourage each child to make a collage by gluing the items of his choice onto his paper. Display all of the completed projects on a black background along with the title "Kwanzaa!"

Dayle Timmons—Special Education Pre-K
Alimacani Elementary School • Jacksonville, FL

My First Kwanzaa Book
Written by Deborah M. Newton Chocolate
Illustrated by Cal Massey
Published by Scholastic Inc.

A Kwanzaa Celebration—A Pop-Up Book
Written by Nancy Williams
Illustrated by Robert Sabuda
Published by Simon & Schuster

Let's Tie It All Together

Link the cultures of your room together with this culminating, cooperative activity. Have youngsters make paper chains using construction-paper strips in colors that represent each of the three holidays—blue, gold, and white for Hanukkah; red, green, and white for Christmas; and red, green, and black for Kwanzaa. Link the chains together and hang them to represent the unity in your room throughout the holiday season.

Carolyn Macdonald—Preschool • Kiddie Haven Daycare • Brockton, MA

Out Of The Blue

Look in the sky! It's a bird. It's a plane. It's the sun, moon, and stars! Move youngsters' thoughts onward and upward with these sky-high learning ideas.

ideas by Lucia Kemp Henry

Why is the sky blue?
The sun's light looks white but is really made of many colors. When the light shines on dust and tiny drops of water in the sky, it is scattered. The blue light is scattered more than any other color. This makes the sky look blue.

Things In The Sky

The warmer weather and springtime winds of March make it the perfect time to take your class on an outdoor stroll to observe the sky. As youngsters look into the wild, blue yonder for natural and man-made items, their feet will be on the ground, but their enthusiasm is sure to take flight!

When you return to the classroom, write on a large piece of blue bulletin-board paper as youngsters list items they saw in the sky. Have them also suggest things they might see in the sky at another time such as at night. Follow up your walk and brainstorming session with the following classification ideas.

Sky-High Classification

To prepare for the following classification activities, duplicate two sets of the picture cards on pages 52 and 53 onto heavy paper. Color and cut out the cards. Glue flannel to the back of one set of cards. Punch a hole near the top of each card in the second set; then string each card with a length of yarn to make a necklace.

Following your sky-watching stroll, discuss the weather and space-related, animal or insect, and man-made items illustrated on the flannel-backed cards. Challenge your group to classify the items in similar categories and place them on a flannelboard.

Once the group is familiar with the classifications, give each child a necklace. Play a lilting musical selection as youngsters move about the room and sort themselves into three groups based on the pictures on their necklaces.

What are clouds made of?
Clouds are made of tiny drops of water in the air. We see a cloud when many tiny drops join together.

The Right Atmosphere

Keep youngsters' sights set high by creating just the right atmosphere in your room. Enlarge each of the patterns on pages 52 and 53 onto tagboard. Give each student or pair of students a design to paint. When the paint is dry, cut out the design. Punch a hole near the top of each one; then tie on a length of clear fishing line. If desired, label the back of each design with its name and the artist's or artists' names before hanging it from the ceiling. For additional decorating ideas, see the literature feature on page 100. Up, up, and away!

What is a rainbow?
A rainbow is made when sunlight shines through and bounces off drops of water in the air. The light is spread apart into the colors of the rainbow.

Way Up High

Focus on weather and space-related things in the sky with this simple poem. If desired, give each of six children a necklace to wear (see "Sky-High Classification") that corresponds to an item named in the poem. Ask each of the children to recite the appropriate line as you chant and move.

Up High In The Sky

Teacher: Things up high in the sky,
(Chorus) Things that we can see.
          Up…up…up, way up high,
          Far from you and me!

Children: Sun up high in the sky.   *Make circle with arms above head.*
          Moon up high in the sky.   *Make circle with arms above head.*
          Stars up high in the sky.   *Open and shut hands above head.*
          Clouds up high in the sky.   *Wave arms above head.*
          Rain up high in the sky.   *Wiggle fingers above head.*
          Rainbow up high in the sky.   *Move arms in an arch above head.*

(Repeat chorus.)

What causes the rain?
When a cloud gets full of water drops, it gets too heavy for the air to carry. The water drops fall down as rain.

Birds And Bugs In Flight

Turn your sky watchers' attention to animals and insects that fly in the sky by decorating these headbands. Collect a supply of stickers and stamps featuring birds and insects. From blue construction paper, cut a headband for each child. Have each child decorate his paper with the stickers and stamps; then staple together the ends of the headband. Encourage youngsters to wear their headbands as they participate in the following song and movement activities.

They Can Fly!

Before singing this song, ask youngsters to name creatures that can fly in the sky. Include each of their suggestions in a verse of the song.

(sung to the tune of "This Old Man")

They've got wings. They can fly.
They can fly up in the sky.
[Birds] can fly so very, very high.
[Birds] can fly up in the sky.

> **How do birds fly?**
> As a bird flaps its wings, air is pushed back and down. The bird flies forward and up.

Flying High

Give youngsters plenty of open space for movement as they pretend to fly like creatures in the sky. As you recite each verse of the following poem, encourage the children to vary their flight patterns to match the movement of each different animal or insect.

Fly up high.
Fly down low.
Flap your bird wings
As you go!

Buzz up high.
Buzz down low.
Buzz your bee wings
As you go!

Float up high.
Float down low.
Float like a butterfly
As you go!

Fabulous Flying Machines

Your little ones will be fascinated with machines that fly in the sky. Collect pictures of planes, helicopters, blimps, hot-air balloons, and even space shuttles to share with the group. After your discussion, display the pictures in a workshop center along with plenty of lock-together construction materials such as DUPLO® bricks. Add a supply of craft sticks to serve as propellers and clay for connecting the propellers to the blocks. Encourage youngsters to create their own versions of flying machines to add to your display.

How does a plane fly?
A plane's engines lift it into the air. Airplanes can fly because their wings are shaped like a bird's wings.

Simple Sky Gliders

Ready for takeoff? Make these simple gliders for youngsters to decorate and fly outside. To make a glider, cut two rectangles that measure 6" x 1" and 6" x 2" from a Styrofoam® meat tray. Round the corners of the rectangles; then cut a slit in the center of the more-narrow rectangle. Slide the wider rectangle through the slit. Secure a large paper clip on the nose of the glider. Personalize each child's glider with a permanent marker; then provide him with stickers to decorate his flyer. To watch it glide, push the flyer up and away!

Uplifting Sky-Related Books

To find books related to sky-high topics written for a preschooler's level, try these stories authored and illustrated by Frank Asch.

Moondance
Published by Scholastic Inc.

Moongame
Published by Simon & Schuster

Mooncake
Published by Simon & Schuster

Skyfire
Published by Simon & Schuster

Picture Cards

Use with "Sky-High Classification" on page 48, and "The Right Atmosphere" and "Way Up High" on page 49.

clouds

sun

rainbow

stars

moon

raindrops

Use with "Sky-High Classification" on page 48, and "The Right Atmosphere" and "Way Up High" on page 49.

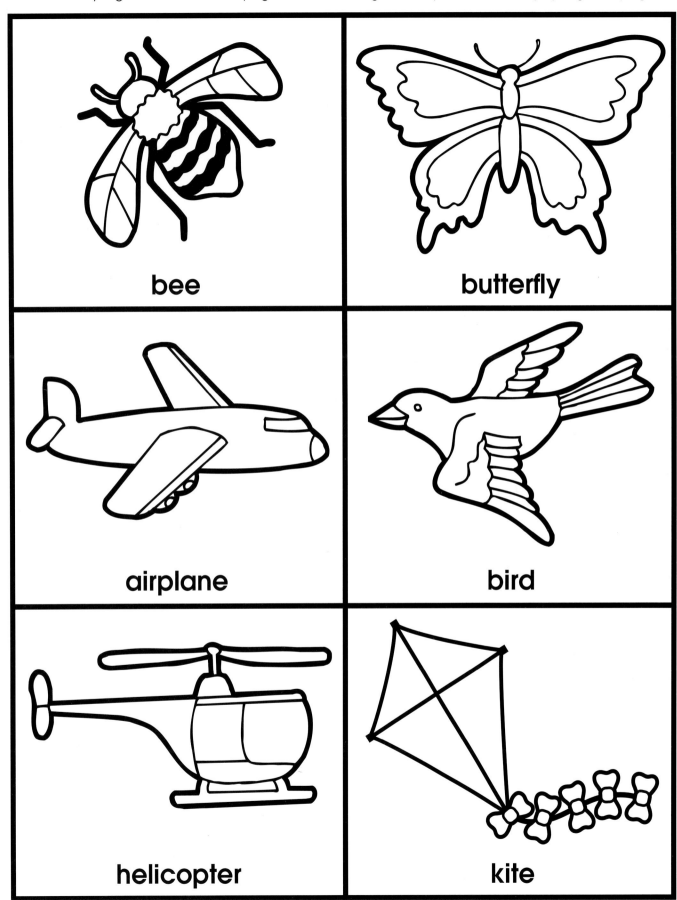

bee

butterfly

airplane

bird

helicopter

kite

A Day At The Beach

Need a winter break? Bring the sensations of the sun, the sand, and the sea to your classroom learning centers with these balmy ideas. Come on in—let's spend a day at the beach!

ideas by Carrie Lacher

Set A Maritime Mood

Wash away the winter blues and sparkle student interest when you transform your classroom into a seaside setting. Before your Beach Day, contact local travel agencies to ask for donations of travel posters featuring sunny beach locales. Display the posters on your classroom walls and windows. Next hang strips of blue and green crepe paper from your ceiling to give the feeling of ocean waves in motion. Add the warmth of sparkling sunshine by hanging strips of silver Mylar® or metallic ribbon. In the background, play some lively calypso music or a recording of the sounds of the surf (available from nature stores and some craft stores). Surf's up!

Stories By The Sea

Greet your little beachcombers at the door on Beach Day with a bucketful of beach supplies. Welcome them to the sand and surf by giving each child a personalized pair of sunglasses and a visor to wear. Ask each child's permission to rub a small amount of tropical-scented tanning lotion on his hands and arms. When you have gathered the class for your group time, invite youngsters who have visited the beach to share their experiences. (Or, if desired, invite them in advance to bring pictures and videos to share.) Help youngsters who haven't visited the beach to set sail into your day by sharing some of the following sea stories. Each of these books contains simple text and illustrations or photographs that are sure to encourage seaworthy discussion.

One Sun: A Book Of Terse Verse
Written & Photo-Illustrated by Bruce McMillan
Published by Holiday House, Inc.

At The Beach
Written & Illustrated by Anne & Harlow Rockwell
Published by Simon & Schuster Books For Young Readers

A Beach Day
Written & Illustrated by Douglas Florian
Published by Greenwillow Books

Sensory Area

Down In The Nitty-Gritty

A day at the beach means a day in the sand! Thrill little ones with an opportunity to feel sand between their fingers and toes at your beach-themed sensory area. In addition to your sand table, fill several large tubs or even a wading pool with sand; then thoroughly dampen the sand with water. Supply visitors with pails, scoopers, sand molds, and shells. To help keep the sand moist, place a small spritz bottle of water in the area. Encourage little ones to work cooperatively to build castles. For super sandy fun, invite children to remove their shoes and socks and wiggle their bare feet in the sand. Challenge them to draw designs with their toes. Keep a tub of warm water and beach towels nearby. What a scoop of ticklish fun!

Painting Center

"Sand-Sational" Painting

Add this nautical concoction to your painting center, and it's sure to get plenty of beach exposure. To make the paint, thoroughly mix together one part flour with two parts salt. Slowly add liquid tempera paint in equal proportion to the salt-flour mixture. Stir the mixture until it is lump-free and the consistency of thick cake batter. Pour this mixture into paint cups and place them in your painting center. Provide tagboard or recycled cardboard for use as canvases with this seashore paint. Encourage each painter to spread a thick layer of paint onto his canvas. Allow the completed paintings to dry for several days. Youngsters will be dazzled by the magic of the salty paints—a seaside sparkle in every picture!

Play Dough Center

Scented, Seaside Play Dough

Place this supersmooth, sea-sparkly play dough in a center along with seashells and nautical-themed cookie cutters. Your classroom will soon be awash with the scents of the seashore!

3 cups flour
1.5 ounces cream of tartar
3/4 cup salt
3 tablespoons cooking oil
3 cups water
1 tablespoon coconut extract
yellow food coloring
gold glitter

Combine the first five ingredients in a large pot. Whisk together until free of lumps. Stir in the coconut extract and yellow food coloring. Stir the mixture constantly over medium heat until it pulls away from the sides of the pot and forms a large ball. Knead the ball on a lightly floured board until the dough is silky smooth. Knead in the desired amount of gold glitter. When the mixture has cooled, store it in an airtight container.

Bathing Beauties

Something's fishy about this beachwear, but it's just what the weather calls for during your winter getaway! To make bathing "suits" for your dramatic play area, ask parents to donate children's old and used bathing suits (or check your thrift store for bargain beachwear). Purchase an adult-sized, beige or brown T-shirt for each suit collected. Cut each bathing suit along the side and bottom seams. Pin the front and back of each suit to a shirt; then sew them in place. During your Beach Day, youngsters who dress in these bathing suits are sure to catch a wave of fun!

Debbie Hugli—Pre-K • Carousel Preschool • Downey, CA

Swing And Sway

Bring a splash of colors to your music or listening area with these sparkling, ocean streamers. To make a streamer, cut out the inside circle from a plastic margarine-tub lid. To the remaining plastic ring, tie lengths of blue, green, and metallic ribbon or cellophane. In this activity center, place recordings of gentle, instrumental melodies or ocean-related tunes, such as "Gentle Sea" (from *Movin'* by Hap Palmer; Educational Activities, Inc.) or "Hawaiian Hukilau Dance" (from *Folk Dance Fun* by Georgiana Stewart, Kimbo®). Little ones will soon be afloat with maritime music and movement!

Constructing Castles...And Other Sandy Structures

A day at the beach would be incomplete without building a sand castle, so use this tip to add the texture of beach sand to your block area. Trace one side of each block (in a small set) onto sandpaper. Cut along the outline on the sandpaper; then use masking tape or clear-drying glue to adhere each sandpaper shape to its matching block. Add a pail of shells to the center. Invite your youngsters to build sand structures using the blocks and the shells. Watch out for that...WAVE!

Beach Picnic

The weather outside may be frightful, but a picnic inside will make your Beach Day perfectly delightful! Spread beach towels on the floor in your group area. If desired, prop open several beach umbrellas. Serve up some Sandy Sandwiches and Magical Mermaid Potion (recipes below); then sing a rousing chorus of "Down By The Shore." Ahhh…isn't it about time for a seaside snooze?

Sandy Sandwiches

Invite your little ones to help you make these sandwiches with just a bit of crunchy sand (toasted wheat germ). To make one, use a cookie cutter to cut a shell shape from a slice of whole wheat bread. Squeeze some honey onto this shape; then sprinkle it with the "sand." Get ready to crunch!

Magical Mermaid Potion

In advance, fill several ice-cube trays with water; then squirt a drop of blue food coloring into each cube. Put the trays in the freezer. Ask your class to help as you use warm water to prepare a pitcher of powdered lemonade-flavored drink. Have students take turns pouring one 12-ounce can of lemon-lime soda into the lemonade. Add about eight drops of yellow food coloring. For each child, pour a serving of this drink into a clear plastic cup. Then invite each child to drop one or two blue ice cubes into his yellow potion and stir it with a tropical straw. Watch the mermaid magic happen!

Down By The Shore

(sung to the tune of "Down By The Bay")

Down by the shore
In the sand and the sun,
I like to dive
And splash and run.
And as the waves
Roll out and in,
I'll get warm in the sun
And have lots of fun.
Down by the shore!

Say, "Cheese!"

Picture this—gift, learning, and management ideas that use photos. That's what you'll find when you zoom in on this unit full of ideas from preschool teachers. Say, "Cheese!"

Safety Note: Because of the chemicals used with instant photography, avoid using Polaroid® film for projects that suggest cutting photos. Laminate any cut Polaroid® pictures before allowing children to use them.

Film Favors

With these tips, using photos in your classroom doesn't have to be time-consuming or expensive. Consider asking parents for donations of film. Take several pictures of each child; then have double prints developed. Make photocopies or color copies of the pictures so that you'll always have a snapshot handy. When you use photos in your classroom, you're sure to like what develops!

Attractive Smiles

These sweetheart magnets make heartwarming gifts for Valentine's Day. To make one, have a child color or paint a construction-paper heart shape. Cut a photo of the child into a smaller heart shape; then let the child glue the picture to the center of the heart. Laminate the heart; then attach a strip of magnetic tape to the back. These magnets are sure to attract the smiles of loved ones!

Kim Richman—Preschool, The Learning Zone
Des Moines, IA

Puzzling Pictures

Add interest to your puzzle collection in a flash. If you've already taken an individual picture of each child, have 5" x 7" duplicates developed from the negatives. Laminate each picture; then cut it into several puzzle pieces. Store the pieces for each puzzle in a resealable bag labeled with the pictured child's name. Each puzzle set also makes a great holiday or birthday gift for a youngster in your class.

Christine Dise—Four-Year-Olds, Pottstown YMCA
Pottstown, PA

Through The Year

Decorate your door with this wreath of smiling faces. Each month cut a classroom supply of a seasonal shape from tagboard. Ask each student to decorate her shape using various art supplies. To each child's shape, attach a circular photo (or color copy of a photo) of the child. Attach the shapes to a wreath along with a seasonal bow before hanging it on your door. Welcome to our class!

Debbie Monts de Oca—K–4 Preschool
St. Paul's Episcopal School, Winter Haven, FL

Picture Pops

Make these manipulatives for use with circle-time activities. To make one, tape a Popsicle® stick to the back of a child's picture. Glue the picture to a piece of tagboard that is identical in size. Write the pictured child's name on the tagboard. Use the classroom set of picture pops with management needs such as taking turns in a game or getting in line. Or use them with language activities such as the following:

During circle time, hold up one of the picture pops so that the child's name is facing the group. Say to the child, "[Child's name, child's name], whom do you see?" Hold up a second picture pop with the picture side facing the group for the child to look at. The child then responds by saying, "I see [child's name] looking at me." Give the first child his picture pop to hold. Turn the second child's card around so that the name is facing the group. Continue in the same manner until each child is holding his picture pop.

Terrie Barr—Three-Year-Olds, Sonshine Preschool, Fillmore, CA

Picture-Perfect Nametags

Prepare these nametags in advance, and youngsters who create artistic masterpieces in your classroom will be able to independently put their names on their work. Down the left side of a sheet of paper, glue a small photo of each child. Write each child's name twice beside her picture. Duplicate a supply of the page; then cut the pages so that each child has a set of nametags that show her picture, and a supply with her name only. Store the tags in a hanging shoe organizer. When a child completes a work of art, she can find one of her nametags—using the picture if necessary—and attach it to her work. "I did it all by myself!"

Sally Greiner—Early Childhood Special Needs
Metzenbaum School, Chesterland, OH

59

Survey Says...

Make a smooth transition from center time to group time with photo magnets. Collect a juice-can lid for each child in your class. To make a photo magnet, use a lid to trace a circle onto a child's picture. Cut a circle from the picture that is slightly smaller than the outline; then glue it to the rimmed side of the lid. To the back of the lid, attach a piece of magnetic tape.

To use the magnets, write the words "yes" and "no" on a magnetic board. Give each child a magnet as he arrives at your group area. Pose a question for him to answer by placing his magnet on the board under one of the words. When every child has arrived and placed his magnet on the board, discuss the results. Survey says...success!

Terry Steinke—Preschool, Emmaus Lutheran School
Indianapolis, IN

Snapshot Opposites

Learning about opposites? Capture the fun on film; then include the pictures in a class book. Take pictures as volunteers strike poses that demonstrate opposites. For example, ask one child to stand at the top of the stairs and another to stand at the bottom. Or ask one child to lie down and another to stand up. Encourage youngsters to suggest additional photo opportunities. Mount each developed photo on a sheet of construction paper; then bind the sheets into a book. Invite the class to help as you add text to your publication. This book is sure to be enjoyed from start to finish!

Joan Mason—Pre-K, Discovery Point, Alpharetta, GA

Who's Smiling?

Your little ones will be all smiles as they mix and match these photo puzzles. Mount a close-up photo of each child on a separate index card. Cut each card horizontally just above the child's smile. Mark the back of both pieces with matching letters or numerals. Laminate the cards for durability. To use the puzzles, a child looks at a card showing a child's smile and tries to guess who is smiling. He then finds the matching card. For fun, encourage youngsters to mix and match the cards. A picture is worth... a thousand smiles!

Carol Pochert—Four- And Five-Year-Olds, ABC Kids Care
Grafton, WI

We learned about WIND!

Teresa dances like the wind.

We flew our streamers outside in the wind.

A Picture Is Worth...

Use pictures as valuable tools for strengthening the home-school connection. Simply capture the activities of your classroom on film. As you arrange the developed pictures into scrapbooks, include descriptions of the activities as well as the learning objectives. Send the scrapbooks home to give parents and caregivers a glimpse into their children's everyday world. It's the next best thing to being there!

Nancy Barton—Four-Year-Olds, Bethel Lutheran Preschool
Manassas, VA

Prints Charming

Introduce each parent to his child's classmates by sending home a picture book displaying all of your little darlings. Take a picture of each child in your class. To prepare the book, glue each child's developed photo onto a 9" x 6" piece of construction paper. Print each child's name on his page. Laminate the pages; then bind them together. Don't forget to include a picture of you and your assistant. What a class!

Tracy Tavernese—Four-Year-Olds
Holy Child School, Old Westbury, NY

Jeremy

Pam Crane

Visual Reminders

Need a visual reminder of each child's transportation, medication, or other important information? Purchase a classroom supply of clear plastic, magnetic frames. Slip a different child's photo into each frame. When you receive a note from home, use the appropriate child's photo to display the note on a magnetic surface. A quick glance will remind you of your little ones' needs!

Sandra W. Scott
Asheville High School Child Care
Asheville, NC

I will pick up Sarah at 12:00 today.

Mrs. Jordan

61

The Big Picture

Use photos to help little ones see the big picture of your daily schedule. Take pictures of youngsters involved in daily activities such as snack and outdoor time. Laminate the developed pictures for durability. Then display them at youngsters' eye level. If youngsters are familiar with your daily routine, give them the opportunity to sequence the pictures. Looks like a picture-perfect day!

Mary Wisniewski—Preschool, Twinbrook School
Hoffman Estates, IL

I'm Here!

To make taking attendance a simple matter and help youngsters practice name recognition, try this management tip. Write each child's name on and attach a different sticker to the back of each child's photo. Each morning arrange the pictures on a table so that the names and stickers are showing. As each child arrives, have him locate his name and turn his picture over. Names still showing on the table will indicate at a glance who's absent.

Michelle Miget—Four-Year-Olds, Humboldt Preschool
St. Joseph, MO

A Place For Everything

Cleanup time will be a snap when you use this idea to help little ones return everything to its place. When you have arranged your classroom centers as desired, take a picture of each one. Mount each developed photo on a piece of tagboard and place it in the corresponding center. As youngsters clean up, encourage them to refer to the photo for the proper placement of classroom materials.

Kitty Moufarrege—Three-Year-Olds
Foothill Progressive Montessori Preschool, La Canada, CA

Discovery Center

Picturesque Placemats

Prepare these placemats to help each child find his own space at snacktime. To make a placemat, glue a child's photo onto a large piece of construction paper. Write the child's name in bold letters near the photo; then ask the child to decorate his mat using crayons, markers, or paint. On the back of the placemat, write information you would like for the child to learn, such as his phone number and address. Laminate each mat. Before snacktime, arrange the mats as desired. Can you find your special place?

Lori A. Lafratta—Preschool, Garden Gate Preschool
West Seneca, NY

Maggie

615 Shutterbug Road
643-5016

My friends like to paint.
photo by Benji

A Child's Point Of View

Photos can be valuable learning tools in the preschool classroom, but what about the camera? Have you considered placing a camera in each child's hands to find out what she finds interesting or meaningful enough to capture on film? Share some of the following suggested books with small groups of youngsters. Discuss the photos and speculate why the photographer chose to take each picture. What did the photographer want to remember or want others to see? How does each picture make you feel? Also allow children to look at coffee-table books for adults. Opportunities to develop language and thinking skills will abound as a pair of youngsters—or youngsters and an adult—peruse the photographs. Finally give your little ones the opportunities to take several (or more!) pictures of the world from their viewpoints. Refrain from giving specific instructions (other than how to use the camera) so the children will feel free to choose their own subject matter. When the pictures have been developed, place them in a scrapbook along with the names of the young photographers. Camera, Camera, what do you see?

Polaroid® Education Program

Need a clear picture for using photography in your classroom? The Polaroid® Education Program presents *A Child's Eye View: Instant Imagery In The Early Childhood Classroom.* This three-hour, hands-on session provides early childhood educators and daycare providers like yourselves with the tools and skills needed to incorporate photography into your classrooms and centers. The course covers how to use cameras and instant photography to develop self-esteem, document student achievement, teach basic skills, and more. Each participating teacher receives a Polaroid® camera and application materials. For information concerning fees and the minimum number of participants, contact Polaroid® Education Program, 201 Burlington Road, Bedford, MA 01730-1434 or call (617) 386-5090. You'll be able to jazz up your curriculum in an instant!

The Camera's Eye

Books Photo-Illustrated By Tana Hoban:
Circles, Triangles, And Squares (Simon & Schuster Children's Books)
Colors Everywhere (Greenwillow Books)
Dots, Spots, Speckles, And Stripes (Greenwillow Books)
I Walk And Read (Greenwillow Books)
Is It Red? Is It Yellow? Is It Blue? (Greenwillow Books)
Over, Under And Through (Simon & Schuster Children's Books)
Round & Round & Round (Greenwillow Books)
Spirals, Curves, Fanshapes, And Lines (Greenwillow)

Books Written By Ann Morris And Photo-Illustrated By Ken Heyman:
Bread, Bread, Bread (Lothrop, Lee, & Shepard Books)
Hats, Hats, Hats (Lothrop, Lee, & Shepard Books)
Houses And Homes (Lothrop, Lee, & Shepard Books)
Loving (Lothrop, Lee, & Shepard Books)
On The Go (William Morrow & Company, Inc.)

Books Photo-Illustrated By Margaret Miller:
Guess Who? (Greenwillow Books)
Now I'm Big (Greenwillow Books)

In A Patch Of Grass

In a patch of grass so cool and green, many little creatures can be seen! Take a closer look at things in the grass with the art, movement, and discovery ideas in this springtime unit.

ideas by Lucia Kemp Henry

We saw one black bug...then we saw lots more crawling all around it!

Tiptoe Through The Green Grass

Tickle, tickle, tickle. The best way to get a feel for this topic is with your toes! In advance, carefully examine a patch of lawn near your classroom for items that may be dangerous to bare feet. Then gather a supply of hand magnifiers, grab your camera, and take your little ones on a grassy field trip. When everyone is settled onto the previously examined area of nature's carpet, invite your children to take off their shoes and socks. Encourage them to explore the grass by feeling it with their feet. Invite them to use the magnifiers to look for critters that may be crawling or hopping in the grass. Take pictures of several children at a time as they explore. Before you return to your classroom, record youngsters' observations. Later rewrite the observations and display them on a board along with the photos and several rows of fringed-paper grass.

I See The Green Grass

Following your field trip, teach youngsters this fingerplay.

I see the green grass	*Look down and point to the ground.*
Under my feet.	*Lift up one foot at a time.*
It tickles my toes,	*Wiggle toes.*
And it smells so sweet.	*Sniff and smile.*
It feels so soft,	*Stroke arm with fingertips.*
Like a bed, you know.	*Hands under face as if sleeping.*
I see the green grass—	*Look down and point to the ground.*
Grow, grass, grow!	*Raise hands while wiggling fingers.*

A Busy Place!

Watch out—there's lots of life underfoot. Using the patterns on page 68, create flannelboard pieces to help introduce your little ones to animals that live and find their food in the grass. Duplicate the patterns onto white construction paper. Color and cut out each animal; then laminate each one, if desired. Attach self-adhesive flannel to the back of each piece. As you recite each verse of the following poem, add the appropriate animals to your flannelboard.

Things In The Grass

In a patch of grass
So cool and green,
Many little creatures
Can be seen!

Insects are here!
A **grasshopper** green,
A **bug,** and a **butterfly**
Can be seen!

Little birds are here
In the grass so green.
A **robin** and a **sparrow**
Can be seen!

Furry things are here
In the grass so green.
A **mouse** and a **chipmunk**
Can be seen!

Amphibians are here
In the grass so green.
A little **frog** and a big **toad**
Can be seen!

Crawly things are here
In the grass so green.
A **snail** and an **earthworm**
Can be seen!

In a patch of grass
So cool and green,
How many creatures
Have *you* seen?

Now You See Me, Now You Don't

Not all animals are easily spotted in the grass. That's because they take advantage of their natural ability to be *camouflaged*, or hidden, in the grass. To demonstrate to your little ones how some animals and insects hide in the grass, prepare a creature hunt. Duplicate the frog, toad, snail, and grasshopper patterns on page 68 several times onto white, brown, and green construction paper. Cut out the patterns. Take a group of children outside to a grassy area. Ask them to close their eyes as you scatter the white and brown cutouts. When the children open their eyes, ask them to seek the hidden creatures. When all of the cutouts have been found, repeat the game using the green cutouts. Ask youngsters which creatures were harder to find—the white and brown ones, or the green cutouts that matched the grass. Animal hide-and-seek...that's camouflage!

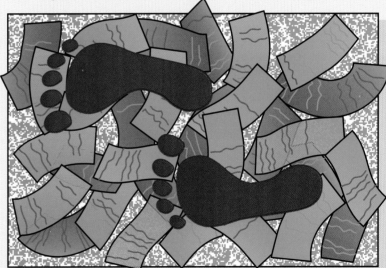

Barefoot In The Grass

Students will put their best feet forward when making these lovely lawn collages. To create a collage, a child sponge-paints green liquid paint onto a large sheet of white construction paper. When the paint is dry, he glues strips of green crepe paper onto the paper. Finally he removes his shoes and socks, and steps into a shallow tray of washable, brown liquid paint, then onto the collage. (To ensure that he leaves footprints behind *only* on the collage, keep towels and a bucket of warm, soapy water nearby.) Looks like something silly was afoot here!

All Sorts Of Creatures

Goodness gracious! The grass is just full of all sorts of creatures. Use the patterns on page 68 to make a sorting activity that you can place in a science center or take outside with you during playtime. Collect as many as 11 cleaned frozen-juice cans. Cover each can with a strip of light green paper. Add a strip of fringed, green paper to the can to resemble grass. Duplicate the patterns on page 68 at least four times. Color and cut out the patterns. Mount one or more different creatures on each can. If desired, label each can with the name(s) of the creature(s) shown. Mount the remaining creatures onto craft sticks. To use, a child sorts the sticks and places each set in the can that displays the matching creature.

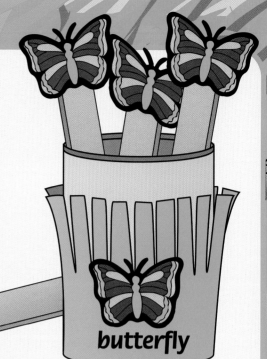

It's The Little Things

As you sing this song about little things in the grass, encourage your little ones to move all around! Have youngsters practice moving like each of the suggested creatures. Sing the first verse; then modify the following verse as indicated. Get "grass-hoppin' "!

Little Things Are In The Grass
(sung to the tune of "Mary Had A Little Lamb")

Little things are in the grass, in the grass, in the grass.
Little things are in the grass, moving all around.

[Tiny toads hop] in the grass, in the grass, in the grass.
[Tiny toads hop] in the grass, moving all around.

Little snails slide…
Earthworms wiggle…
Butterflies glide…
Ladybugs bounce…
Tiny frogs jump…
Little mice run…
Chipmunks scurry…

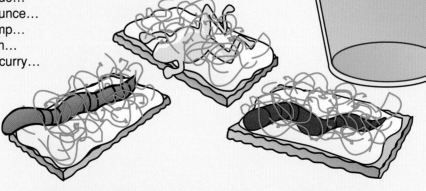

Gobble These Green Grass Goodies!

Youngsters are sure to enjoy making and grazing on these grass goodies! To make a little patch of grass, spread soft cream cheese on a cracker. Then sprinkle a little alfalfa-sprout "grass" atop the cheese. If desired, add a Gummy Worm®, frog, or bug to the patch of grass. Serve small cups of grass juice—lime-flavored drink—with the grass goodies.

Grassroots Support

If your students' parents often inquire about the learning topics in preschool, then this take-home activity is just what you need for your grassroots supporters. For each child, duplicate the patterns on pages 68 and 69 onto white construction paper. Ask each child to color his creatures; then assist him in cutting them out along the bold lines. To store the creatures, cut out the pocket pattern along the bold lines. Fold the pocket where indicated; then tape along the sides. Provide each child with a 2" x 7" strip of green paper to fringe, then glue to the front of his pocket. Have the child personalize his pocket before putting the creatures inside and taking the pocket home.

Green Grows The Grass

The grass is always greener—when it grows inside your classroom! To prepare for this grass-growing project, collect a clean, plastic yogurt cup or pint-sized milk carton for each child. If using milk cartons, cut off the tops. Purchase a small bag of potting soil and quick-sprouting grass seed from a garden store. Personalize each child's cup or carton by writing her name on a strip of masking tape and attaching it to the container. Direct each child to fill her container with soil, then gently press a spoonful of seeds into the dirt. Next have her water the seeds with a spray bottle so as not to disturb the seeds. Place the containers near a window. Encourage youngsters to spray their seeds daily and to observe the changes. In about a week, each child will have her own little patch of grass. Just before sending the projects home, place a Gummy Worm® in a plastic, pop-apart egg for each child. Tuck an egg into each patch of grass. Surprise! The green grass does grow all around!

Read And Grow

Tuck these books into a planter full of green, plastic grass. During nice weather, take the planter outside, settle youngsters onto a grassy spot, and read!

In The Tall, Tall Grass
Written & Illustrated by Denise Fleming
Published by Henry Holt and Company, Inc.
(Additional ideas for using this book are on pages 102–103.)

Mowing
Written by Jessie Haas
Illustrated by Jos. A. Smith
Published by Greenwillow Books

Brown Cow, Green Grass, Yellow Mellow Sun
Written by Ellen Jackson
Illustrated by Victoria Raymond
Published by Hyperion Books for Children

A House Of Leaves
Written by Kiyoshi Soya
Illustrated by Akiko Hayashi
(This book is out of print. Check your library.)

The Green Grass Grows All Around
Illustrated by Hilde Hoffman
(This book is out of print. Check your library.)

Patterns

Use with "A Busy Place!" and "Now You See Me, Now You Don't" on page 65, "All Sorts Of Creatures" on page 66, and "Grassroots Support" on page 67.

Dear Parent,

We are learning about things in the grass. Help your child's learning grow with this "Things In The Grass" creature collection. Here are some suggestions:

- Ask your child to name the creatures. The creatures included are: grasshopper, ladybug, butterfly, robin, sparrow, mouse, chipmunk, frog, toad, snail, and earthworm.
- Find ways that you and your child can sort the animals. For example, sort the creatures that can fly and those that cannot fly, or sort the creatures with two legs and those with four or six legs.
- Ask your child to count out a specific number of creatures onto the pocket's grass.
- Hide the creatures in your child's room. Have him/her find the creatures and return them to the pocket.
- Encourage your child to help you create stories about the creatures.

Have fun with things in the grass!

©The Education Center, Inc. • THE MAILBOX® • Preschool • April/May 1997

fold

Name

Glue grass here.

Things In The Grass

Pocket Pattern
Use with "Grassroots Support" on page 67.

The Ins And Outs Of Opposites

Stop and take a look at this assortment of sensational activities designed to help your youngsters experience opposites. Then *go* to your classroom and have fun from start to finish!

ideas by Carrie Lacher

Hands Off? Hands On!

To give your little ones a real feel for opposites, fill your sensory table with a collection of opposite sensations for sorting. For example, in an empty sensory table you might place soft items (feathers, cotton balls, and pom-poms) and rough items (Styrofoam® blocks, sandpaper). On a different day, fill your table with items that are big and little, black and white, or quiet and noisy. Now that's one idea you can really dig!

Edible Opposites

This baking project is sure to tantalize youngsters' taste buds and take them from feeling empty to feeling full. Have volunteers assist as you use a rolling pin to roll a package of purchased sugar-cookie dough onto a floured surface. (Set aside a small portion of the dough for comparisons after the cookies have baked.) Present a collection of big and little cookie cutters. Give each child an opportunity to use a small and a large cutter to cut out two cookies. Place the cookie shapes on a pan and bake according to package directions. Give each child a small ball of cookie dough so that he can compare the soft, cold dough to his warm, crisp cookies. If desired, accompany your sweet treat with a sour surprise such as lemonade. Opposites are delicious!

Shake It To The Left, Shake It To The Right

These shakers are so much fun, the first time you use them to learn about opposites probably won't be the last! In advance make a pair of shakers for each child. To make one shaker, fill an empty plastic film container with rice, beans, or popcorn kernels. Hot-glue the lid to the container. During a group time, give each child two shakers. Allow time for everyone to explore the shakers; then instruct them to stop. Repeat the opposite instructions "Stop" and "Go" as long as the fun continues. Then have your students use their shakers to give these opposite commands a try: left and right, up and down, fast and slow, quiet and loud, front and back.

Over-Under Art

To help youngsters understand the opposites *over* and *under,* give them the opportunity to contribute to two class murals. Cut two bulletin-board paper lengths to match the length and width of a table. Tape one length to the tabletop. Tape the other length to the underside of the table, trimming the paper if necessary to accommodate the table legs. Arrange pillows under the table. Encourage children to use crayons to decorate the paper taped over the table, and to lie or sit on the pillows while decorating the paper under the table as well. Michelangelo would be proud!

Shall We Dance?

Invite your little ones to give opposites a whirl with this spirited dance about fast and slow. In advance choose two musical selections: one with a fast tempo, and one with a slow tempo. Direct youngsters to stand in an open area so that they have plenty of personal space. Give each child a scarf or streamer to move while dancing. Encourage the children to move freely about the area as you play the fast, then the slow selection. When your dance time is over, ask individual children to describe the differences in the music and talk about which of the tempos they preferred for dancing. For a change of pace, try other movements such as walking, stomping, or clapping to both musical selections.

A Cool Idea!

Mix up a large batch of play dough using your favorite recipe. Then use the dough to give your little ones a hands-on opposite experience. Divide the dough and shape it so that you have two balls for each child. Place half of the balls in a freezer for about 30 minutes. Just before removing the balls of dough from the freezer, heat the remaining balls in a microwave for a few seconds. (To prevent accidental burns, be sure to knead each microwaved ball of play dough before giving it to a child.) Give each child a cold and warm ball of dough to manipulate. If desired, provide a collection of big and little cookie cutters and rolling pins to extend the sensory fun.

Is It Smooth? Is It Rough?

Prepare several containers of different colors of fingerpaint. Add a small amount of sand to some of the colors. Provide each child with a large sheet of fingerpainting paper and encourage him to fingerpaint with each of the different colors. Which colors feel smooth? Which feel rough?

Pam Crane

71

Outdoor Opposites

Tired of staying inside? Choose from these learning ideas that take place outside!

Warm "Splish," Cold Splash

Fill one large plastic tub with warm water and a second tub with ice-cold water. Place the tubs outside along with scoopers and pourers. Invite several children at a time to experience the hot-cold water play. Encourage them to name other things that can be hot, cold, or both at different times.

Stop And Go

Stop traffic with this outdoor suggestion that gives youngsters gross-motor exercise as well as practice following directions. In advance prepare a stop-and-go sign by cutting a large octagonal shape from red poster board and a circle from green poster board. Label the octagon "Stop" and the circle "Go." Tape a ruler to the back of one of the shapes; then glue the shapes together back-to-back.

While outside invite a group of youngsters to play a stop-and-go movement game. Introduce your sign, making sure that the children can correctly identify both sides. Then announce a type of movement such as clapping, running, or hopping. Flash the "Stop" and "Go" sides of your sign to indicate to the group when to stop and when to resume the directed movement.

Opposite Obstacle Course

Your youngsters will find loads of opportunities to experience opposites on the playground. To organize the fun, set up an opposite obstacle course of large appliance boxes and traffic cones around your existing playground equipment. Arrange the boxes and cones; then demonstrate the path of the course, showing your little ones how to go—for example, in and out of a box, to the left and right of the cones, under a bar, up a ladder, down a slide, and more. With this great idea, nothing will get in the way of opposite learning fun!

Carmen Carpenter—Pre-K, Children's Discovery Center
Cary, NC

"Bee" Polite!

Please allow me to introduce myself. I'm Miss Bea Polite, a queen bee of impeccable manners. May I help you keep your hive buzzing with good manners? Very well! Let's get started, shall we?

ideas contributed by Miss Bea Polite and Lisa D. Cowman

It's Nice To Meet You!

Get "buzzy" teaching your little ones about manners by making a Miss Bea look-alike. To make one, gather a nine-inch, orange foam ball; a straw hat; two black pipe cleaners; two practice golf balls; and black and pink Slick® fabric paints. To make Miss Bea's antennae, paint the plastic golf balls black. Fold each pipe cleaner in half and twist it. Insert one end of each pipe cleaner into a golf ball, and the other end into the top of the straw hat. Paint facial features on the foam ball. When the paint is dry, gently press the ball into the hat.

During a group time, bring Miss Bea out for a flyby. Modeling your most appropriate manners, introduce Miss Bea to each child by saying, "Miss Bea, this is [Child's name]. [Child's name], this is Miss Bea Polite." Encourage each child to respond by saying, "It's nice to meet you!" When all formal introductions have been made, explain to your group that your honored guest has arrived so that your class can learn about manners. Ask volunteers to explain what they think it means to be polite and have them give examples of good manners. If desired, record their examples. Then conclude by reminding your children that Miss Bea will be using her eyes and antennae to watch and listen for good manners in your classroom. When she does indeed observe politeness, allow her to buzz a word of praise in that child's ear.

Miss Bea's Recommended Reading

To help your little ones better understand mannerly behavior, Miss Bea Polite recommends reading aloud and discussing the following books:

Say Please
Written & Illustrated by Virginia Austin
Published by Candlewick Press

Perfect Pigs: An Introduction To Manners
Written & Illustrated by Marc Brown
and Stephen Krensky
Published by Little, Brown and Company

What Do You Say, Dear? and *What Do You Do, Dear?*
Written by Sesyle Joslin
Illustrated by Maurice Sendak
Published by HarperCollins Children's Books

Monster Manners
Written by Bethany Roberts
Illustrated by Andrew Glass
Published by Clarion Books

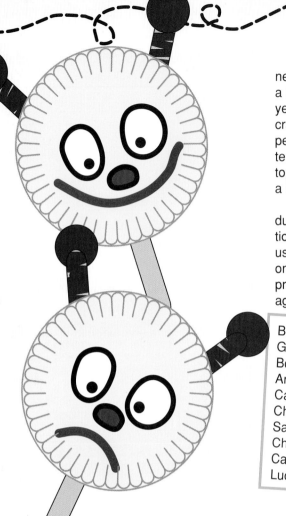

If you'd like your little ones to begin making choices about mannerly behavior, keep this activity in mind. First have each child make a Miss Bea bee puppet. To make one, draw a smiling face on one yellow paper plate and a frowning face on a second plate. Color two craft sticks black. Cut two small circles from black construction paper; then glue a circle to one end of each craft stick to represent antennae. To the back of one plate, tape the craft-stick antennae at the top of the plate. Tape another craft stick to the bottom of the plate for a handle. Glue the backs of both plates together.

When each child has made a puppet, have him use his puppet during this group-time activity. Using each of the following suggestions, describe a situation in which proper or improper manners were used. Direct each child to display either the happy or sad expression on his puppet to indicate if Miss Bea Polite would approve or disapprove of the behavior. After using the following suggestions, encourage volunteers to contribute scenarios of their own.

Beatrice Butterfly said, "Pass the flowers, *please.*"
Gracie Grasshopper said, *"Thank you,"* when she was given a treat.
Bobby Bumblebee bumped his brother off the beehive.
Arnie Ant waited his turn in line.
Carl Caterpillar crunched quietly.
Chrysy Caterpillar chatted with her mouth full.
Sammy Spider played with his food.
Christopher Cricket chirped while another cricket was chirping.
Casey Cricket chirped, *"Excuse me,"* before interrupting.
Lucy Ladybug borrowed a leaf without asking.

A Honey Of A Game!

This honey of a game will give your little ones practice using the magic words "please" and "thank you." In advance, cut a honeycomb shape from yellow construction paper; then add details with a marker. Remove Miss Bea Polite's straw hat and place it in a chair that is near, but facing away from your group area. To play, seat the class on the floor. Ask a volunteer to sit in the chair, wear the hat, and pretend to be Miss Bea. Place the honeycomb under the chair. Ask Miss Bea to close her eyes; then quietly choose another child to tiptoe to the chair and take the honeycomb. The child then returns to the group and sits on the honeycomb. Ask Miss Bea to open her eyes and face the group. Recite this chant:

(Class)	Miss Bea Polite, you're very sweet.
	May we *please* have a honey treat?
(Miss Bea)	Miss Bea Polite says, "Yes, you may."
(Class)	*"Thank you, thank you,"* we all say.

Give Miss Bea several chances to guess who took the honeycomb before revealing the child, if necessary. The child who took the honeycomb then becomes the new Miss Bea. Continue play until each child has been the queen bee.

"Bee-utiful" Behavior

Miss Bea Polite recommends making a batch of these bee stickers to remind youngsters to use good manners. Or use the stickers as rewards for children who make an effort to show exceptional etiquette. Simply use a black marker to draw stripes on a set of yellow dot stickers. Encourage a child to press a sticker on his hand or clothing. Your room is sure to be buzzin' with "bee-utiful" behavior!

Sweet Table Manners

Place a container of Honeycomb® cereal in your housekeeping area along with napkins, small paper plates, and a spoon. Set Miss Bea on the center of your housekeeping table. Encourage each child at the center to have a seat at the table, obtain a napkin and a plate, and serve himself a spoonful of cereal. Remind youngsters that Miss Bea will be watching for polite table manners such as keeping mouths closed while chewing, using napkins to wipe mouths and hands, taking turns, saying "Please" and "Thank you," saying "Excuse me" before leaving the table, and cleaning up properly.

Tea-Party Time

Celebrate good manners with a tea party! To prepare for your party, collect dress-up items such as scarves, hats, and ties. Also purchase the ingredients, utensils, and paper supplies needed to make and enjoy honey buns and tea (directions below). Prepare a giant invitation from Miss Bea Polite; then ask an adult volunteer to deliver it to your class on the morning of the day you've planned for your party. Read the invitation aloud. Discuss the manners that will be necessary at the party, relating them to these opposites: clean/dirty, neat/messy, polite/rude, smile/frown, quiet/loud. Invite each child to dress up using the gathered items of clothing. Then let the celebration begin!

It's Tea Party Time! Come celebrate good manners with Miss Bea!

Honey Buns And Tea

Miss Bea suggests serving these treats at your tea party. Use any biscuit dough (including canned) and a small, round canapé cutter to make miniature biscuits. Bake the biscuits; then slice and top them with different kinds of honey (clover, sage, orange blossom, etc.). Accompany the biscuits with decaffeinated mint tea.

Wet, Wild, And Wonderful

Dive into summer with this splashy unit about things in the water. Come on in—the water's fine!

pond

bathtub

pool

Water, Water, Every...Where?

To start your unit, get youngsters' feet wet—so to speak—by asking where water can be found, such as in a bathtub, a swimming pool, a puddle, an aquarium, a pond, a lake, a river, and an ocean. Using a crayon, record their answers in large writing on a length of white bulletin-board paper. Next brainstorm a list of animals or things that might be found in each different body of water. Encourage each child to draw one or more items on the paper with crayons. Cover an area of the floor with newspapers; then place the paper on the newspaper. Invite the group to paint over the entire sheet of paper with large brushes and watered-down blue paint. This group project will be wet and could be wild, but the resulting mural is sure to be wonderful!

The More, The Merrier

Ready to cool off? Jump in the water! In advance bring a small wading pool into your classroom along with beach towels, water goggles, flippers, inflatable floats, and other items that would add to make-believe water fun in your dramatic play area. During a storytime, invite your little ones to sit in and around the pool. Read aloud *Joe's Pool* by Claire Henley (Hyperion Books For Children)—a story about a boy, a cool pool, and lots of hot friends.

After the story, make a splash with this group chant and counting activity. Invite a volunteer to stand in the wading pool. Chant the first verse and clap as indicated. Invite a second child to stand in the pool, and modify the chant appropriately. Continue in this manner until you have a full pool; then begin a "splishy-splashy" countdown. Chant the verses in reverse order, asking a different child to hop out during each verse.

One in the water;
Everybody's cool!
Splish! *(Clap!)*
One in the water!

Two in the water;
Everybody's cool!
Splish! Splash! *(Clap! Clap!)*
Two in the water!

Three in the water;
Everybody's cool!
Splish! Splash! Splish! *(Clap! Clap! Clap!)*
Three in the water!

Water-Safety Song

Chances are that your little ones will be spending lots of time in a swimming pool, a lake, or an ocean this summer. Use this song as a springboard for teaching youngsters about water safety.

Hooray For Safe Water Play
(sung to the tune of "Hickory Dickory Dock")

Hip, hip, hip, hooray—
For fun and safe water play.
These are the rules
We learn in school.
We promise to obey!

Swim with a buddy or pal.
Make sure that a grown-up's around.
Don't push or run.
Protect from the sun.
The water's a fun playground!

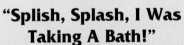

"Splish, Splash, I Was Taking A Bath!"

Who's in the water *every* day? Kids taking baths! Set up this center, and your bathing beauties will find themselves doing some very relaxing reading. Paint a large rectangular box white to resemble a bathtub. Fill the tub with packing peanuts. Be sure to include a plastic tub pillow, towels, sponges, and empty shampoo and soap containers in the center. Supply the center with the water-related books suggested throughout this unit and on page 79. To inspire youngsters to spend some time in the center, seat your little ones on the floor, settle yourself in the tub, and read aloud *King Bidgood's In The Bathtub* by Don and Audrey Wood (Harcourt Brace And Company) or *The Beast In The Bathtub* by Kathleen Stevens (Gareth Stevens Inc.).

Dear Parent,
Rub-a-dub-dub! Have lots of learning fun in the tub with these animal shapes. You can wet them, wash them, and stick them to the wall or tub! Just dive in with these suggestions:
• Ask
• To

Rub-A-Dub-Dub!

There's learning fun in the tub! Help parents turn bath time into a learning time by providing them with these activity kits. If funds allow, make one kit for each child. Or prepare several kits for children to take home on a rotating basis. To make one kit, trace and cut out two or more of each animal pattern on pages 80 and 81 from various colors of Fun Foam™. Store the shapes in a resealable plastic bag. Color, cut out, and laminate a copy of the parent note on page 80; then slip it into the bag. Send the bag home with a child. What a way to pool your resources!

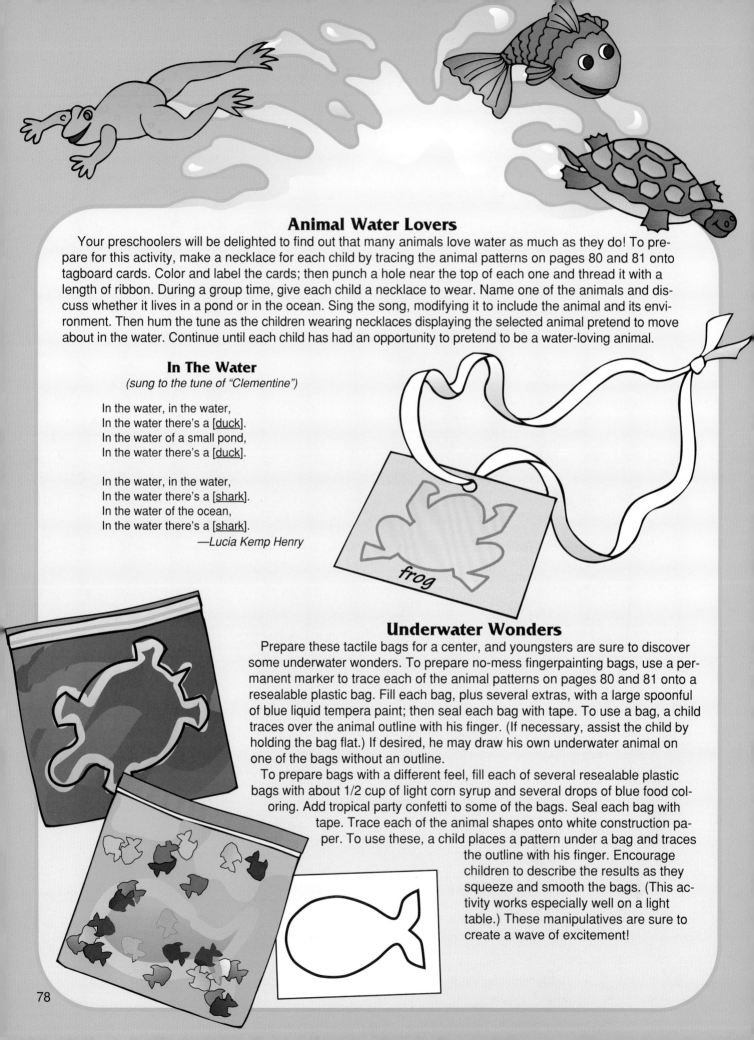

Animal Water Lovers

Your preschoolers will be delighted to find out that many animals love water as much as they do! To prepare for this activity, make a necklace for each child by tracing the animal patterns on pages 80 and 81 onto tagboard cards. Color and label the cards; then punch a hole near the top of each one and thread it with a length of ribbon. During a group time, give each child a necklace to wear. Name one of the animals and discuss whether it lives in a pond or in the ocean. Sing the song, modifying it to include the animal and its environment. Then hum the tune as the children wearing necklaces displaying the selected animal pretend to move about in the water. Continue until each child has had an opportunity to pretend to be a water-loving animal.

In The Water
(sung to the tune of "Clementine")

In the water, in the water,
In the water there's a [duck].
In the water of a small pond,
In the water there's a [duck].

In the water, in the water,
In the water there's a [shark].
In the water of the ocean,
In the water there's a [shark].
—Lucia Kemp Henry

Underwater Wonders

Prepare these tactile bags for a center, and youngsters are sure to discover some underwater wonders. To prepare no-mess fingerpainting bags, use a permanent marker to trace each of the animal patterns on pages 80 and 81 onto a resealable plastic bag. Fill each bag, plus several extras, with a large spoonful of blue liquid tempera paint; then seal each bag with tape. To use a bag, a child traces over the animal outline with his finger. (If necessary, assist the child by holding the bag flat.) If desired, he may draw his own underwater animal on one of the bags without an outline.

To prepare bags with a different feel, fill each of several resealable plastic bags with about 1/2 cup of light corn syrup and several drops of blue food coloring. Add tropical party confetti to some of the bags. Seal each bag with tape. Trace each of the animal shapes onto white construction paper. To use these, a child places a pattern under a bag and traces the outline with his finger. Encourage children to describe the results as they squeeze and smooth the bags. (This activity works especially well on a light table.) These manipulatives are sure to create a wave of excitement!

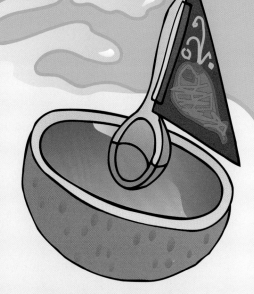

Boats Afloat

People and animals aren't all you'll find in the water. Introduce youngsters to some of the man-made objects in the water by reading aloud and discussing *Boats* by Anne Rockwell (Puffin Books), *Boats* by Byron Barton (HarperCollins Children's Books), or *Boat Book* by Gail Gibbons (Holiday House, Inc.). Then invite youngsters to cruise into creativity as they explore the boat-making possibilities at your water table. Prepare a boat-builders workshop that includes pictures of boats (as found in the suggested books) and these items: cardboard tubes, margarine tubs, Ivory® Soap bars, foam meat trays, milk cartons, foam egg cartons, sponges, straws, rubber bands, construction paper, scissors, tape, clay, toothpicks, yarn, a hole puncher, crayons, and craft sticks. Encourage youngsters to experiment—even to sink a few ships—until they make some boats that float. Need navigation? Here are some suggestions:

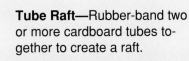

Tube Raft—Rubber-band two or more cardboard tubes together to create a raft.

Margarine-Tub Sailboat—Press a ball of clay in the bottom of a margarine tub. Insert a straw in the clay; then tape a decorated paper sail to the straw.

Soap Boat—Attach a decorated paper sail to one end of a craft stick. Insert the other end of the craft stick into the top of the bar of soap.

Egg-Cup Boats—Cut apart the individual cups of a foam egg carton. Float the cups in the water.

Meat-Tray Barges—Punch a hole in opposite ends of each of several foam meat trays. Connect the trays with yarn to make a barge.

Lori Kent
Hood River, OR

Shipshape Snacks

When your sailors get hungry, have them dock at your classroom cooking center to make some shipshape snacks. In advance cut ten navel oranges in half. Remove the pulp and squeeze the juice from the orange halves; then place them on a tray. Follow the directions on a three-ounce package for preparing blue, berry-flavored gelatin. Pour the gelatin into the orange halves; then place the halves in the refrigerator for at least four hours. To make a snack, a child uses markers to decorate a construction-paper triangle. He then tapes the triangle to the handle of a plastic spoon before inserting the spoon into the gelatin. "Tummy-ho"!

More Buoyant Books About...

Swimming
Edward In Deep Water
Written & Illustrated by Rosemary Wells
Published by Dial Books For Young Children

Animals In The Water
In The Small, Small Pond
Written & Illustrated by Denise Fleming
Published by Henry Holt And Company

Splash!
Written & Illustrated by Ann Jonas
Published by Greenwillow Books

Boats
I Love Boats
Written & Illustrated by Flora McDonnell
Published by Candlewick Press

Parent Note
Use with "Rub-A-Dub-Dub!" on page 77.

Dear Parent,
Rub-a-dub-dub! Have lots of learning fun in the tub with these animal shapes. You can wet them, wash them, and stick them to the wall or tub! Just dive in with these suggestions:

- Ask your child to find the matching animal shapes.
- Talk about how the shapes are alike and different.
- Help your child sort the shapes by color.
- Place a set of shapes on the wall. Ask your child to give each shape a partner.
- Count aloud as you put a number of shapes on a wall. Ask your child to count aloud as he or she removes them.
- Use the shapes to measure the length and width of the bathtub.
- Have your child help you tell a story using the shapes.

"Splish, splash!" You're learning in the bath!

Animal Patterns
Use with "Rub-A-Dub-Dub!" on page 77, and "Animal Water Lovers" and "Underwater Wonders" on page 78.

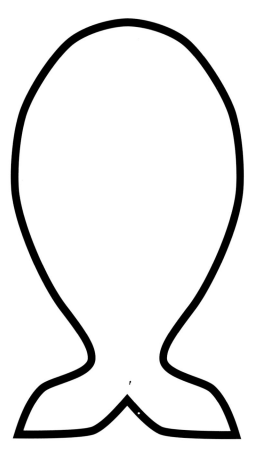
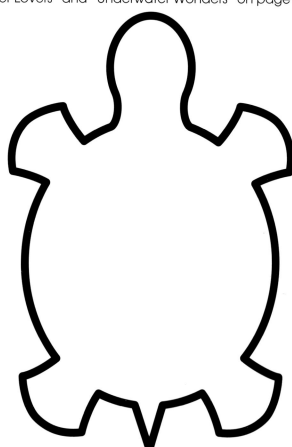

Animal Patterns

Use with "Rub-A-Dub-Dub!" on page 77, and "Animal Water Lovers" and "Underwater Wonders" on page 78.

THE GREATEST DAY ON EARTH

Hur-ry, hur-ry! If your classroom is feeling like a three-ring circus these days, step right up! Here's a big-top unit that's bursting with learning-center ideas for a Circus Day that you, your little ones, and some adult volunteers are sure to enjoy. Ladies and gentlemen, children of all ages (especially three- and four-year-olds), the show is about to begin!

Hear Ye! Hear Ye!

Prepare circus tickets that serve first as announcements, then as nametags for your big day. Program a copy of the ticket (page 86) before duplicating a classroom supply plus extras onto colorful paper. If desired, use the tickets to help organize the rotation of children through your circus of centers by dividing the class into groups and duplicating each group's tickets onto a different color of paper. Use decorative-edged scissors to cut out each ticket; then personalize the tickets and pass them out prior to your Circus Day. Build excitement by encouraging each child to arrive at school on the designated day with his ticket in hand.

> **HEAR YE! HEAR YE!**
> Austin McClure
> (child's name)
> is invited to
> Circus Day
> under the big top
> in Ms. Berry 's room.
> (teacher)
> Bring this ticket to school
> on 6/2/97 .
> (date)

Under The Big Top

You'll be able to convert your classroom into a circus arena with the greatest of ease when you use these fun suggestions:

- To create the feeling of a big-top circus tent, drape crepe-paper streamer lengths from the center to the corners of your classroom ceiling. Or tape pairs of bulletin-board paper lengths together along one side. Punch holes at one end of each panel; then tie yarn through the holes. Make several panels in this manner and hang them from the ceiling. As a final option, suspend a parachute from your ceiling.
- Drape strings of colorful Christmas-tree lights around your room.
- Enlarge several of the animal patterns on pages 86–87 onto large pieces of cardboard. Paint the animals; then tape them to chairs or boxes so that they are freestanding. Display them throughout your room.
- Suspend balloons from your ceiling, keeping them out of youngsters' reach.
- Locate a puppet stage where it can be used first as a ticket counter, then as a concession stand during snacktime.

After setting the stage, prepare your choice of the learning-center ideas described on pages 84–85. Soon you'll have a learning environment worth roaring about!

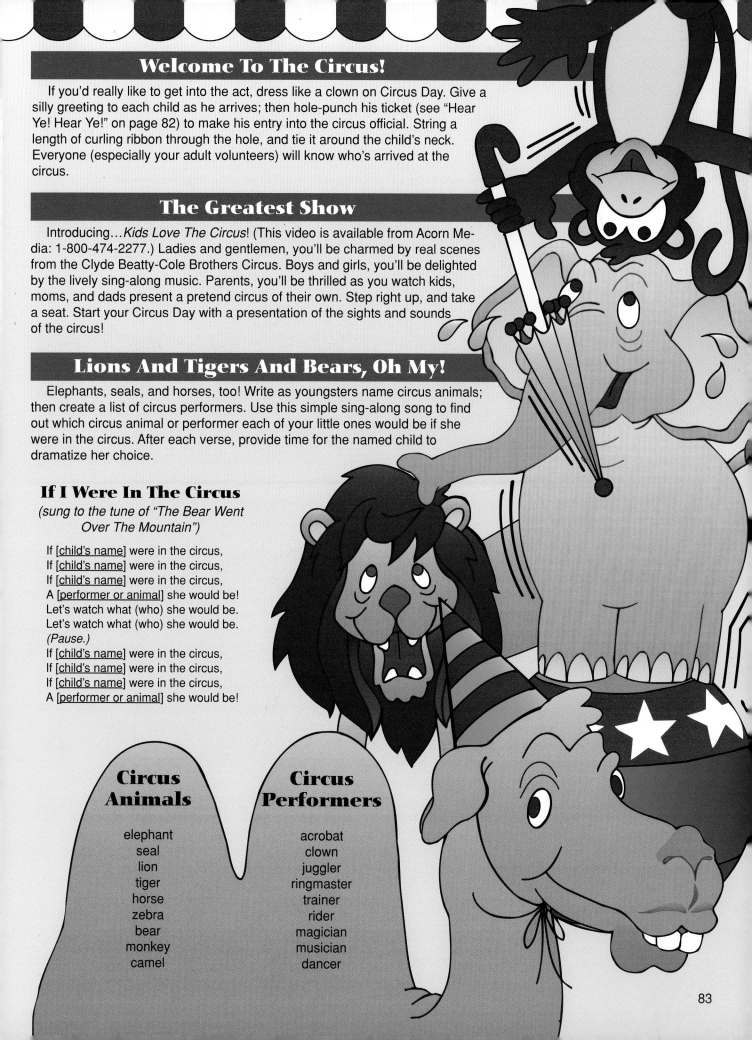

Welcome To The Circus!

If you'd really like to get into the act, dress like a clown on Circus Day. Give a silly greeting to each child as he arrives; then hole-punch his ticket (see "Hear Ye! Hear Ye!" on page 82) to make his entry into the circus official. String a length of curling ribbon through the hole, and tie it around the child's neck. Everyone (especially your adult volunteers) will know who's arrived at the circus.

The Greatest Show

Introducing…*Kids Love The Circus*! (This video is available from Acorn Media: 1-800-474-2277.) Ladies and gentlemen, you'll be charmed by real scenes from the Clyde Beatty-Cole Brothers Circus. Boys and girls, you'll be delighted by the lively sing-along music. Parents, you'll be thrilled as you watch kids, moms, and dads present a pretend circus of their own. Step right up, and take a seat. Start your Circus Day with a presentation of the sights and sounds of the circus!

Lions And Tigers And Bears, Oh My!

Elephants, seals, and horses, too! Write as youngsters name circus animals; then create a list of circus performers. Use this simple sing-along song to find out which circus animal or performer each of your little ones would be if she were in the circus. After each verse, provide time for the named child to dramatize her choice.

If I Were In The Circus
(sung to the tune of "The Bear Went Over The Mountain")

If [child's name] were in the circus,
If [child's name] were in the circus,
If [child's name] were in the circus,
A [performer or animal] she would be!
Let's watch what (who) she would be.
Let's watch what (who) she would be.
(Pause.)
If [child's name] were in the circus,
If [child's name] were in the circus,
If [child's name] were in the circus,
A [performer or animal] she would be!

Circus Animals

elephant
seal
lion
tiger
horse
zebra
bear
monkey
camel

Circus Performers

acrobat
clown
juggler
ringmaster
trainer
rider
magician
musician
dancer

Top–Cat Center

Youngsters interested in acting like or training wild animals are sure to enjoy visiting this top-cat center. Purring, prancing, and pawing can take place on a plastic jungle gym that's located in an open area of the room. Prepare a hoop of fire for tiny tigers to jump through by securing red and orange ribbons or paper streamers to a plastic hoop. An interested trainer can take control with a whip of yarn tied to a cardboard tube. And after performing, lions and tigers may want to retreat to large boxes cut to resemble cages. Roar! Let's see more!

Cooperative Clowning Around

Clowning around will get applause at this creative center. To prepare, cut a large circle from white felt. Then cut an assortment of geometric shapes and shapes that resemble clowns' hair from various colors of felt. Encourage youngsters who visit the area to observe pictures of clowns as found in books about the circus. Then have them work together with the felt pieces to create their own crazy clown. Let's give a round of applause for cooperation.

The Circus Train

How do all of the circus animals and performers come to town? On the circus train! To stimulate imaginative play in the block area, supply the area with a collection of shoebox train cars, cardboard rolls, and crayons. Duplicate a supply of the animal patterns on pages 86 and 87 onto white construction paper; then cut them out. Encourage youngsters who visit the center to color the animals of their choice, then tape them onto portions of cardboard rolls or blocks. Now that the circus train and a host of animals have arrived, isn't it time to build the big top? Youngsters at this center are sure to keep busy!

The Elephant's Feet Sound Like A Drum

Duplicate, color, and cut out a set of the animal patterns on pages 86 and 87 for use in a music center that is stocked with a variety of rhythm instruments. Encourage children to match each animal to an instrument. There are many possibilities at this center, so be sure to encourage creative thinking!

A Balancing Act

Set up an area of your room where your children can practice their balancing abilities. Place a piece of lumber, a strip of masking tape, or a length of rope on the ground to represent a tightrope. Encourage a child to walk on the imaginary tightrope forward, backward, sideways, while balancing a beanbag on her head, and while holding an umbrella that has safety spokes.

To make a pair of stilts, use rope and two empty food cans. Near the top of each can, puncture two holes. Thread a five-foot piece of rope through both holes in each can. Tie the ends of rope together so that when a child is standing on the cans and holding both ropes, the ends are at his waist. Encourage a child to stand on the cans and practice walking around the room. Stand tall and proud—you're in the circus now!

Get Your Peanuts! Get Your Popcorn!

Students will be hungry for more and more fun when they work behind a puppet-theater concession stand. Fill separate large plastic tubs with popcorn and unshelled peanuts. Encourage exploration as students use containers and large spoons to scoop and pour the items into small paper bags and popcorn boxes. For added fun, provide toy money and a measurement scale. Since peanuts and popcorn present choking concerns, ask youngsters not to eat while exploring. Instead invite them to a supervised area where they can sit and enjoy these traditional circus treats.

Animal–Cracker Math

Duplicate and cut out multiple sets of the animal patterns on pages 86 and 87. Empty the contents of at least five boxes of animal crackers into a bowl. Remove the tops from the boxes; then attach a paper flag displaying a different numeral from one to five to each box. Place the boxes, the animal patterns, and the crackers in a center. Suggest these activities to reinforce math concepts:

- To develop one-to-one correspondence, ask a child to place a desired number of animal patterns on the table. Ask another child to give each animal pattern an animal-cracker partner.
- Encourage a child to fill each box with the number of crackers indicated on its flag.
- Challenge a child to sort the animal crackers or patterns, then place them in the boxes by type.

Reward each child for a job well done by inviting him to a cooking center to make the following animal-cracker snack.

Circus Parade

Here's a parade of circus animals that's also a tasty treat. To make your own parade, spread a generous amount of creamy peanut butter onto the rounded sides of several vanilla wafers. Press an animal cracker into the peanut butter on each of your wafers. Rum, tum, tum…here comes the parade. Rum, tum, *tummy*…there goes the parade! Delicious!

Funny Faces

Send each child home with a smile and a painted design on his face. For each different color of paint, mix 2 parts cornstarch, 1 part cold cream, and several drops of food coloring together into a smooth cream. To apply, use small paintbrushes to paint the design of a child's choice onto his face.

Class Acts

Contributors to this Circus Day unit: Carol K. Budsock, Kinderwrap, Summit Child Care Centers, Summit, NJ • Ann Endorf—Preschool, Open Arms Christian Preschool, Bloomington, MN • Gail Johnson, Morgan Park Academy, Chicago, IL • Jeanne Price—Preschool, Tomorrow's World Inc., Ephrata, PA • Maria York—Preschool, Holy Trinity Christian Preschool, Streator, IL

Three–Ring Reading

Display these and other circus books in your reading area. Or read a title aloud to provide an intermission from youngsters' circus activities.

Circus
Written & Illustrated by Lois Ehlert
Published by HarperCollins
    Children's Books

The Circus
Written & Illustrated by Heidi
    Goennel
Published by Tambourine Books

Peter Spier's Circus!
Written & Illustrated by Peter Spier
Published by Doubleday, and
    Company, Inc.

Circus Ticket

Use with "Hear Ye! Hear Ye!" on page 82 and "Welcome To The Circus!" on page 83.

HEAR YE! HEAR YE!

_____
(child's name)

is invited to

Circus Day

under the big top

in _____'s room.
(teacher)

Bring this ticket to school

on _____.
(date)

Circus-Animal Patterns

Use with "Under The Big Top" on page 82, "The Circus Train" and "The Elephant's Feet Sound Like A Drum" on page 84, and "Animal-Cracker Math" on page 85.

Use with "Under The Big Top" on page 82, "The Circus Train" and "The Elephant's Feet Sound Like A Drum" on page 84, and "Animal-Cracker Math" on page 85.

Irresistible Ice Cream

"I scream. You scream. We all scream for ice cream!" Scoop up a gallon of learning fun with these flavorful activities that are sure to keep youngsters "ice-screaming" for more!

ideas contributed by Carrie Lacher

What's The Scoop?

Get your ice-cream theme off to a smooth start by gathering your little ones together for a mouthwatering discussion about this delicious topic. In advance, mount a giant bulletin-board-paper ice-cream cone and scoop onto a flat surface such as your easel or a bulletin board. During a group time, ask volunteers to explain what they think ice cream is made of and how they think it is made. Record their explanations on the giant scoop. Then share a book that details the chilly facts about ice cream. *Ice Cream* by William Jaspersohn (Macmillan Publishing Company) provides black-and-white photos along with informative text that you can paraphrase and share with your children. For a really chilly treat, read aloud and discuss *Make Mine Ice Cream* by Melvin Berger (the big book, small book, and teaching guide for this photo-illustrated title are available by calling Newbridge Communications, Inc., at 1-800-867-0307). Youngsters will soon have their taste buds ready for an ice-cream extravaganza!

Ice cream is made of milk and chocolate that you put in a frozen box.
Mariza

Ice cream is made of pink milk, white milk, and chocolate milk. It has stripes.
Ellis

From Cow To Cream...A Sweet Story

Now that your little ones know the scoop about how ice cream is made, encourage them to review the sequence of the sweet story while playing in your block area. Label each of five cards with a different numeral from one to five. Spray-paint or cover with paper three boxes; then label and decorate each box to resemble an ice-cream factory, a grocery store, or an ice-cream parlor. Place the cards, the boxes, two toy trucks, and a herd of plastic cows in the center. Encourage children playing in the area to use the numeral cards and props, along with blocks, to create a scene that shows the sequence from cow, to dairy truck, to factory, to truck, to grocery store or ice-cream parlor. Want some ice cream? Get "moo-ving"!

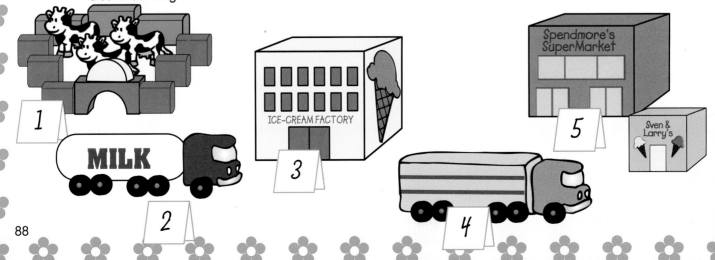

Flavorful Favorites

Our surveys indicate that three ice-cream flavors reign supreme—vanilla, chocolate, and strawberry. Conduct a taste test to determine which of these flavors is the most popular with your youngsters. In advance, glue a large, construction-paper cone shape to the bottom of a sheet of painting paper for each child. Stock your painting center with paints that represent the three flavors of ice cream that will be tasted—white (vanilla), brown (chocolate), and pink (strawberry). For added fun, add a few drops of the appropriate flavorings or extracts to each color of paint.

When it's time for your taste test, serve samples of the three suggested flavors of ice cream in individual paper cups. Then have each child use the paint that represents the flavor of his choice to paint a giant scoop. When the paint is dry, cut around the shape of each painted scoop and label the cone with the painter's name. Punch a hole in the top of each scoop and add thread for hanging it. Sort the cones by flavor; then hang each group in a different corner of your room. To tabulate the results, ask each child to stand under his cone. Together count aloud the children in each group. And the most popular flavor is….

One Scoop, Two Scoops, Three Scoops, Four!

Tiny tongues will be tantalized when you treat them to this chilly chant. As you begin the chant, place a tan, felt cone shape onto your flannelboard. As you continue the chant, top the cone with a white, a brown, a pink, and—finally—an orange felt scoop of ice cream. Repeat the chant and invite youngsters to clap along to the frosty-freeze beat.

A Chilly Chant

First we need a cone,
Nice and crunchy.
Then we need some ice cream,
Sweet and yummy.
Scoop 'em on; stack 'em up;
Up to the sky.
We love ice cream; my, oh my!

First comes vanilla,
Rich and sweet.
Then comes chocolate,
A delicious treat.
Here's some strawberry;
Orange sherbet, too.
A super-duper scooper cone
Just for you!

One scoop, two scoops,
Three scoops, four.
We love ice cream.
Let's have some more!

Dreamy Dramatic Play

Wouldn't a trip to an ice-cream parlor be delicious? If it's possible to take your group to an ice-cream shop, take instant pictures of the surroundings while you're visiting. When you return, look at the pictures with your group, and ask for youngsters' input on items that are needed to set up a pretend ice-cream shop in your dramatic play area. Or, if you won't be able to take a trip, begin by gathering and displaying the listed items during a group time. As your little ones review the gathered materials, ask them to help you decide how to use them to establish your ice-cream shop. This dramatic-play idea will have your little ones doing some "scooper-duper" planning, and the resulting center is sure to be "dairy" fun.

white baseball caps
clean, empty ice-cream containers of various sizes
clean, empty, plastic ice-cream-topping containers
painted Styrofoam® balls
play dough
plastic dishes
ice-cream cones made from heavy brown paper
ice-cream scoopers
plastic spoons
checkered tablecloths
a toy cash register and toy money

Sing A Song For Ice Cream

Ice cream shows up in lots of delectable forms—such as a milk shake, a sundae, a float, and an ice-cream sandwich. Ask parents to send to school clean and empty ice-cream-product packages and containers. Gather your students together to look carefully at the packages and brainstorm frosty ways that ice cream can be enjoyed. Add the containers to your class ice-cream shop, to a writing center, or even to your block-building area; then sing and dramatize this sweet song.

A Sweet, Chilly Treat
(sung to the tune of
"Did You Ever See A Lassie?")

Oh, I love to lick my ice-cream cone,
Ice-cream cone, ice-cream cone.
Oh, I love to lick my ice-cream cone—
A sweet, chilly treat!
  First I lick it on the left side;
  Then I lick it on the right side.
Oh, I love to lick my ice-cream cone—
A sweet, chilly treat!

Oh, I love to slurp my milk shake,
My milk shake, my milk shake.
Oh, I love to slurp my milk shake—
A sweet, chilly treat!
  First I slurp it with one straw;
  Then I slurp it with two straws.
Oh, I love to slurp my milk shake—
A sweet, chilly treat!

Oh, I love to eat my sundae,
My sundae, my sundae.
Oh, I love to eat my sundae—
A sweet, chilly treat!
  First I eat up the top scoop;
  Then I eat up the bottom scoop.
Oh, I love to eat my sundae—
A sweet, chilly treat!

Ice Cream In A Bag

Add this remarkable recipe to your list of ways that ice cream can be enjoyed. To make ice cream in a bag, pour one-half cup of milk, one-fourth teaspoon of vanilla, and one tablespoon of sugar into a pint-size resealable plastic bag. Seal the bag tightly. Then half-fill a gallon-size resealable plastic bag with crushed ice and add one-half cup of salt. Place the pint bag inside the gallon bag; then tightly seal the gallon bag. Have a pair of children take turns wearing mittens (yes, mittens!) and shaking the bag. After about five minutes, the ice cream should be ready to share.

An end-of-the-year party   Our classroom   June 6 noon

Please bring: chocolate sprinkles

It's time to banana split!

It's Time To Banana Split!

Go bananas by hosting a banana-split party to celebrate the end of the year! For each child's family, prepare an invitation by cutting a banana boat, a banana, and three ice-cream-scoop shapes from construction paper. Glue the shapes together as shown to resemble a banana split. Program the banana-split invitation with your party's date, time, and any requests for needed items. Send an invitation home with each child. On the day of your party, arrange the ingredients and utensils on a table; then invite everyone to create her own banana split.

Pin The Scoop On The Cone

Top off your banana-split party with this version of a familiar party game. To prepare, cut a large ice-cream-cone shape from brown bulletin-board paper. Cut enough construction-paper ice-cream scoops for each parent and child who will be attending the party. Mount the ice-cream cone on a bulletin board that is at students' level or on an outside wall. To begin play, a volunteer is blindfolded (or asked to close his eyes) and given an ice-cream scoop that has a piece of tape or Sticky-Tac on the back. As the group gives him encouragement and verbal directions, the blindfolded volunteer attempts to place the scoop above the cone. Remove the blindfold from the volunteer; then, as a group, give him a cheer!

You're super! You're "duper"! You're quite an ice-cream scooper! Yea, Carlos!

Kindergarten Bound!

Are you the proud teacher of four-year-olds who are bound and ready for the big "K"? Send them off to kindergarten with these fun ideas.

ideas contributed by Linda Ludlow—Preschool, Bethesda Christian School, Brownsburg, IN

Packed With Fun

It's true that you'll want your preschoolers to take what they've learned with them to kindergarten, but you'll also want them to take plenty of happy memories. With this idea, each youngster can pack a crafty suitcase full of preschool memorabilia. Using the pattern on page 93, cut a suitcase shape for each child from a folded 12" x 18" sheet of construction paper. Fill each suitcase with a supply of paper that measures 6" x 9 1/2". Staple along the fold of the suitcase. Personalize the suitcase and label it "Kindergarten Bound." When each child has used markers, stickers, or paint to decorate his suitcase, help him pack the pages using the following suggestions:

- Tape extra photos of preschool events on the paper inside the suitcase. Ask each child to dictate as you write his description of the event shown in each photo.
- Direct each child to ask his classmates to autograph the paper in his suitcase.
- Write a personal note of congratulations inside each child's suitcase.
- Ask each child to draw on one page a picture of himself as a preschooler. On another page, have him draw a picture of himself as a kindergartner. Write as he describes why he is ready for kindergarten.

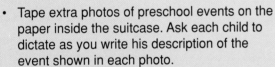

Kindergarten Countdown

Color one star each day...Kindergarten's only ten days away!

10 9 8 7 6 5 4 3 2 1

Today's the big day! I'm in grade K!

Kindergarten, Here We Come!

Once your little ones are packed with pride, send them on their way with a song!

(sung to the tune of "Twinkle, Twinkle, Little Star")

Kindergarten, here we come!
We know we'll have lots of fun.
Lots of things to make and do.
Reading, writing, counting, too.
Kindergarten, here we come!
We know we'll have lots of fun.

Countdown To Kindergarten

Along with any end-of the-year materials that you send home, give each child a countdown calendar to use just prior to when she will enter kindergarten. For each child, duplicate a copy of the countdown calendar provided on page 134. To use her calendar, a child begins to color one star a day ten days before her first day of school. She's sure to feel like a big star when the "K-day" arrives!

Place on fold.

BOOK FEATURES

CLAP YOUR HANDS

Written & Illustrated by Lorinda Bryan Cauley
Published by G. P. Putnam's Sons

Give a round of applause to a book so bouncy and full of life it's sure to become a class favorite. Move into a brand-new year with these story-extension activities. How do you get your hands on *Clap Your Hands*? In hardback (ISBN 0-399-22118-2) it's available from G. P. Putnam's Sons: 1-800-847-5515. The paperback and big book with audiocassette are available from Scholastic Inc.: 1-800-724-6527.

ideas contributed by Lori Kent and Grace Morris

JUMP RIGHT IN!

Ask the children to pay special attention to the humorously illustrated characters' feet as you read aloud *Clap Your Hands.* At the conclusion of the story, ask your preschoolers if they noticed what all of the animals and children in the book have in common. When they discover that the characters are all shoeless, invite your little ones to take off their shoes. Then jump right into a game of Simon Says using the text as your guide. Stomp your feet. Simon says, "Stomp your feet!"

SHH! IT'S A SECRET

Show youngsters the page on which the animals are shown sharing secrets. Then lead your little ones in a round of whispers. Select a phrase from the text to whisper into one child's ear. Have that child whisper the same phrase into his neighbor's ear. Continue around the circle until every child has heard the secret. Ask the last child who heard the phrase to say it aloud. If the phrase has changed in meaning, let youngsters in on the secret. Then join together in moving as the selected phrase suggests. Get ready for some silliness, but shh! Better keep it a secret!

LAUGH LINES

This group activity will grab youngsters' attention and tickle their funny bones. Remind students of the line in the rhyme that reads, "I'll tickle you if you tickle me!" Ask your little ones to sit in a circle so that each child is facing the back of the child in front of him. Sit in the circle opposite the direction of the children so that you are facing a child. As you sing the following song, tickle the nose, knees, toes, and tummy of the child you are facing. Encourage the remainder of the group to gently tickle the backs of the children in front of them. At the end of each verse, ask the child you are facing to exchange places with you so that you are facing a new child and he is facing another child's back. Continue in this manner until each child has been tickled by you. Get ready for giggles!

TICKLE TIME
(sung to the tune of "Mary Had A Little Lamb")

Gather round and make a line.
Make a line, make a line.
Gather round and make a line,
'Cause now it's tickle time.
Tickle on your little nose,
Little knees, little toes.
Tickle on your tummy, too.
It's tickle time for you!

CLAP YOUR COLORFUL HANDS

Call youngsters' attention to the page that reads, "Rub your tummy, pat your head. Find something yellow, find something red." Then play a color-recognition game that will really keep things moving. From construction paper, cut several hand shapes in each of the colors named below. To play the game, ask a group of students to stand in a circle. Spread the cutouts on the floor. Say the first two lines of the poem, inserting a child's name in the second line. Encourage the group to move as described; then have the selected child pick up an appropriately colored cutout and take it back to his place in the circle. Recite the poem in order or randomly, repeating colors and children's names as desired. Continue play as long as interest dictates or until each child has had at least one turn.

Rub your tummy; pat your head.
[Child's name], find a hand that's red.

Wave your hand and say, "Hello."
[Child's name], find a hand that's yellow.

Show a smile; give a wink.
[Child's name], find a hand that's pink.

Stand up straight. Start to lean.
[Child's name], find a hand that's green.

Spin around in a circle.
[Child's name], find a hand that's purple.

Tap your head. Tap your shoe.
[Child's name], find a hand that's blue.

IF WE COULD MOVE LIKE THE ANIMALS

The books listed under "More, More, More!" are sure to be the ticket to even more movement fun and games. As you read each book, consider keeping a list of the animals mentioned and the descriptions of how they move. Encourage youngsters to practice moving like their favorite animals. So that all of the animal imitations won't look alike, ask youngsters to decide if the animal is heavy or light. Is it fast or slow, or can it be both? What are the characteristic movements of the animal? For example, a cat might lick its paw and clean its ear.

When youngsters have had plenty of time to experiment with moving like animals, play an animal guessing game. Collect pictures of animals from coloring books, workbooks, clip art, or magazines. Mount each picture on a construction-paper card. Turn the cards facedown on the floor. Ask a volunteer to select a card and act like the animal pictured. Go ahead...let your little ones go wild with animal movement fun.

MORE, MORE, MORE!

Pretend You're A Cat
Written by Jean Marzollo
Illustrated by Jerry Pinkney
Published by Dial Books For
   Young Readers

Slither, Swoop, Swing
Written & Illustrated by Alex Ayliffe
(Check your local library.)

Jiggle Wiggle Prance
Written & Illustrated by Sally Noll
Published by Greenwillow Books

Quick As A Cricket
Written by Audrey Wood
Illustrated by Don Wood
Published by Child's Play (International) Ltd.

Cover of *Clap Your Hands* by Lorinda Bryan Cauley. ©1992 by Lorinda Bryan Cauley. By permission of G. P. Putnam's Sons, a division of The Putnam & Grosset Book Group.

Ten, Nine, Eight

**A Caldecott Honor Book
Written And Illustrated By Molly Bang
Published By Scholastic Inc.**

The countdown to bedtime is a warm and soothing ritual in Molly Bang's award-winning picture book. *Ten, Nine, Eight* is available in paperback and as a big book with a teaching guide (Scholastic Inc.: 1-800-325-6149).

ideas by Lucia Kemp Henry

Counting Down

Ask youngsters to help you read the book aloud by counting down as you read each page of the text. Ask them to say the number *ten* with loud voices. Have them lower the volume of their voices with each page so that the number *one* is said in a whisper.

Wiggling Toes And Sleepy Smiles

After introducing the story to youngsters and involving them in reading the text aloud, teach them these suggested movements to accompany the story. Encourage your little ones to perform the movements as you reread the text.

10…*Wiggle toes.*
9…*Hold finger to lips and say, "Shh."*
8…*Make a square with fingers and thumbs; peek through square.*
7…*Stoop down and touch shoes.*
6…*Point above head; look up.*
5…*Count five imaginary buttons on shirt.*
4…*Close eyes and yawn.*
3…*Make a kissing sound.*
2…*Pretend to hug someone.*
1…*Smile and pretend to sleep.*

Tucked Under The Covers

This display idea will keep everyone cozy. Cut a classroom supply of large squares from various colors of construction paper. Direct youngsters to decorate the squares with sponge shapes and tempera paint. When the squares have dried, mount them on a bulletin board or wall in the arrangement of a quilt. Then cut circles from skin-toned construction paper. Have a child use various art supplies such as paper, yarn, crayons, and markers to decorate the appropriate color of circle so that it resembles his face. Tuck the faces under the top of the quilt. Add a title such as "Sleep Tight!" to complete the display.

Bedtime Friends

Most youngsters have a special stuffed animal, doll, or toy that they like to sleep with. Review the page illustrating the young girl's bedtime friends. Then ask youngsters to invite their special bedtime friends to visit your classroom for a day. On that day, take an instant photo of each child holding her special friend. Mount each child's photo on a construction-paper bed shape. Write on each child's shape as she dictates a sentence about her bedtime friend. If desired, bind the pages together with a bed-shaped cover. Title the book "Our Bedtime Friends."

Time For Bed, Everybody!

Gather a collection of small, stuffed toys to use with this bedtime counting activity. Make a set of ten beds by covering ten shoeboxes with paper. Cut ten miniature headboards from construction paper; then label each one with a different numeral from one to ten. Mount a headboard to each shoebox bed. To use, encourage a child to identify the number on a bed's headboard, and to put the corresponding number of toys into the bed. Good night. Sleep tight!

The Stuffed-Toy Connection

Read aloud your choice of these additional sleepy-time titles all about bedtime friends.

Ten Out Of Bed
Written & Illustrated by Penny Dale
Published by Candlewick Press

Good Night!
Written by Claire Masurel
Illustrated by Marie H. Henry
Published by Chronicle Books

Bedtime, Everybody!
Written & Illustrated by Mordicai Gerstein
Published by Hyperion Books For Children

Time For Bed

Tuck your little ones in with the dreamy bedtime unit on pages 20–25.

Cover of *Ten, Nine, Eight* by Molly Bang. ©1983 by Molly Garrett Bang. By permission of Greenwillow Books, a division of William Morrow & Company, Inc.

99

It Looked Like Spilt Milk

Written & Illustrated by Charles G. Shaw
Published by HarperCollins Children's Books

Sometimes it looked like Spilt Milk, a Rabbit, a Birthday Cake—even a Cloud. But it was really just a series of simple and timeless illustrations by Charles G. Shaw. The repetitive language and intriguing shapes of this book are sure to draw youngsters in and leave them floating on clouds of imagination. *It Looked Like Spilt Milk* is available in hardcover, paperback, board book, and big-book versions by calling the publisher at 1-800-331-3761.

ideas by Barbara Meyers

Keep Your Head In The Clouds

Before reading the book aloud, go the extra mile to create a classroom environment that is sure to keep youngsters' heads in the clouds. To transform your reading center into Cloud Central, drape a white sheet over a beanbag; then tuck and tie the ends of the sheet under the beanbag. To make a supply of stuffed clouds for your ceiling, cut pairs of large, unusually shaped clouds from white bulletin-board paper. (If desired, enlarge and cut out the shapes from the book.) Staple the edges of each pair almost completely, stuff each pair with plastic bags, and staple the openings shut. Punch a hole in each cloud; then hang it from the ceiling using clear fishing line.

Cloud Clues

Invite youngsters to float over to your group area. Encourage them to guess what your storytime selection is about by giving them the clue that it is white. Encourage your youngsters to name things that are white as you list them. For a second clue, tell children that the subject of your story is fluffy. As you read through the previously brainstormed list, circle items that could be fluffy as well as white. For a final clue, tell students that the story's subject can be found in the sky. When your little ones have concluded that the book you will read is about a cloud, share *It Looked Like Spilt Milk.* Conclude your storytime by naming other items that could have been illustrated in the book.

It Looked Like Spilt Milk

by Charles G. Shaw

Classy Cloud Big Book

Follow up your group discussion by making this classy cloud big book. Provide each child with a large sheet of blue construction paper and a round sponge. Direct her to dip the sponge in a tray of white tempera paint, then press it onto her paper to create a design. Write as she completes these sentences: "Sometimes it looked like a [Name of object]. But it wasn't a [Name of object]." Prepare a cover for your book along with a final page that reads "It was just a Cloud in the Sky." Then bind the cover, students' pages, and last page together, and share the book with your group. Youngsters will be puffed up with pride!

Changing Shapes

This action song is sure to keep your little cloud watchers on the move.

(sung to the tune of "Twinkle, Twinkle, Little Star")

Floating clouds up in the sky,
Changing shapes as you pass by.

Point up.
Make motions with arms and hands.

Floating by without a sound.
Won't you come and touch the ground?

Move arms and hands slowly in air.
Gently touch the ground.

Floating clouds up in the sky,
Changing shapes as you pass by.

Point up.
Make motions with arms and hands.

Here A Cloud, There A Cloud

Inflated white balloons are just what you'll need for this cloud-chasing activity. Invite several children to an open area. Tell each child to pretend he is the wind; then give him an inflated white balloon to represent a cloud. Challenge him to use his hands to keep the cloud in the sky and on the move. To add the joy of a musical experience, play gentle instrumental music (such as a waltz) in the background. Youngsters will feel sky-high while participating in these cloud capers.

Whipped-Creamy Clouds

Following these simple recipe directions will provide your little ones with a delicious cloudlike treat. Provide each child with a piece of waxed paper and a spoon. To make a treat, a child scoops a large spoonful of nondairy whipped topping onto her waxed paper. She then uses her spoon to create a cloud shape. Freeze each child's cloud; then serve them.

Cloudy Cleaners

Every cloud—and cloud-related activity—has a silver lining. The benefit of this idea is that after plenty of hands-on fun, your tables will be clean and your room filled with the breezy scent of spring. To conclude your celebration of clouds, squirt a generous amount of shaving cream on each of your classroom tables. Encourage your little ones to fingerpaint with the foamy clouds. As an added perk, cloud cleanup is just a wipe away!

Cloud One, Cloud Two, ...Cloud Nine!

Recycle old bed pillows by sprinkling them with a little imagination and sky dust so that when they're randomly arranged on the floor, they'll become clouds. Encourage your little ones to be planes or birds as they fly around the cloud formation. Remind them not to step on any clouds—they wouldn't want to make it rain!

Get Carried Away!

Get carried away by reading aloud these cloud-related books.

Little Cloud
Written & Illustrated by Eric Carle
Published by Philomel Books

Dreams
Written & Illustrated by Peter Spier
(This book is not in print. Check your library.)

In The Tall, Tall Grass

Written & Illustrated by Denise Fleming
Published by Henry Holt and Company, Inc.

Ahhh…a warm, sunny afternoon. Just the perfect time to take a crunchy-munchy trip through the grass with a fuzzy caterpillar. Your little ones are sure to warm up to this award-winning nature tale with its rambunctious rhyme and bright, bold illustrations. A hardcover, paperback, or big-book version of *In The Tall, Tall Grass* can be ordered by calling the publisher at 1-800-321-9299.

ideas contributed by Lisa Leonardi

Sway, Swing, Children Sing

Need some rhythm and rhyme? It must be read-aloud time! Share *In The Tall, Tall Grass* with your young nature lovers. Then sing the following modification of the author's words (below) to the tune of "The Wheels On The Bus." As youngsters sing each verse, encourage them to swing and sway, hip and hop, and slip and slide. Your little ones will have a wild time as their imaginations take them into the tall, tall grass.

The caterpillars at lunch go crunch and munch,
Crunch and munch,
Crunch and munch.
The caterpillars at lunch go crunch and munch,
In the tall, tall grass.

The hummingbirds that sip go dart and dip…
The bees that hum go strum and drum…
The wings of the bird go crack and snap…
The ants that lug go pull and tug…
The snakes that glide go slip and slide…
The moles that scratch go ritch and ratch…
The beetles that hurry go skitter and scurry…
The tongues of the frogs go zip and zap…
The floppy-eared bunnies go hip and hop…
The fireflies that glow go stop and go…
The bats that swoop go lunge and loop…

A-Hunting We Will Go

Fill an empty sensory table with plastic grass. Tuck plastic critters such as bugs, frogs, and snakes, along with decorative birds, into the grass. Provide children who visit the area with hand magnifiers and encourage them to embark on a quest for things that creep and crawl in the grass. Ask the children to draw their findings. Label the pictures; then display them near the center.

Crunch, Munch, Cookies For Lunch

If all that hunting leaves youngsters hungry, make them happy with these caterpillar cookies. Obtain a 22.3-ounce box of Duncan Hines® sugar-cookie mix. To prepare the dough, add yellow food coloring to the liquid ingredient; then follow the directions provided on the package for making drop cookies. Using a permanent marker, personalize a section of aluminum foil for each child. To make his caterpillar cookie, a child rolls four small balls of dough, then arranges the balls on his foil so that they touch. He then presses two miniature chocolate chips in the ball on one end to resemble eyes. Place the child's foil on a baking pan and bake as directed. Allow the cookies to cool until they are crisp. (This recipe makes about 15 cookies.) Invite each child to find his caterpillar. Just listen to your happy bunch crunch!

Barry Slate

Calls From The Wild

Since it's a well-known fact that kids love to make noise, have your students liven up your classroom with some nature soundalikes! Using the following suggestions, assign a noisemaker or commercial rhythm instrument to represent each of the 12 busy animals in the story. Then give an instrument to each child in your group. As you read each page aloud, request that a child play his instrument upon a cue (such as a wink or nod). Conclude your story with the cumulative sounds of the critters. If desired, repeat the activity, this time audiotaping the fun. Place the tape in a listening or music center along with the book and one of each different type of instrument. Hark! It's the call of the wild!

creatures	sound suggestions
caterpillars	crinkle waxed paper, rub ribbed rhythm sticks together
hummingbirds	tap a spoon on a jar, tap a triangle
bees	strum a toy guitar, strum an Autoharp®
bird	clap hands, tap rhythm sticks
ants	rub hands together, scratch a guiro tone block
snakes	shake a tub of dried beans, shake a maraca
moles	rub sandpaper together, rub sand blocks together
beetles	jingle a set of keys, shake a tambourine
toads	tap two blocks, shake a handled castanet
bunnies	tap a box, tap a drum
fireflies	ring jingle bells
bats	blow a party-favor noisemaker, slide a mallet on a set of step bells

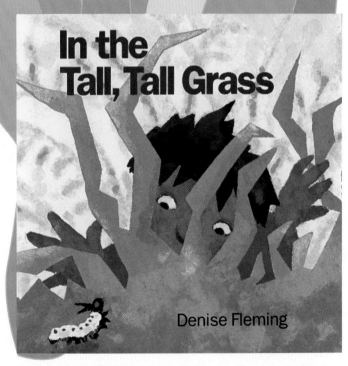

Cover of *In The Tall, Tall Grass* by Denise Fleming. ©1991 by Denise Fleming. By permission of Henry Holt and Company, Inc.

A Change Of Scenery

Suppose the author chose to title her story *In The Deep, Deep Ocean?* What animals would she have included in her book? Pose this question to your little ones, making a list of ocean animals as your children name them. Then ask your students to help you make a list of animals that might be included in a book titled *In The Wild, Wild Jungle.* If desired continue the activity by listing animals that might live in a pond, a forest, or a desert. Provide youngsters with old issues of nature magazines. Ask each child to find and cut out several animals. As a group, sort the animals by possible habitat. Write the name of each habitat you have chosen on a different sheet of construction paper. Then ask youngsters to glue the pictures onto the appropriate sheets of paper. Follow up your discussion of animal habitats by reading aloud these additional titles by Denise Fleming (published by Henry Holt and Company, Inc.): *In The Small, Small Pond; Where Once There Was A Wood;* and *Barnyard Banter.*

Jump, Frog, Jump!

Written by Robert Kalan
Illustrated by Byron Barton
Published by Scholastic Inc.

Here's a book that will lead to "un-frog-gettable" movement, counting, and language fun! Ready to dive into reading? The paperback and big book with teaching guide and audiocassette are available from Scholastic Inc.: 1-800-724-6527. Hop to it!

"Read-it! Read-it!"

Read aloud the title of the book, and show youngsters the front and back covers. Ask the group to name the characters that they think will be in the story. Flip through the pages of the book, encouraging youngsters to find the characters and make suggestions about the story's plot. Then return to the beginning of the book and read the story aloud. If sharing the book inspires some jumping, get moving with the following activities.

Jump, Frogs!

You'll leap for joy as your students learn to recognize colors, letters, or numerals with this indoor game. To prepare, cut out a classroom supply of green poster-board lily pads that are large enough for youngsters to sit on. Label each lily pad with a numeral, a letter, or a colorful splash of paint; then laminate the pads, if desired. To play, randomly place the lily pads on the floor of an open area. Direct youngsters to hop around the pads as you play a lively instrumental selection. Stop the music and say, "Jump, frogs, jump!" On this cue, the children jump onto a pad and sit down. Next direct the children seated on specifically labeled pads to jump up. For example, you might say, "If you are seated on the color red [letter *F*, number 3]—jump, frog, jump!" Play the music and encourage the jumping to begin again!

Kristen Sharpe—Preschool, Kristen's Corner
Mansfield, MA

"Hoopity-Hoppity"

Youngsters can "take the plunge" with this simple outdoor movement suggestion. For fun, prepare several sets of construction-paper characters that resemble the frog's animal predators—the fish, the snake, and the turtle. Arrange several plastic hoops about a foot apart around a playing area; then place the creatures on the ground near the hoops. Encourage the children to pretend to be frogs and hop from one lily-pad hoop to another without falling in the "water." Increase the distance between hoops according to youngsters' abilities. How did the frog get away? Jump, frog, jump!

Hands-On "Hoppiness"

You'll be oh so "hoppy" when you observe youngsters extending the fun of the story using manipulatives. Obtain frog, fly, fish, snake, and turtle counting objects from science and discount stores. (Or call Concepts To Go, Early Childhood Activities at 1-800-660-8646 for ordering information or a catalog.) To encourage creative use of the manipulatives, cut a large felt pond and lily-pad shapes. Ask youngsters to use the objects to retell the sequence of the story. Or lead them in creating new stories that develop counting, sorting, and patterning skills. With manipulatives, youngsters will have a pool of possibilities!

Barbara Meyers
Fort Worth Country Day, Fort Worth, TX

Froggie Went A-Reading

If your little ones enjoy *Jump, Frog, Jump!,* they'll flip over these additional books about frogs that hop, dance, leap, tiptoe, twirl, and even fly!

Hop Jump
Written & Illustrated by Ellen Stoll Walsh
Published by Harcourt Brace & Company

April Showers
Written by George Shannon
Illustrated by Jose Aruego & Ariane Dewey
Published by Greenwillow Books

Tuesday
Written & Illustrated by David Wiesner
Published by Clarion Books

Write, Frog, Write!

After you've had an opportunity to share the previously suggested books with your little ones, pull out a pad (paper, not lily) and enlist the help of your children in creating a class book. Ask youngsters to list different ways that they can move, such as twirl, spin, march, crawl, stomp, and more. Then provide each child with a large sheet of construction paper. Direct him to draw a frog in the movement of his choice. Write on his page as he dictates a completion to the phrase, "[Movement], frog, [movement]!" Bind the pages between titled covers; then share the book during a class storytime. To extend the fun, pause after each page to allow the children to move in the corresponding manner.

Frogs On A Log

Make a splash with this three-dimensional display that your young artists can help you create. Use green and blue bulletin-board paper to create a background that resembles a pond. Crumple a large length of brown bulletin-board paper. Spread the paper flat; then roll it loosely to resemble a log. Mount the log onto the background, along with large, student-painted frogs. If desired, include the animal cutouts prepared for " 'Hoopity-Hoppity' " on your display.

Barbara Meyers
Fort Worth Country Day
Fort Worth, TX

March, frog, march!

We read
Jump, Frog, Jump!
Let's leap to the library
to find more
"un-frog-gettable"
books!

Parents Take The Plunge

Have you been "pond-ering" how to encourage families to read together? These student-made magnets will remind parents to leap to the library. To make one frog magnet, paint a small plastic lid (as from a sour-cream container) and two baby-food-jar lids green. When the paint is dry, hot-glue the jar lids near the edge of the plastic lid to resemble a frog's head and eyes. Paint black dots in the centers of the jar lids, and a red smile on the plastic lid. To the rim of the plastic lid, glue a strip of magnetic tape. Near the bottom of the frog's face, glue a tagboard card with a motivating message similar to the one shown. Go ahead, parents—take the plunge!

Alma Kay Borgen—Preschool
Amherst Own Child Care
Amherst, WI

MOUSE PAINT

Written & Illustrated by Ellen Stoll Walsh
Published by Harcourt Brace & Company

As this cat-and-mouse tale unfolds, a trio of rambunctious rodents splashes and dances its way through red, yellow, and blue paint. Read aloud *Mouse Paint;* then follow up the story with these color-mixing lessons that are full of whiskers and whimsy. *Mouse Paint* is available in hardback, paperback, as a board book, and as a big book from Harcourt Brace & Company: 1-800-543-1918.

ideas by Lisa Leonardi

Mouse Hide-And-Seek

To prepare for a scampering round of mouse hide-and-seek, cut a classroom supply of mouse shapes from white construction paper (pattern on page 108). Using tape or Sticky-Tac, hide the cutouts against the white back-grounds of your room—such as white walls or bulletin boards. Ask each of your little ones to pretend he is the cat in the story and encourage him to prowl around your room in search of a mouse. When he finds one, have him re-move the adhesive and write his name on one side with crayon. Later invite each child to visit your art center to give his mouse a dip (see "Taking A Dip").

Taking A Dip

If your little ones are still pretending to be cats, have them lie down to take a nap like the cat in the book. Remind them that in the story, when the cat went to sleep, the mice climbed into the mouse paint. In an art center, fill each of three jars with watered-down red, yellow, or blue paint. Then, as the group rests, invite one child at a time to tiptoe over to your art center with his mouse cutout. Encourage him to dip his mouse in the jar of his choice, then pat it dry with a paper towel. Next encourage the child to dip the mouse into one of the two remaining colors. Repeat the drying process. When each child has had an opportunity to take his mouse for a dip, awaken the group from their catnap and gather them to-gether. Discuss the results of each mouse's mischief.

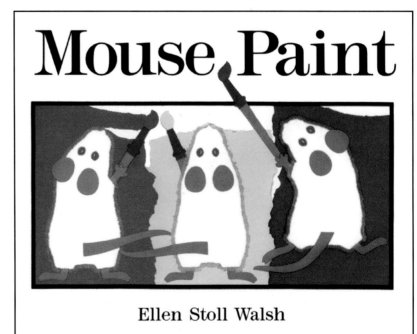

Mouse Paint

Ellen Stoll Walsh

The Pitter-Patter Of Painted Feet

Your youngsters are guaranteed to jump feetfirst into this activity that encourages them to pretend to be mice instead of cats. To prepare for this slightly messy mouse activity, spread a protective covering over the floor near your painting area. Fill a tub with warm, soapy water and set some old towels nearby. Fill three different paint pots with red, yellow, and blue paint. Fill three different pie pans with the same colors. Select some lively music to back up the fun.

As a group, discuss the pages that show each paint-covered mouse dancing in a puddle. Ask each child to remove her shoes and socks, roll up her pants, and pretend to be a mouse. Direct her to use a brush to paint a red, yellow, or blue puddle on a large piece of paper. Next have her step in the pie pan containing one of the two remaining colors. As music plays, have her dance with painted feet on her paper, swirling the colors together to create a secondary color. When she is finished, have her wash and dry her feet. Now that's a masterpiece that's quite a "feet!"

Sugar And Spice And Everything Mice!

These colorful treats are a "mouse-ful!" Bake or purchase a classroom quantity of sugar cookies. Give each child a cookie on a sheet of waxed paper. Drop a spoonful of white icing onto his sheet. Have him decide which secondary color he would like his mouse to be. If he's not sure which two colors of food coloring to add to his icing, let him check the pages of *Mouse Paint*. Once he has added several drops of each color to his icing, have him blend the colors with a craft stick, then spread the icing on his cookie. Finally have him add raisin eyes and a nose, pretzel-stick whiskers, and gumdrop ears. Your little "mouseketeers" won't be able to resist these tasty mouse morsels!

A Collection Of Colors

Culminate your activities as the mice did at the end of the story—by painting a mural. Enlarge the mouse pattern on page 108 onto the bottom corner of a length of white bulletin-board paper. Visually divide the paper into thirds. Using the appropriate colors of markers, label each third *red + yellow = orange, blue + yellow = green,* or *red + blue = purple.* Provide your little ones with red, yellow, and blue paint and paintbrushes. Encourage them to paint the mural, using the primary colors of paint to create secondary colors. Be sure to leave the mouse white...just in case the cat comes back!

Mouse Parents

Encourage parents to join in the "color-ific" fun! Duplicate a copy of the parent note on page 108 for each child. Encourage youngsters to color the mice on the notes before sending them home.

Mouse Pattern

Use with "Mouse Hide-And-Seek" and "Taking A Dip" on page 106 and "A Collection Of Colors" on page 107.

Parent Note

Use with "Mouse Parents" on page 107.

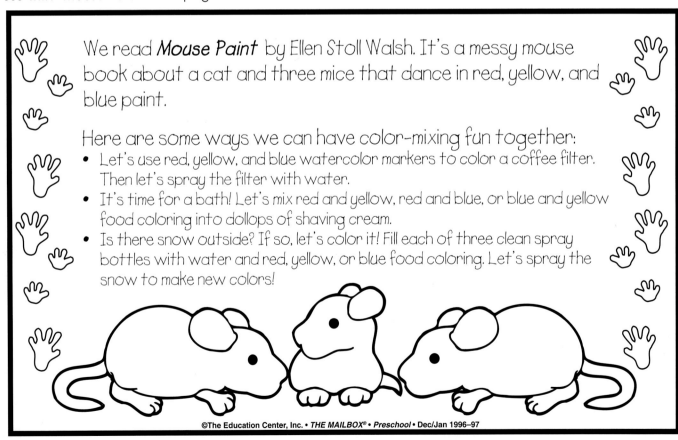

We read **Mouse Paint** by Ellen Stoll Walsh. It's a messy mouse book about a cat and three mice that dance in red, yellow, and blue paint.

Here are some ways we can have color-mixing fun together:
- Let's use red, yellow, and blue watercolor markers to color a coffee filter. Then let's spray the filter with water.
- It's time for a bath! Let's mix red and yellow, red and blue, or blue and yellow food coloring into dollops of shaving cream.
- Is there snow outside? If so, let's color it! Fill each of three clean spray bottles with water and red, yellow, or blue food coloring. Let's spray the snow to make new colors!

ONCE UPON A STORY...

Once Upon A Story...

Here are my eyes...

Here is my mouth for _singing_.

...my hands for _clapping_.

Here Are My Hands

"Here are my hands for catching and throwing."
Here is a book for reading and showing. Read aloud
Here Are My Hands by Bill Martin, Jr., and John
Archambault (Henry Holt and Company). On each of
five sequential days, read the book again. Each day follow the reading by brainstorming how we use one of
the body parts listed below. Program a page to read
"Here are(is) my [body parts] for_____." Duplicate
the page for each child. Ask the child to complete the
page's sentence for you to write. Each day provide her
with the art materials to decorate the page as suggested.
When each child has completed a page for each of the
body parts listed below, bind her pages together
between covers to create her own "Here Are My
Hands" book.

Hands—Have each child dip her hands in paint and press prints on
    the page.
Eyes—Provide each child with the outline drawing of two eyes.
    Have her glue the eyes to the page, then decorate them with
    colored glue and glitter.
Ears—Provide each child with ear shapes to glue on the paper.
    Have her paint them with a cotton swab.
Nose—Provide each child with a nose shape to glue to the page.
    Have her spread glue on the page, then sprinkle spices over the
    glue.
Mouth—Provide each child with a mouth shape to glue on the
    paper. Have her glue white beans on the mouth to resemble
    teeth.

Tanya Rowburrey—Three-, Four-, And Five-Year-Olds
The Learning Place
Milton, FL

We're Going On A Bear Hunt

What's more fun than a bear hunt? Especially when the events are retold by Michael
Rosen and illustrated by Helen Oxenbury
(Simon & Schuster Children's Books). With
this clever craft idea, even your little ones
will be able to retell the events of this popular
adventure. To make a story bear, each child
will need a large, construction-paper bear
shape. Have him fringe a small strip of green
paper, then glue it near the top of the bear to
represent grass; then have him glue a small
piece of blue streamer on the bear to represent
the river. Next direct the child to paint brown
paint to represent the mud, glue on several
small paper tree shapes to represent the forest,
and glue on small pieces of a white doily to
represent the snowstorm. At the bottom of the
bear shape, have him glue on a pom-pom
bear. (To make a pom-pom bear, glue two
brown pom-poms together; then add wiggle
eyes, paper ears, and a paper nose.) If you
have a miniature paw-print stamp, have each
child stamp it on the bear as a finishing touch.
We're going on a bear hunt. What's that? A
BEAR!

Bonnie L. Wyke—Developmentally Delayed
  Three-Year-Olds
Charles W. Bush School
Wilmington, DE

We're going on a bear hunt!

Papa Bear | Mama Bear | Baby Bear

Large | Medium | Small

The Three Bears

Some stories are too long for preschoolers and some stories are too short. But this story—and these versions of the story—are just right! Read aloud *The Three Bears* as retold and illustrated by Byron Barton (HarperCollins Children's Books) or Paul Galdone (Houghton Mifflin Company). Follow up the story with this sorting and seriation activity. For each child, fold a 12" x 18" sheet of construction paper in thirds lengthwise. Label the tops of the sections with "Papa Bear," "Mama Bear," and "Baby Bear," respectively; and the bottoms of the sections "large," "medium," and "small" as shown. Duplicate a classroom supply of the patterns on pages 123 and 124. Provide each child with a set of patterns to color; then assist him in cutting out the pieces along the bold lines. (Depending on the level of the children, it may be necessary to stop at this point and complete the project at a later time.) Have each child glue his colored bear patterns onto the appropriate sections. Then assist him in sorting then gluing the bowls, the chairs, and finally the beds onto the paper. Encourage youngsters to use their completed projects to retell this classic story.

Margo Griffin—Pre-K
Williams School-North
Chelsea, MA

Apple Juice Tea

Celebrate National Grandparents Day in September with this literature-based party idea. Read aloud *Apple Juice Tea* by Martha Weston (Clarion Books). Ask the children to talk about things that they like to do with their grandparents or older friends. Invite the children's parents and grandparents (or older friends) to visit the classroom for an informal "Apple Juice Tea." On the day of the tea, read the story aloud to the gathered children and their guests. Then assist the children in serving the apple juice. If desired have the children also help you prepare muffins or cookies in advance to serve on the day of the tea. It's sure to be a day children, parents, and grandparents will remember!

Bonnie McKenzie—Pre-K and Gr. K
Cheshire Country Day School
Cheshire, CT

See the corresponding book notes on page 122.

Once Upon A Story...

Owen

Now that it's time for Owen to start school, his parents and Mrs. Tweezers believe that he should give up his blanket, Fuzzy. Owen, however, outwits every attempt to retire Fuzzy. In the end, some snipping and sewing save the day. Prior to reading aloud *Owen* by Kevin Henkes (Greenwillow Books), show your children a large piece of yellow felt. Explain that it is your warm-and-fuzzy blanket; then find out what special items your youngsters have that they love and keep with them for comfort. Share the story, providing time afterward for youngsters to share their reactions. Then cut your felt blanket into as many equal sections as you have children. Give one section to each child to keep with him just in case something warm and fuzzy is needed. If desired, use the miniature blankets for movement activities later in the day. Or have children practice their cutting skills by cutting fabric remnants into smaller sections and sharing the pieces with their classmates.

Rhonda Heide
Northmore Elementary School
West Palm Beach, FL

I Want To Be An Astronaut

10–9–8...blast off! Invite your little ones to join the crew of Byron Barton's *I Want To Be An Astronaut* (HarperCollins Children's Books) when they "fly" in a class-made space shuttle. Read the story aloud; then discuss the astronauts' journey. To prepare a class spaceship, cut circular windows and an entry hatch from a large appliance box. Ask youngsters to assist you in painting the box black. When the paint is dry, have them help you mount strips of aluminum foil onto the box. Spray-paint two soda cans silver. Join the cans with a metal spiral removed from a spiral-bound notebook; then hot-glue them to the top of the box. Your ship is now complete. Crew, prepare for liftoff!

Penny Horne—Preschool
University of Maine A. C. A. P. Daycare
Presque Isle, ME

See the corresponding book notes on page 125.

Red Riding Hood's Trail Mix

There's A Nightmare In My Closet

Afraid of the dark? Read *There's A Nightmare In My Closet* by Mercer Mayer (Puffin Books). Certainly many of your children will empathize with the young boy and his fear of what might lurk in the dark of his room. Provide youngsters with an opportunity to share what they are afraid of at night. Discuss the boy's solution to his problem; then help youngsters brainstorm other positive ways to cope with their fears.

Follow up your discussion with this story-extension activity. For each child, tape a light-colored sheet and a black sheet of construction paper together vertically along the left side. Attach a paper brad to the light-colored sheet to resemble a doorknob on a closet door. Personalize each child's door as shown. Encourage each child to use white or colored chalk to draw an imaginary, nighttime monster on his black sheet of paper. If the child desires to describe his fear, write his description on the inside of the closet door.

Betsy Broome—Three- And Four-Year-Olds
Christ Lutheran Preschool
Hilton Head Island, SC

Red Riding Hood

My, what humorous pictures this book has! The better for preschoolers to look at, my dear. *My, what readable text this book has!* The better for preschoolers to listen to, my dear. Share *Red Riding Hood* as retold and illustrated by James Marshall (Dial Books For Young Readers). Then provide youngsters with props—such as a red hooded cape or jacket, a picnic basket, artificial flowers, and Granny's cap (a shower cap)—to use for acting out the story.

If your little actors get hungry, have them step out of the enchanted forest and over to your cooking center to prepare individual picnic baskets of Red Riding Hood's trail mix. For each child, photocopy the picnic-basket pattern (on page 126) onto tan construction paper. Cut on the bold lines; then fold on the dotted line. Glue together the sides of the basket only. Personalize each child's basket. To make trail mix, have each child mix 1/3 cup of toasted oat cereal, one spoonful of chocolate chips, and one spoonful of raisins together in a plastic sandwich bag. Fold and twist the bag closed; then insert the bag into the child's paper basket. Into the woods we go!

Cathy Mansfield—Preschool
Playstation
Trucksville, PA

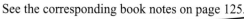

See the corresponding book notes on page 125.

Once Upon A Story...

Chicken Soup With Rice

Read it once. Read it twice. Read it with chicken soup and rice! Serve small bowls of chicken soup with rice to accompany Maurice Sendak's story in verse that features the months of the year and some pretty unusual uses for chicken soup (Scholastic Inc.). As a follow-up, create rice collages. Prepare the rice in advance by soaking it in bowls of water and food coloring for about five minutes. Drain the rice and let it dry overnight. Provide each child with a construction-paper circle to represent a bowl of soup. Encourage each child to squirt or spread glue on his circle as desired, then cover it with colored rice. Any month of the year, art with rice is mighty nice!

Catherine V. Herber—Pre-K
Highland Preschool
Raleigh, NC

The Jacket I Wear In The Snow

The Jacket I Wear In The Snow by Shirley Neitzel (Scholastic Inc.) is the book to read when it's time to wear jackets in the snow. Gather the winter clothing articles named in the book—a jacket, a scarf, a stocking cap, a pair of mittens, a sweater, a pair of jeans, a pair of boots, long underwear, and a pair of socks. Introduce the items as you read the story aloud. Read the story again, asking a different volunteer to put on each item as it is mentioned. Take a group picture. (If you have more than nine children in your class, repeat this step until each child is included in a group photo.) Tape the picture(s) to the inside cover of the book; then place the book in your reading area along with the clothing items.

Chris Foedisch—Four-Year-Olds
Indian Valley Nursery School
Souderton, PA

See the corresponding book notes on page 127.

Snowballs

Celebrate the season of snowballs and snowfolk by sharing *Snowballs* by Lois Ehlert (Harcourt Brace & Company). Use several consecutive days to make wooden snowfolk for youngsters to display in their own yards. Ask a parent volunteer to cut and provide a classroom supply of 3/4-inch boards that are 3 feet long and are cut to a point at one end, as well as smaller lengths of wood that measure 16" x 2 1/2". Have each child use sandpaper to smooth her boards. Assist her in nailing the small wood strip to the large board about one-fourth of the distance from the top. Have her use small paint rollers to paint the lower part of the board white, and the small strip and top of the board black. When the paint is dry, have her paint eyes and a nose, then hot-glue buttons for the mouth. Tie a fabric scrap around the snowperson for a scarf; then nail it in place. Paint the child's name and the date on the back.

Lisa LaLonde—Three-
    And Four-Year-Olds
St. Mary's School For
    The Deaf
Buffalo, NY

The Three Little Pigs

A dab of straw, a handful of sticks, and a brick will set the tone for a reading aloud of your favorite version of *The Three Little Pigs*. After reading the story, ask youngsters to help you decide which parts of the story are real and which are make-believe. Then prepare for some make-believe of your own by making these storytelling headbands. To make headbands for each of the three pigs and the wolf, duplicate the pig pattern on page 128 onto pink construction paper three times and the wolf pattern on page 129 onto gray paper. Number each of the pigs *1, 2,* or *3.* Cut out the patterns; then attach each one to the center of a sentence strip. Tape the ends of each sentence strip together to make storytelling headbands. For loads of "chinny-chin-chin" fun, have students put on the headbands and take turns dramatizing the story.

See the corresponding book notes on page 127.

Once Upon A Story...

Clifford The Big Red Dog

Introduce your little ones to Emily Elizabeth and Clifford with this first-in-the-series title by Norman Bridwell (Scholastic Inc.). Since your children are likely to fall head over heels in love with Clifford, read any of the more than 30 additional Clifford titles that you can get your paws on. Then designate a day as Clifford Day. Ask youngsters to wear red on the special day. Provide each child with a headband made by stapling two red dog-ear shapes to opposite sides of a red construction-paper strip. Use face paint to give each child a black nose. On Clifford Day, read stories about Clifford and watch Clifford videos. Top off your day with Clifford cupcakes. To make one, spread red frosting on a cupcake; then top with chocolate-covered raisins for eyes and a Junior® Mint for a nose.

Sharon Newman—Pre-K
St. Matthew's Episcopal Child Care Center
Warson Woods, MO

CLIFFORD® and CLIFFORD® THE BIG RED DOG® are registered trademarks of Norman Bridwell.

Piggies

Celebrate National Pig Day in March by reading aloud Don and Audrey Wood's humorously illustrated pig tale (Harcourt Brace & Company). For more pig fun, make these mighty fine swine. To make ten little piggies, have a child remove his socks and shoes. Recite the "This Little Piggy Went To Market" rhyme as you paint the bottom of his toes with washable pink liquid paint. Have the child step onto a piece of paper, then into a tub of warm, soapy water. When the paint—and the child's feet—are dry, encourage him to use a marker to add pig features to each of his ten pink toe prints. This little piggy went to preschool and said, "Yeah, yeah, yeah," all the way home!

Sue Lein—Four-Year-Olds
St. Pius X
Wauwatosa, WI

See the corresponding book notes on page 130.

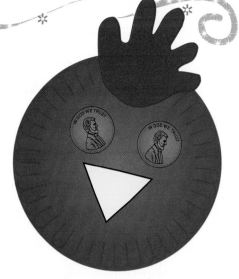

A Color Of His Own

Read aloud this charming story of friendship by Leo Lionni (Alfred A. Knopf Books For Young Readers); then encourage every child to paint a chameleon with a color she creates on her own. Duplicate a classroom supply of the chameleon pattern (on page 131) onto white art paper. For each child, squirt a dollop of shaving cream on her chameleon. Ask her to choose two primary colors of food coloring; then squeeze a small amount of both colors onto the shaving cream. Encourage her to spread the shaving cream over the paper so that the chameleon and its background become the new secondary color. When each child has completed the project, encourage her to find a friend with a matching chameleon.

adapted from an idea by Dana Smith—
    Special Education, Noncategorical Preschool
Donaldsonville Elementary
Donaldsonville, LA

Henny Penny

Goodness gracious me! Go tell the king to find a version of this classic tale of Henny Penny's alarm and Foxy Loxy's charm. Then read the story aloud, encouraging your ducky-lucky listeners to join in. Ask your little ones if they think the sky could really fall. Explain that the *sky* is "air that surrounds the earth." Have the children discuss what could fall from the sky (or clouds in the sky), such as rain and snow.

Follow up a reading aloud or telling of *Henny Penny* by making Henny Penny characters. To make one, have a child paint a six-inch paper plate brown. While the paint is drying, trace the child's hand onto red construction paper and cut out the shape. Have the child glue the hand shape to the top of the plate, a yellow triangle to the center of the plate for a beak, and two pennies to the plate to represent eyes. Watch out for that acorn, Henny!

See the corresponding book notes on page 130.

Once Upon A Story...

Growing Vegetable Soup

When you read aloud *Growing Vegetable Soup* by Lois Ehlert (Harcourt Brace & Company) and name the vegetables pictured, it's almost guaranteed that tummies will be hungry for—what else—vegetable soup! Here's a way to make class soup and a class book to record the experience at the same time. Prior to the day you'll make the soup, gather the vegetables and other ingredients suggested in your favorite vegetable-soup recipe, along with the necessary cooking utensils. Take an instant picture of each child as he slices a vegetable or adds it to your pot or slow cooker. Glue each child's picture to the center of a pot-shaped piece of construction paper. Add this sentence programmed appropriately: "[Child's name] added [vegetable] to the pot." To complete the last page, take a picture of the cooking soup; then glue it to a pot-shaped page along with the phrase, "Vegetable Soup!" Bind the pages together between titled covers. Serve up your soup followed by a hearty reading aloud of your new vegetable-soup book.

Frankie added red peppers to the pot.

Dayle Timmons—Special Education Pre-K
Alimacani Elementary School
Jacksonville, FL

The Very Quiet Cricket

Shh...be very quiet. You'll probably be able to hear chirps of delight with the ending of this special story by Eric Carle (Philomel Books). After reading the story aloud, play this quiet cricket game. Seat youngsters together in a group area. Ask a volunteer to be the cricket; then give him a set of sand blocks or two pieces of sandpaper. To play, the children close their eyes as the cricket hides in the room. At your signal, the group opens their eyes, and the cricket rubs the sand blocks together. Select a second volunteer to locate the cricket by following the sounds. Continue play until each child has been the cricket. Hide-and-go-chirp!

Cathie Pesa—Pre-K
Youngstown City Schools
Youngstown, OH

See the corresponding book notes on page 132.

Are You My Mother?

Here's a "tweet" book to read aloud when taking a break from your preparations for Mother's Day. Share *Are You My Mother?* by P. D. Eastman (Beginner Books). Then follow up the story by making a display using this craft idea. For each child, fold down the opening of a paper lunch bag several times. Have each child take his bag outside to gather leaves, twigs, pine needles, and other natural items that a bird might use to make a nest. Return to the classroom and direct each child to glue his items on the out- and inside of his paper bag to make a nest. Next provide each child with scissors, glue, and a supply of construction-paper scraps and geometric shapes in a variety of colors and sizes. If desired, also provide feathers. Encourage him to use his choice of the materials to make a mother and baby bird. To prepare a three-dimensional display for the projects, mount a construction-paper limb or tree on a bulletin board. Mount each child's nest on the display, arranging his birds in and around his nest. Complete the display with the book's title, if desired.

Donna Austin—Preschool
St. Matthew's Preschool
Lehighton, PA

See the corresponding book notes on page 132.

The Princess And The Pea

What makes a *real* prince or princess charming? Before sharing your favorite version of *The Princess And The Pea*, pose this question to your little ones. Record their thoughts; then extend their ideas by discussing such virtues as kindness, politeness, honesty, gentleness, and others. Tell your little ones to listen to the story to discover the Queen's method for finding out if one is really royalty.

Follow up the fairy tale by giving each of your little ones the opportunity to prove that he or she is also a prince or princess charming. For each child, cut a crown shape from heavy paper. Label each child's crown "Prince Charming" or "Princess Charming" appropriately. Then encourage youngsters to embellish their crowns with a variety of art supplies. Staple each crown to a sentence-strip headband; then collect the completed crowns. As you see a child displaying one of the virtues previously discussed, crown her and announce that she must really be a princess. Soon you'll have a room full of perfectly pleasing princes and princesses!

Once Upon A Story...

The Very Lonely Firefly

Eric Carle's simple story *The Very Lonely Firefly* (Philomel Books) is about one firefly's need—and our own and our preschoolers' needs—to belong to a group. Share this story with your little ones; then help them name groups that they belong to, such as your class, a school, a family, a church, and others. Teach youngsters the song below; then play this game that will give each child in your group a sense of belonging. To play have youngsters stand in a circle with their hands behind their backs. Dim the lights in your room. Ask your little ones to pretend to be fireflies. Give each of two children a flashlight to hold behind their backs. (Provide flashlights that are easily turned off and on.) Have the group sing the song. When the group sings, "See my light flicker," the two children holding flashlights begin to turn them off and on and pair up at the center of the circle. They then give the flashlights to two different children. Continue play until each child has had an opportunity to find a firefly partner.

I'm A Little Firefly

(sung to the tune of "I'm A Little Teapot")

I'm a little firefly;
Look at me!
I'm as happy as I can be.
See my light flicker and shine so bright.
Now watch me fly into the night!

song by Gayle Simoneaux, Ellen Knight, Linda Powell—
    Four-Year-Olds, Pineville Park WEE
Pineville, LA

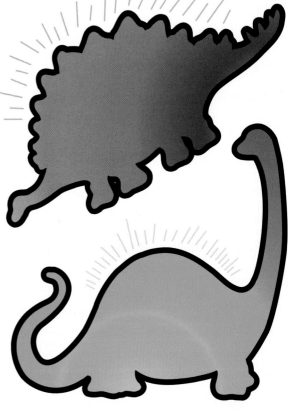

Dazzle The Dinosaur

Read aloud Marcus Pfister's *Dazzle The Dinosaur* (North-South Books); then dazzle your little ones with these dandy dinosaurs. Provide each child with several precut, construction-paper dinosaur shapes and Crayola® glitter crayons. Have him color his shapes; then place them between sheets of paper. To create a dazzling effect, rub a warm iron across the paper. Remove the paper. The melted wax and shimmering glitter make these dinosaurs really dazzling!

adapted from an idea by Cheryl Cicioni—Preschool
Kindernook Preschool
Lancaster, PA

See the corresponding book notes on page 133.

The Teddy Bears' Picnic

Summertime is picnic time, so do as the teddy bears do—prepare a picnic! To get ready for a special storytime, tuck these items into a picnic basket: a tablecloth or blanket, a version of Jimmy Kennedy's *The Teddy Bears' Picnic,* a class supply of several different flavors of purchased teddy bear–shaped snacks, and a class supply of teddy bear–shaped stickers or cutouts. Also in advance, prepare a graph with one column for each different flavor of snack that the group will be tasting.

During a group time, invite youngsters to join you as you spread out the picnic blanket and sit on the floor. Read aloud the story. Then surprise youngsters with the teddy treats. Have each child attach a teddy-bear shape on the graph to indicate his favorite flavor. Finally remind your little ones that at the end of the teddy bears' picnic, the little bears went home to bed. I'm needing a nap, aren't you?

Jennifer Bouse—Preschool
Laurens Community Preschool
Laurens, IA

A promise is a promise!

I promise to share the play dough.

The Frog Prince

A promise is a promise! That's what the frog reminded the princess when she selfishly ran away from her promises to him if he would retrieve her golden ball. Share a version of *The Frog Prince.* Then ask each of your little ones to think of a simple promise that he can make to his other classmates and fulfill at some point later in the day. For example, promising to clean up his snack will mean that everyone has clean tables to use. Or promising to share the swing means that more children can have a turn. Write each child's promise on a separate copy of the frog pattern on page 134. At the end of the day, discuss the promises. Reward each child with a golden ball (an orange) of his own to take home along with the written promise. Parents are sure to be pleased with this valuable lesson—we promise!

121

Book Notes

After reading each of the books mentioned below and on pages 110 and 111, send home copies of the corresponding note.

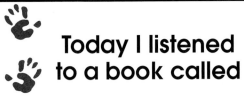

Today I listened to a book called *Here Are My Hands.*

Did you know that hands are for holding and hugging? I'll show you!

Let's play a game! You name a body part and I'll point to or wiggle that part.

©1996 The Education Center, Inc.

Apple Juice Tea by Martha Weston is a story about a girl and her Gran.

Let's have a tea party. Can we invite a grandparent or older friend?

Don't forget: National Grandparents Day is the first Sunday in September.

©1996 The Education Center, Inc.

Want an adventure? Let's go to the library and hunt for *We're Going On A Bear Hunt* by Michael Rosen.

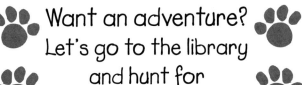

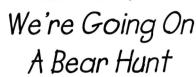

We'll have to go through the grass, through the river, through the mud, through a forest, through a snowstorm, and into a cave. It's a bear! Run!

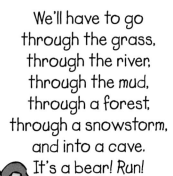

©1996 The Education Center, Inc.

Today I heard the story of *The Three Bears.* Ask me to tell it to you.

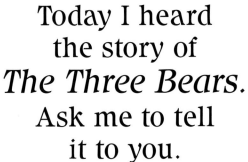

Can you help me find things in our house that are large, medium, and small in size?

©1996 The Education Center, Inc.

---

122   ©The Education Center, Inc. • THE MAILBOX® • Preschool • Aug./Sept. 1996

The Three Bears
Patterns
Use with *The Three Bears*
on page 111.

The Three Bears Patterns

Use with *The Three Bears* on page 111.

©The Education Center, Inc. • *THE MAILBOX* • Preschool • Aug./Sept. 1996

Book Notes

After reading each of the books mentioned below and on pages 112 and 113, send home copies of the corresponding note.

Would you like to hear about a mouse named Owen and his blanket, Fuzzy?

Let's go to the library and check out *Owen* by Kevin Henkes.

©1996 The Education Center, Inc.

Today I heard a story called

I Want To Be An Astronaut
by Byron Barton.

Let's sit outside tonight, look at the stars, and pretend we're astronauts! 10–9–8... Blast off!

©1996 The Education Center, Inc.

There's A Nightmare In My Closet
by Mercer Mayer
is a story with a happy ending.

Are you ever afraid of the dark? Let's think of ways that we can have courage at night.

©1996 The Education Center, Inc.

Ask me to tell you the story of
RED RIDING HOOD.

Then let's make a treat!

Red Riding Hood's Trail Mix
1/3 cup of toasted oat cereal
1 spoonful of chocolate chips
1 spoonful of raisins

©1996 The Education Center, Inc.

Red Riding Hood's Trail Mix

Fold.

name

Book Notes

After reading each of the books mentioned below and on pages 114 and 115, send home copies of the corresponding note.

I learned about the months of the year when we read

Chicken Soup With Rice

by Maurice Sendak.

Let's make soup!
I can help you open the can.
I can help you scoop and pour.
I can help you stir.
I can help you...eat!

Today we helped our teacher read a story with rebus pictures called

The Jacket I Wear In The Snow.

Ask me what I wear in the winter.

Ask me what I wear in the summer.

To celebrate the season of snow, we read

Snowballs

by Lois Ehlert.

Let's flurry to the library to find this and other books about snow.

Ask me to tell you the story of

The Three Little Pigs.

Let's make a snack!

Pigs-In-A-Blanket
Wrap half a hot dog in a portion of refrigerated crescent-roll dough.
Bake and eat. Oink, oink!

Pattern
Use with *The Three Little Pigs* on page 115.

Book Notes

After reading each of the books mentioned below and on pages 116 and 117, send home copies of the corresponding note.

Today we read

Clifford®
The Big Red Dog®
by Norman Bridwell.

Let's make tracks to the library to get our paws on more books about Clifford®.

We went hog-wild today when we read

Piggies
by Don and Audrey Wood!

Want to go to the library to root out some more books about pigs?

 Did you know that chameleons change color?

Ask me about a story called

A Color Of His Own
by Leo Lionni.

Help me find clothes that are all the same color to wear today.

Goodness gracious me!

Henny Penny
says the sky is falling!

I'll tell you the story— just ask!

Let's go outside to look at the sky. What do you see?

©The Education Center, Inc. • *THE MAILBOX®* • *Preschool* • FebMar 1997

Book Notes

After reading each of the books mentioned below and on pages 118 and 119, send home copies of the corresponding note.

Yummy!
Today we read

Growing Vegetable Soup

by Lois Ehlert.

Ask me to name
my favorite vegetables.

How many vegetables
can you name?
Let's count!

©1997 The Education Center, Inc.

Ask me to tell you
the story about

The Very Quiet Cricket

by
Eric Carle.

Close your eyes.
I'll hide, then chirp.
You can come find me!

©1997 The Education Center, Inc.

Are You My Mother?

is a silly story
by P. D. Eastman.

Let's go to the
library to look for
other books
about
moms!

Is Your Mama A Llama?
Deborah Gauarino

The Mother's Day Mice
Eve Bunting

©1997 The Education Center, Inc.

We heard a fairy tale
today called

The Princess And The Pea.

Do you know what makes a
prince or princess charming?

I'll tell you!

A real prince or princess is:
kind, polite,
patient, gentle,
honest ...

©1997 The Education Center, Inc.

Book Notes

After reading each of the books mentioned below and on pages 120 and 121, send home copies of the corresponding note.

Today we heard a story called

The Very Lonely Firefly

by Eric Carle.

Here's a song you can sing with me!

I'm A Little Firefly
(sung to the tune of "I'm A Little Teapot")

I'm a little firefly;
Look at me!
I'm as happy as I can be.
See my light flicker and shine so bright.
Now watch me fly into the night!

©1997 The Education Center, Inc.

Our story today was

DAZZLE THE DINOSAUR

by Marcus Pfister.

Dazzle was special!
I am, too!
Let's talk about how I can use my special abilities to dazzle.

©1997 The Education Center, Inc.

Did you know that the teddy bears have a picnic in the woods?
I know because we read

The Teddy Bears' Picnic

by Jimmy Kennedy.

Let's have a picnic! I can help you decide what to take!

©1997 The Education Center, Inc.

A promise is a promise!

Ask me to tell you about

The Frog Prince

and I will...I promise!

©1997 The Education Center, Inc.

Frog Pattern

Use with *The Frog Prince* on page 121.

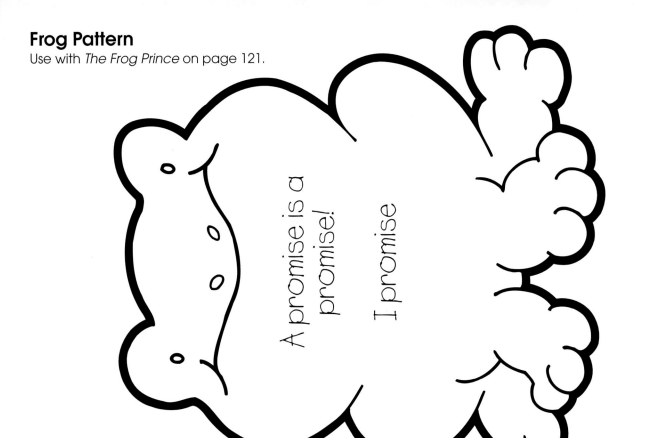

A promise is a promise!

I promise

©The Education Center, Inc. • *THE MAILBOX® • Preschool • June/July 1997*

Calendar Pattern

Use with "Countdown To Kindergarten" on page 92.

Kindergarten Countdown
Color one star each day...Kindergarten's only ten days away!

10 9 8 7

4 5 6

3 2 1 Today's the big day! I'm in grade K!

©The Education Center, Inc. • *THE MAILBOX® • Preschool •* June/July 1997

It's Circle Time!

IT'S CIRCLE TIME!

Circle-Time Song

Invite youngsters to join you in singing this circle-time song to the tune of "This Old Man."

Circle time, circle time—
It's a very special time!
Let's go to the carpet
And we'll have some fun!
Circle time's for everyone!

Janis Woods—Four-Year-Olds, Ridgeland Elementary, Ridgeland, SC

Honey Hunt

For a "beary" special snack and activity that every child is sure to enjoy, have a honey hunt! For each child, prepare a honey pot by gluing yellow construction-paper honey to a paper lunch bag. Label each bag "Honey Pot." Prepare a bear headband for each child by gluing brown, construction-paper semicircles to the top of a stapled sentence strip. As a final preparation, partially fill a zippered plastic bag with Honeycomb® cereal for each child. Hide the bags around the classroom when the children are not present.

Then, during circle time, invite youngsters to put on their bear headbands, pick up their honey pots, and forage for honey! As each child locates a plastic bag of cereal, encourage him to place it in his honey pot and return to the circle area. Then invite your hunters to eat their cereal snacks. Mmmm...I'm as hungry as a bear!

Linda Rice Ludlow—Four-Year-Olds, Bethesda Christian School, Brownsburg, IN

Sign Language

Help young children practice their budding communication and fine-motor skills when you teach them sign language as part of your circle-time routine. (If you're not familiar with sign language, check out a book from your local library.) Begin by teaching the sign-language alphabet. After you've taught the letters, sign the children's names and ask youngsters to identify whose name you are spelling each time. In addition to the alphabet, youngsters will enjoy learning and using the signs for simple words such as yes, no, or drink.

Dawn Moore–Preschool, Mount View Elementary, Thorndike, ME

136

"I'm The Baker!"

Bake up a batch of visual-discrimination skills with this fun group activity. To prepare, trace a class supply of cookie-cutter shapes onto poster board. Cut out the shapes. Decorate one side of each poster-board cookie. During circle time, have each child select a cookie cutter from among those you used to trace the cutouts. Hold up the undecorated sides of the cutouts one at a time, each time asking, "Whose cookie cutter made this cookie?" Invite the child who holds the corresponding cookie cutter to respond, "I'm the baker!" Ask him to then identify the object represented by the outline shape. Turn the cutout around to reveal the poster-board cookie's decorated side. Give the cutout to the child to hold until the end of the game. For a tasty variation, try playing this game with real cookies!

Karen Eiben—Preschool, The Kids' Place, LaSalle, IL

"That's My Name!"

What's in a name? Some circle-time fun! Print each child's name on a colored sentence strip or a strip of bulletin-board paper. Laminate the strips for durability. Begin each morning's routine by holding up the children's name strips one at a time. Encourage each child to greet you when he sees his name card. Then return his greeting. Vary this morning ritual by requesting a seasonal hello, such as "Gobble, gobble!" or "Ho, ho, ho!" Or ask the children to answer a question of the day—such as "What is your favorite color?"—when they see their names. Little ones will pay attention to roll call and quickly learn to recognize their own and their classmates' names.

Cheryl Kizer Ireland—Four- And Five-Year-Olds, St. Edward–Epiphany, Bon Air, VA

Share Bear

A special teddy bear will add a sense of closure to your end-of-the-day circle time. Designate a favorite stuffed teddy as "Share Bear." When you gather students at the end of the day, give each child an opportunity to hold Share Bear and describe a favorite activity of that day. Each youngster will leave your care with a happy memory to then share with Mom or Dad!

Elaine M. Utt—Two-Year-Olds, La Petite Academy, Tampa, FL

IT'S CIRCLE TIME!

Christmas Countdown Calendar

Start a new tradition in your classroom by creating a Christmas countdown calendar. To make the calendar, you'll need a large tree shape cut from green tagboard, a classroom supply of construction-paper ornaments, a paper star for the top of the tree, individual pictures of your students, and one class photo. Use transparent tape to fasten the tops of the ornaments and the star to the tree so that one ornament can be removed on each day of the countdown. Number the ornaments. Under each ornament, attach a child's photo to the tree. Under the star attach the class photo to the tree.

Begin your countdown as many days from Christmas vacation as you have numbered ornaments on your tree. Each day remove the largest-numbered ornament to reveal a child's picture. To honor the pictured child, invite him to pick out the book for storytime or to help with a special task. On the last day before vacation, lift the star to reveal the class photo. Christmas vacation is here!

Diane DiMarco—Three- And Four-Year-Olds
Country Kids Preschool
Groton, MA

Join In The Circle

Make the transition to circle time easier by singing these inviting lyrics. Announce circle time by singing the first verse. Sing the second verse as many times as necessary until the whole group is seated. Ask the children to suggest movements—such as stomping or waving—for the action verses. Sing the final verse with a big smile!

(sung to the tune of "Give Me That Old-Time Religion")

Come and join in the circle.
Come and join in the circle.
Come and join in the circle.
Oh, come and sit with me.

[Child's name] is sitting in the circle.
[Different child's name] is sitting in the circle.
[Different child's name] is sitting in the circle.
They came to sit with me.

[Clap your hands] in the circle.
[Clap your hands] in the circle.
[Clap your hands] in the circle.
Oh, come and [clap] with me.

We're all sitting in the circle.
We're all sitting in the circle.
We're all sitting in the circle.
I'm glad you're here with me.

Marcia Specht—Special Education Pre-K
Dutch Lane Elementary School, Hicksville, NY

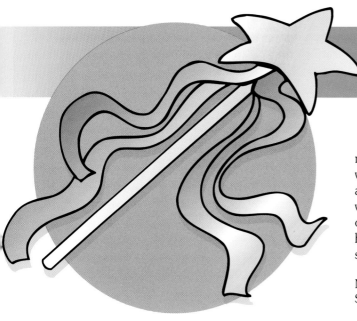

Magical Sharing

Encourage turn-taking during group sharing time by using this magical word wand. To make this simple tool, cover a star cutout with foil. Tape metallic streamers to the bottom of the star; then attach it to a wooden dowel. Explain to your students that the wand gives its holder magical powers to tell a special story while others listen quietly. When a child finishes his story, have him hand the wand to a child whose listening was enchanting. This spectacular idea works magic with manners.

Mary Ledyard—Preschool, Holy Rosary Central School
Steubenville, OH

Zookeeper, Zookeeper

The predictable text of *Brown Bear, Brown Bear* by Bill Martin Jr. (Henry Holt and Company) lends itself well to an innovation with a zoo theme. In advance make a classroom supply of puppets by gluing pictures of a zookeeper and zoo animals to craft sticks. Keeping the zookeeper puppet for yourself, give one puppet to each child seated in a circle. Begin with the verse, "Zookeeper, Zookeeper, what do you see?" On this cue the first child holds up his puppet and names his animal by reciting, "I see a [zebra] looking at me." The whole class then says, "[Zebra, zebra], what do you see?" Continue in this manner until each child has had a turn. When it is the zookeeper's turn again, say, "I see children looking at me. Children, children, what do you see?" Have the group review the name of each animal puppet and end the story with, "That's what we see."

Dana Smith—Noncategorical Preschool
Donaldsonville Elementary
Donaldsonville, LA

End-Of-The-Day Recap

Gather your little ones around you, and have each of them re-call what she did in school today. Start a slap/clap rhythm and encourage your youngsters to join in. Then chant, "Hey, [insert child's name], what do you say? What did you do in school to-day?" As the rhythm continues, the child tells something about her day. Continue in this manner until each child has had an opportu-nity to respond. It's a great way to find out what youngsters con-sider memorable.

IT'S CIRCLE TIME!

Acts Of Kindness

Promote kindness in your classroom with this heartwarming idea. Cut a large heart shape from bulletin-board paper; then attach it to a wall in your room. Duplicate a supply of small heart shapes onto colored paper; then cut them out. During your group time, discuss the word *kindness*. Explain that the class will fill the big heart with the small hearts by doing kind things for one another. As you see a kind act, write it on a small heart shape. Ask the child who did the act of kindness to attach the heart to the big heart.

To spread the kindness message, send home a note describing the activity along with several small heart shapes. Ask parents to catch their little angels doing kind deeds and describe the deeds on the hearts. Be ready for hearts in little hands and smiles on parents when you greet them at your door.

Beth Walker—Four- And Five-Year-Olds
Brevard Community College Childcare Center
Melbourne, FL

Act Of Kindness...
Liza helped Mrs. Cannon at recess.

Act Of Kindness...
Grover David helped his mommy sort the socks.

Act Of Kindness...
Josh helped Karen with the books.

Act Of Kindness...
Payton gave her brother a big hug!

Leaping Leprechauns!

Review March's unpredictable weather while playing this musical circle-time game. In advance, cut five large shamrock shapes from green construction paper. On another sheet of paper, draw a symbol to represent each type of weather (*sunny, rainy, windy, snowy,* and *cloudy*). Cut out and glue a symbol to the middle of each shamrock cutout. To play the game, arrange your children in a circle. Place the shamrock cutouts facedown in the middle of the circle. Direct a volunteer leprechaun to go to the middle of the circle. Sing the following song as the leprechaun performs her own jig. When indicated, pause and instruct the leprechaun to choose a shamrock to show to everyone. Then sing the last line to describe the weather shown on the shamrock. Continue until everyone has had a turn to be the leprechaun.

Leprechaun, Come Out To Play
(sung to the tune of "Jimmy Crack Corn")

Leprechaun, come out to play.
Leprechaun, come out to play.
Leprechaun, come out to play. *Pause. Child picks up shamrock.*
It is a [sunny] day.

Marcia Miller
Merritt Elementary
Mt. Iron, MN

140

Circle Seating

Here's a fun way to assess your little ones' color- and shape-recognition abilities and create a favorable seating arrangement at the same time. In advance, cut geometric shapes from colored construction paper; then laminate them for durability. When it's circle time, arrange the shape cutouts in a circle on the floor. Invite each child to your group area by asking her to find and sit on a specific shape. For example, say, "Courtney, find an orange circle." For a challenging variation, add numerals or letters to the shapes. A transition time full of learning!

Christa Wimberly—Four-Year-Olds
All Saints Preschool
Albuquerque, NM

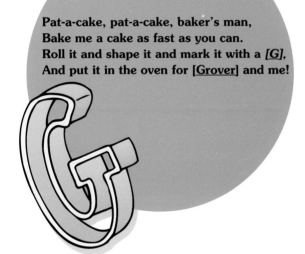

Pat-a-cake, pat-a-cake, baker's man,
Bake me a cake as fast as you can.
Roll it and shape it and mark it with a [G],
And put it in the oven for [Grover] and me!

Bake Me A Name

First names are delicious in this circle-time game. Gather wooden, plastic, magnetic, or cookie-cutter letters. Put the letters in a bag or bowl. Review the traditional rhyme "Pat-A-Cake" with your little ones. Then have one child draw a letter from the bag or bowl. Ask whose name begins with the selected letter. Lead the group in reciting the rhyme again—this time replacing the "B" and "Baby" with the chosen letter and a child's name that begins with that letter. Continue until all of your children's names have been inserted into the rhyme.

Terry Steinke—Preschool
Emmaus Lutheran School
Indianapolis, IN

"Egg-ceptional" Singing

Need a time filler? Just crack open one of these eggs! To prepare, ask your little ones to name their favorite circle-time songs and fingerplays. Write each title on a small piece of paper; then tuck each piece into a plastic egg. Keep the eggs in an Easter basket in your group area. When you need a quick time filler, just ask a child to crack open an egg. Read the title aloud; then sing the song. To ease transitions, this "eggs-cellent" idea just can't be beat!

Jane FitzSimmons-Thomez—Preschool
St. Mary's Preschool
Owatonna, MN

The Bunny Hop Song

IT'S CIRCLE TIME!

Category Catch

All you'll need are a beanbag and some thinking caps to play this fun association game! Seat your children in a circle. Name a category, such as *foods, animals,* or *toys.* Select a child in the group, say his name, and toss him the beanbag. Ask him to name an item from the category; then have him say another child's name and toss the beanbag to that child. When the category has been exhausted, change topics. Play until interest wanes. Here…catch!

Blooming Bingo

Sunshine is sure to fill your room during this blooming bingo game. To prepare, cut six flower petals and six squares from each of six different colors of construction paper. Also cut six strips of green paper to represent stems. Store each set of same-colored petals in a separate resealable plastic bag and store all of the squares in a paper bag.

To play this game with six children, give a stem to each child in the group. Ask each child to choose a set of same-colored petals to use as markers. Pick a square from the bag. Have the children name its color. Instruct the child who has the corresponding color of petals to place one petal on her stem. Each time a child completes a flower—by placing all six petals on her stem—she announces, "Blooming Bingo!" Continue picking squares until each child has completed her flower. Everyone's a winner!

Sheri McGarvey—Pre-K
Garrett's Way
Newtown Square, PA

142

Our
Tall
Tale

by
Mrs. Ger
Class

Once upon a time there was a giant frog.

Cooperative Storytelling

Promote imaginative thinking with a tale that your students help you create. Start the story by saying, "Once upon a time there was a...." Pause and ask a student volunteer to name a character. Continue the story, pausing whenever possible to let the children contribute. As an extension, encourage students to draw illustrations for the story. Write the corresponding text on the pages and bind them together for sharing with families. The imagination is an amazing thing!

1•2•3   4•5•6

How Many?

Get your little ones' blood flowing and hearts pumping by doing exercises that practice counting skills. Ask a student volunteer to call out a number from one to ten. Pick an exercise that's appropriate for the volunteer's number. Perform the exercise as a class, counting each repetition aloud. Then ask another volunteer for a number. A great way to shape the body and the mind!

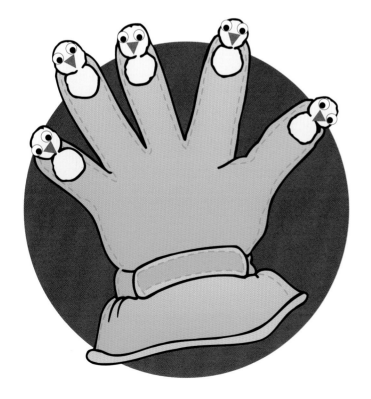

Give The Ducks A Hand

Capture your children's attention with this handy duck puppet. Make the puppet in advance by using a gardening glove; ten small, yellow pom-poms; ten small wiggle eyes; and five orange, felt triangles. Hot-glue two of the pom-poms to each fingertip on the palm side of the gardening glove. Glue wiggle eyes and a felt bill to the head of each duck. Once the glue has dried, the ducks are ready to "perform." Slide your hand in the puppet and sing "Five Little Ducks" with your children. Each time a duck is lost, fold a finger toward your palm. When no ducks are left, your hand should be in a fist. Later place the puppet in a center for youngsters to use. Quack, quack, quack, quack!

Jami Dash—Preschool Handicapped
Middlesex County Education Services Commission
Edison, NJ

IT'S CIRCLE TIME!

Shake It To The Shapes

Your little ones will get into the groove as they practice their shape-recognition skills with this idea. To prepare, cut large geometric shapes from construction paper or poster board. Laminate the shapes if desired. Punch a hole in each shape; then hang it from the ceiling with a long piece of string so that the shape is within children's reach. To use the hanging shapes, ask a volunteer to call out the name of a shape while the group dances to a playful tune. Invite your youngsters to bop over to the designated shape and dance under it. Let's dance!

Ellen Palmer—Two- And Three-Year-Olds
Noah's Ark Day Care Center
Haverhill, MA

Seashore Skills

Youngsters will enjoy practicing basic skills if they can do it by the shore. Using bulletin-board paper, create a simple scene similar to the one shown. Cut out a supply of beach-related objects—such as fish, sand buckets, seagulls, crabs, and kites. Place the scene on the floor, seat youngsters around it, and dive into circle time with the activities listed below.

- Show a numeral card and ask a volunteer to place the corresponding number of cutouts on the scene.
- Group the cutouts in sets of one to five. Have students count aloud as a volunteer practices one-to-one correspondence by pointing to all of one type of cutout.
- Place a collection of cutouts on the scene. Describe one cutout for a volunteer to find and take away.

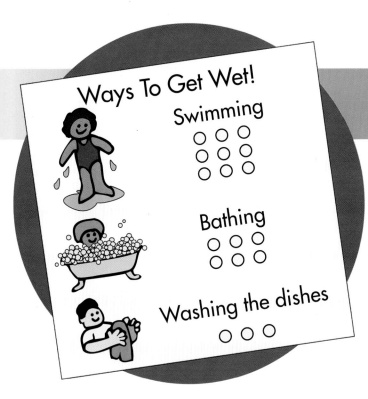

Ways To Get Wet!

Swimming

○ ○ ○
○ ○ ○
○ ○ ○

Bathing

○ ○ ○
○ ○ ○

Washing the dishes

○ ○ ○

Water Fun

Water is sure to be the main ingredient in many of summer's activities. Brainstorm with your youngsters a list of ways to get wet. Record the name of each activity on a sheet of chart paper and draw a simple picture cue beside it. Then ask each child to indicate which water-related activity is her favorite by placing a round sticker beside the appropriate name. Compare the results of this simple graph when finished. The wetter the better!

What's Bugging You?

Use a puppet to get the behavior bugs out of your classroom. Design a simple bug puppet using construction paper and a paper bag. Occasionally during circle time, offer to let one child at a time manipulate the puppet as a way to share what's bugging him. During the session, model to youngsters how to respond to those who are bugged—with reassuring words, problem-solving strategies, and understanding remarks. Giving students the opportunity to talk about problems in a positive manner may even prevent disruptive and inappropriate behavior. What a great way to fill your classroom with hugs, not bugs!

Karen Eiben—Preschool
The Kids' Place, LaSalle, IL

All Around The Castle

Here's a delightful game that will fit like magic into a fairy-tale thematic unit. Seat youngsters in a circle to represent the castle wall. Select two volunteers from the group—one to be the dragon and one to be the knight. As the group sings the song below, the knight chases the dragon around the circle. When the dragon hears "The dragon thought it was all in fun," he stops, turns toward the knight, and roars as indicated in the song. The knight then turns and runs away. Request that the dragon and knight select replacements from the group before returning to the circle. Continue in this manner until each child has had the opportunity to be the knight or the dragon.

(sung to the tune of "Pop! Goes The Weasel")

> All around the castle,
> The knight chased the dragon.
> The dragon thought it was all in fun.
> "Roar!" went the dragon.

Sharon H. Lloyd—Prekindergarten Early Intervention
Edith I. Starke Elementary
DeLand, FL

Head, Shoulders, Knees, & Toes

Head, Shoulders,

These Feet Were Made For Movin'!

Take a good look at those feet. Don't be shy! Take your shoes and socks off and wiggle all ten of those toes! Ask youngsters to name ways that they can move their feet such as tiptoe, march, and stomp. After youngsters put their shoes on, lead them in this action poem that provides great practice for stopping, starting, and making body shapes. As an extension to this activity, ask students to tiptoe as you play a steady beat softly on a drum. Play louder as they march; then play loudest as they stomp.

> Tiptoe, tiptoe, all around.
> Tiptoe now without a sound.
> Lightly, softly, on your toes.
> Stop right now and strike a pose. *(Pause)*
>
> Now let's march. We're straight and tall.
> Let's all march around the hall.
> March around and lift your knees.
> Ready? Everybody freeze! *(Pause)*
>
> Now let's stomp, no time to lose.
> Heavy feet are what we'll use.
> Stomp and stomp with all your might.
> Now sit down and say, "All right!"

Dr. Grace Morris, Southwest Texas State University, San Marcos, TX

The Alphabet...By Us!

Here's an alphabet book created by special design... and lots of cooperation. Spread a white sheet on the floor; then have small groups of students lie on the sheet in the configuration of each alphabet letter. Photograph each letter as it is made. When the prints are developed, mount each picture on a sheet of construction paper. Around each photo, attach stickers or glue magazine pictures of items that begin with that letter. Laminate the pages for durability; then bind them between covers. *A* is for...all right!

Tracy Dodson—Three-Year-Olds
Grandma's House Daycare
Wauwatosa, WI

Knees & Toes

Movement Ideas For Preschoolers

Pick A Part

Play this simple game as your little ones learn to identify body parts. Provide each child with a seasonal, construction-paper cutout. As you name a body part, ask each student to place his cutout on that part of his body. Encourage volunteers to be the leaders in this game of following directions. Ready now? Put an apple on your head. Put an apple on your feet!

Keitha-Lynn Stewart—Four-Year-Olds
Little Kids Day Care
Sissonville, WV

This Is What I Can Do

Need to keep your little ones moving? Here's a catchy rhyme we'd like to pass on to you!

This is what I can do.	*Leader demonstrates a*
	movement—stomping feet, etc.
Everybody do it too!	*Group copies leader's*
	movement.
This is what I can do.	
Now I'll pass it on to you!	*Point to new leader.*

grrr

Busy Bear

This action rhyme will exercise students' listening skills as well as their ability to stop and start on cue. Using rhythm sticks, tap four steady beats as indicated after each line. Encourage your little ones to add movements during your tapping, stopping their movements when you stop tapping. As youngsters become familiar with the rhyme, recite and tap faster. Start slow—then look at those busy bears go!

Busy Bear, Busy Bear, turn around. x x x x
Busy Bear, Busy Bear, jump up and down. x x x x
Busy Bear, Busy Bear, walk to me. x x x x
Busy Bear, Busy Bear, bend your knee. x x x x
Busy Bear, Busy Bear, on your toes. x x x x
Busy Bear, Busy Bear, touch your nose. x x x x
Busy Bear, Busy Bear, hop around. x x x x
Busy Bear, Busy Bear, sit on the ground. x x x x

149

Twinkle Toes, The Turkey

Twinkle Toes, the turkey, will keep students moving while helping them learn to follow directions. To prepare Twinkle Toes, enlarge and laminate a large turkey character and a supply of colorful, construction-paper turkey feathers. On one side of each feather, write simple directions such as "Hop three times" or "Clap softly." To the opposite side of each feather, attach the hook side of a piece of Velcro®. To the tail of the turkey, attach the loop side of as many Velcro® pieces as you have feathers. Attach the feathers to the turkey; then mount the turkey on the lower portion of a wall.

To play, ask a volunteer to select a feather to remove from the turkey's tail. Ask the child to identify the color of the feather. Read aloud the directions written on the feather; then ask the volunteer to lead the group in the action. Continue in this manner until each child has selected a feather, or play the game whenever a time filler is needed.

Diane DiMarco—Three- And Four-Year-Olds
Country Kids Preschool
Groton, MA

Twinkle Toes

Musical Cars

Honk, honk! Rattle, rattle, rattle. Crash. Beep, beep! This motorized version of musical chairs is versatile enough to teach youngsters colors, numeral or letter recognition, and social skills. To prepare for a game of musical cars, cut pairs of car shapes from different colors of poster board or laminated construction paper. Label each pair with a numeral or letter; then tape them together at the top only. For each different color of car, cut a matching circle to resemble a steering wheel. Label each wheel with a letter or numeral to correspond with those written on the cars.

To play, arrange as many chairs in a circle as you have children. Slip the cars over the backs of the chairs. Provide each child with a steering wheel. Direct the group to "drive" around the cars as you play music. When the music stops, have each child match either the color of his steering wheel or the letter or numeral on his steering wheel to a car. If more than one child matches a car, encourage youngsters to carpool by sharing the seat.

adapted from an idea by Laurie Curti—Three-, Four-, And Five-
   Year-Olds With Communication Disorders
Sutherland Elementary
Palm Harbor, FL

Knees, & Toes

Flash Dance

Heard of flashlight dancing? Well, it's soon to be the latest craze on the preschool dance floor. Turn off several lights so that your room is dim but not dark. Then turn on a flashlight and some lively music. Encourage youngsters to move in a manner similar to the movement of the flashlight. For example, if the light is moving rapidly up and down, the children might bounce. If the light is making a circular motion, the children might move their arms, legs, or whole bodies in a circle. Flashlight dancing...what a feeling!

Vicky Long—Preschool
Del Norte Baptist Weekday School
Albuquerque, NM

Funny Scarecrows

Got a field that needs guarding? Enlist the help of your youngsters as they participate in this fun fall poem. Ask your floppy friends to name a different body part to wiggle each time you recite the rhyme.

> The funny, funny scarecrow
> Guards the fields all day.
> He (She) waves his (her) floppy, floppy [arms]
> To scare the crows away!

Lucia Kemp Henry

Leaf Toss

Whirling, swirling leaves will leave your little ones all aflutter! So will this group movement activity that requires a flurry of cooperation. Space your children evenly around a large sheet or a parachute. Instruct each child to hold the sheet tightly with both hands. Place a supply of real leaves or decorative fabric leaves (from a craft store) in the center of the sheet. Challenge the group to move the sheet slowly at first, then faster until all of the leaves have flipped up and floated to the ground. Ask the group to put down the sheet, gather the leaves, and begin again. Whee!

Susan Burbridge—Four-Year-Olds
Trinity Weekday School
San Antonio, TX

151

Action Alphabet

This action-packed alphabet idea is bound to get your little ones moving. When introducing or reviewing each letter of the alphabet, stimulate youngsters' minds and bodies when you associate a movement with the letter. For example, have youngsters dance around a giant *D* cutout, jump over a *J* cutout, or even parade around a *P*.

Jack Be Nimble!

Jack be quick! Jack jump over the candlestick! For this movement activity, you'll want to prepare a "flaming" candlestick. Locate a can that has a plastic lid (an empty infant-food formula can works well). Cover the can with construction paper. Cut a small slit into the center of the lid. Insert a construction-paper or tissue-paper flame into the slit. Place the can on the floor in an open area. As a class re- cite the rhyme, re- placing *Jack* with a child's name. Invite the named youngster to jump over the candlestick. For variety, ask a child to run around or march over the candle- stick when it is his turn.

Susan Anker—Pre-K
Normandy Park School
White Bear Lake, MN

The Numbers-Rumba Dance

This movement suggestion to accompany Raffi's song titled "Numbers Rumba" (*Rise And Shine;* Troubadour Records, Ltd.) will help chil- dren practice following directions while identify- ing the numerals 1, 2, and 3. On each of a classroom supply of large index cards, write the numeral 1, 2, or 3. Ask the children to form a group circle; then give each child a card. As the music is playing, encourage each child to hold up his card and dance in the center of the circle when his number is mentioned. When the song is over, have the children exchange cards and start over again. Let's rumba!

Jannie Bassford—Four-Year-Olds
St. Andrews School
Edgewater, MD

Knees, & Toes

Penguin Pals

When wearing these winter costumes, your own flock of little ones will enjoy moving about as the penguins do. To make a penguin costume, paint a large grocery bag with black tempera paint. When the paint is dry, cut a hole in the bag's bottom that is large enough to accommodate a child's head. To create armholes and flippers, cut rounded flaps from two of the side panels. Add a white, construction-paper oval and orange, construction-paper feet to the front of the bag to complete the penguin's formal attire. Then encourage youngsters to put on their costumes and waddle their way around your room.

adapted from an idea by Alma Kay Borgen—
    Preschool
Amherst Own Child Care
Amherst, WI

Seasonal Streamers

Use cardboard tubes and curling ribbon to create movement wands that youngsters can use to celebrate every season of the year. When learning about winter, paint tubes white. When the tubes are dry, punch several holes in one end of each tube and attach two-foot-long pieces of white, blue, and silver curling ribbon. Have youngsters hold the tubes and pretend to move like the snow or winter wind. When learning about spring, tie different colors of curling-ribbon lengths to painted tubes to create rainbows. Or add blue and silver lengths to create rain. When learning about summer, tie yellow and orange lengths to prepared tubes to create rays of sunlight. And when learning about fall, tie autumn-colored lengths to prepared tubes to create falling leaves. Winter, spring, summer, or fall—creative movement is always in season!

adapted from an idea by Judy Schlicker—
    Pre-K And Gr. K
Brownstown, IN

Head, Shoulders,

Get In And Out Of Shapes

Each season or holiday, use masking or colored tape to create large shapes on the floor. Reinforce positional words and the importance of following directions as you direct groups of children to stand in a shape, walk around a shape, hop inside a shape, and so forth. Now you're really in shape!

adapted from an idea by Marsha Feffer—Four-Year-Olds
Bentley School
Salem, MA

My Space

Help youngsters develop spatial awareness with this simple rhyme. If possible provide each child with a plastic movement-activity hoop (smaller than a Hula-Hoop®) to hold around her waist while reciting the poem. Ask youngsters to put their hoops on the ground and find a different hoop to stand in before reciting the poem again.

I stretch my hands out to my sides.
I make my body big and wide.
I turn around right in my place.
This is my very own,
　　personal space.

Dr. Grace Morris
Southwest Texas
　State University
San Marcos, TX

Pop!

Add some pop to your group time with this imaginative balloon-blowing activity. Have youngsters stand in a group circle; then ask them to hold hands and move toward the center of the circle so that they are standing shoulder to shoulder. Ask the group to pretend that it is a giant balloon. Have each child in the group take one step backward each time you take a breath and pretend to blow up the balloon. Keep blowing until the group has stretched to its original position. Tell the group balloon to "pop" so that the children, like the pieces of a balloon, can fall to the floor. Ready for another balloon?

Doris Porter—Headstart
Anamosa, IA

Knees, & Toes

Movement Ideas For Preschoolers

A Tisket, A Tasket

A green-and-yellow basket and a stamped envelope are just what you need for this group game. (If you are unable to locate a green-and-yellow basket, weave green and yellow ribbons or paper strips into a plain basket.) Seat youngsters in a circle on the floor. Drop the letter (envelope) into the basket and give it to a volunteer leader. Have the leader hold the basket and skip, walk, hop, or otherwise move around the outside of the circle as the group sings the familiar tune "A Tisket, A Tasket." When the group sings, "On the way I dropped it," the leader drops the letter by a child in the group. Play continues as the child who receives the letter puts it back in the basket and becomes the new leader.

Laura McDonough—Integrated Special
    Education Preschool
Brightwood School
Springfield, MA

Heavy Traffic

Start your engines! This activity is sure to keep traffic moving in your classroom. Provide each child with a cardboard pizza or cake base to serve as a steering wheel. Encourage youngsters to move about your room as you read the following poem. For added fun, pair youngsters. Give one child a steering wheel and ask the second child to put his hands on his partner's shoulders. Direct the first child to steer as the second child moves along with him.

I'm a bright and shiny car,
So beautiful to see.
I certainly don't want to crash
And get a scratch on me.

As I travel down the road,
I'm careful not to bump.
I drive around the other cars
And never go "kerthump"!

Dr. Grace Morris
Southwest Texas State University
San Marcos, TX

155

Head, Shoulders,

It's All In The Wrist

Here's a handy way to help your little ones learn the concept of left and right. Ask parents to purchase enough terry-cloth, elastic hair bands for you to have a class supply. During movement activities, such as a singing of "The Hokey Pokey," have each child place a band on his right wrist. (To avoid confusion, have youngsters wear the holders on the same wrist for every movement activity.) Remind youngsters that their right wrists have holders and their left wrists do not. If an activity directs the movement of right or left legs, have each child put his arms by his sides. Remind him that the right leg is the one that the holder is touching. Move to the left, move to the right!

Amy Deml—Preschool
Mary Of Lourdes Community Preschool
Little Falls, MN

An Encouragement

Some children may be shy during movement activities, especially when asked to be leaders. Here's a tip for encouraging such children to join in the fun. Provide the child with a rag doll to hold during the activity. Encourage her to move the doll, instead of her own body, as the activity directs. You'll find this to be a useful tool for drawing a shy child into any action song.

Dr. Grace Morris
Southwestern Texas State University
San Marcos, TX

Musical Shapes

Come on, everybody! Step inside the circle, squeeze into the square, and round up into the rectangle! Your youngsters will enjoy this group activity that reinforces shape recognition and develops cooperation. To prepare, use colored tape to create large geometric-shaped outlines on the floor of an open area. (Make sure the outlines are big enough for a small group of children to stand inside.) Gather a group of youngsters in the area; then play a musical selection. Direct your little ones to hop, jump, walk, or otherwise move around the area. Stop the music; then name a shape. Encourage all of the children to gather inside the specified shape, helping each other by holding hands or by putting arms around each other. Your class will really be in shape now!

Janet S. Vaughn—Preschool Director
First Congregational Church Preschool
LaGrange, IL

Movement Ideas For Preschoolers

Toss And Move

Prepare this giant movement gameboard in advance and obtain a beanbag, and you'll have an indoor/outdoor game ready for use at a moment's notice. To prepare the gameboard, use a marker to visually divide a length of bulletin-board paper into 12 sections. Enlarge the movement pictures on page 158, if desired; then duplicate the pictures twice. Color and cut out the pictures. Mount one picture inside each section on the paper.

To play, place the gameboard on the floor in an open area. Give a volunteer the beanbag and direct him to toss it onto the gameboard. Announce the movement shown and written on the square in which the beanbag lands. Encourage the group to move around the gameboard in that manner. When the group has traveled once around the gameboard, give the beanbag to a different volunteer. Play until each child has had an opportunity to toss the bag, or until interest wanes.

adapted from an idea by Suzanne Fosburgh
  —Four- And Five-Year-Olds
De Pere Cooperative Nursery School
De Pere, WI

Here A Hand, There A Hand, Here A Foot, There A Foot!

Oh, my! This version of the game Twister® is sure to be a hands-down favorite! To prepare, cut a large rectangle from a white shower-curtain liner. Use a permanent marker to visually divide the rectangle into six sections. Cut hand and foot patterns from heavy paper. Trace the patterns onto the rectangle so that there is a pair of hands and a pair of feet in each section. Using permanent markers, color the hands and feet in each section the same primary color—using the same color in the two sections in each column. Use the patterns to cut as many hands and feet from red, blue, and yellow construction paper as there are on the gameboard. Store the cutouts in a bag.

To play the game with a small group of children, first request that the children remove their shoes so that little fingers and toes will not be hurt if stepped on. Select a cutout from the bag. Have a volunteer place the corresponding body part on the matching section of the gameboard. Play until each child in the group has had several turns.

Grace Daniels—5- To 11-Year-Olds, Multiply Disabled
  Winfield Street Elementary School
Corning, NY

157

Movement Pictures

Use with "Toss And Move" on page 157.

walk

run

hop

march

gallop

tiptoe

Songs & Such

SONGS & SUCH

Rise And Shine!

Rise, shine, and start out each morning with this perky song.

(sung to the tune of "Rise And Shine")

Rise and shine and sing out this morning, morning.
Stretch up now and sing out this morning, morning.
Proud and tall now, *(clap)*
Sing out this morning, morning.
Happy to be here!

adapted from an idea by Anna Majorie—Pre-K and Gr. K
Marrero, LA

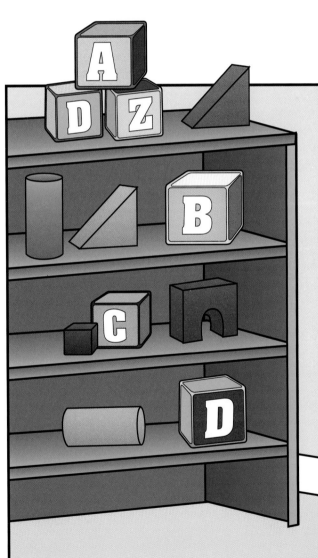

The Cleanup Song

Heigh-ho! The best way to go about cleaning is by singing a song. Ask youngsters to help you create additional verses appropriate for your classroom setting.

(sung to the tune of "The Farmer In The Dell")

Everyone, clean up.
Everyone, clean up.
Heigh-ho, way to go!
Everyone, clean up.

The blocks go on the shelf.
The blocks go on the shelf.
Heigh-ho, way to go!
The blocks go on the shelf.

Now the room is clean.
Now the room is clean.
Heigh-ho, way to go!
Now the room is clean.

Joannie Netzler—Three-Year-Olds
A Special Place
San Jose, CA

It's Snacktime!

This song's the signal. It must be snacktime!

(sung to the tune of "Frère Jacques")

Time for snack now.
Time for snack now.
Munch, munch, munch.
Crunch, crunch, crunch.
We will eat a little.
Just a little nibble.
Munch, munch, munch.
Crunch, crunch, crunch.

Sheri Dressler—Pre-K, Woodland School, Palatine, IL

And Bingo Was His Name-O!

Here's a way to add letter F-U-N to a singing of the favorite song "B-I-N-G-O." Label one side of each of five paper bags with a different letter from the word *BINGO*. Label the opposite side of each bag with a mouth shape and the word "Shh!" To the bag labeled "B," attach construction-paper dog-ear shapes. To the bag labeled "O," attach a paper tail. To the bottom of four bags, attach paper paws.

During a group time, open the bags and place them in sequential order on the floor so that the letters are facing the group. (Put a block in each bag to steady it.) As you sing each verse of the song, turn the appropriate bag around so that the word "Shh!" is facing the group. Later place the bags in a music center for students to enjoy on their own.

Melinda Davidson—Preschool/Integrated Special Needs Teacher
Brockton Early Childhood Program
Brockton, MA

What A Wonderful Day!

Close your day in a positive way with this zippy little song.

(sung to the tune of "Zip-A-Dee-Doo-Dah")

Zip-a-dee-doo-dah! Zip-a-dee-ay!
My, oh my, what a wonderful day!
Preschool is fun—lots of learning and play.
Zip-a-dee-doo-dah! Zip-a-dee-ay!

It's time for me to go now.
I'll be back on [Tuesday].
It'll be another fun day.

(Repeat chorus.)

SONGS & SUCH

Mr. Pumpkin And Mr. Turkey

Mr. Pumpkin and Mr. Turkey had better beware!
Harvesttime is coming and that is that!

(sung to the tune of "Frère Jacques")

Mr. Pumpkin,
Mr. Pumpkin,
Round and fat.
Round and fat.
Harvesttime is coming.
Harvesttime is coming.
Yum, yum, yum.
That is that!

Mr. Turkey,
Mr. Turkey,
Round and fat.
Round and fat.
Carving time is coming.
Carving time is coming.
Yum, yum, yum.
That is that!

Michelle Johnson and René Jenkins
Lakeland, FL

The Leaves Are Falling Down

Ask each child to finger-paint a leaf cutout using his choice of red, orange, yellow, or brown paint. To make necklaces, punch a hole and thread a length of yarn through the top of each leaf. Have youngsters wear their necklaces. Encourage each child to spin around and "fall" to the ground when the color of his leaf is sung.

(sung to the tune of "The Farmer In The Dell")

The leaves are falling down.
The leaves are falling down.
Red, orange, yellow, and brown.
The leaves are falling down.

Amy Ubelhart—Preschool
Lil Bumpkins Daycare
Shavertown, PA

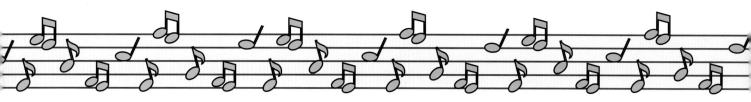

Safety Song

Teaching your little ones the basics of safety? If so then watch out for an opportunity to sing this safety song.

(sung to the tune of "Santa Claus Is Coming To Town")

You'd better watch out,
When crossing the street.
Look left and right
Before moving your feet.
Look and listen closely;
Then cross.

Sharon Spadaro—Preschool And Gr. K
Highland School, Inc.
Marianna, PA

A Song For All Seasons

For every season, there is a verse to this song. Introduce youngsters to the first verse now that autumn has arrived; then teach them the following verses in winter, spring, and summer.

(sung to the tune of "When The Saints Go Marching In")

Oh, when the leaves fall off the trees,
Oh, when the leaves fall off the trees,
We know that it must be autumn,
When the leaves fall off the trees.

Oh, when the snow begins to fall,
Oh, when the snow begins to fall,
We know that it must be winter,
When the snow begins to fall.

Oh, when the birds begin to nest,
Oh, when the birds begin to nest,
We know that it must be springtime,
When the birds begin to nest.

Oh, when the sun gets oh so hot,
Oh, when the sun gets oh so hot,
We know that it must be summer,
When the sun gets oh so hot.

Betty Silkunas
Lansdale, PA

SONGS & SUCH

Funny Valentine

(sung to the tune of "Did You Ever See A Lassie?")

Here's a funny little valentine, a valentine, a valentine,
A happy little heart with a message for you.
It says something special. I bet you can guess it.
My funny little valentine says, "I love you!"

Cheryl Cicioni—Preschool
Kindernook Preschool
Lancaster, PA

Be My Valentine

(sung to the tune of "Clementine")

Won't you be my valentine,
Be my valentine today?
For you are my special friend.
Be my valentine today!

Linda Rice Ludlow—Preschool
Bethesda Christian Schools
Brownsburg, IN

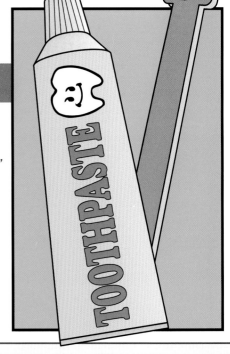

Brush, Brush, Brush Your Teeth

(sung to the tune of "Row, Row, Row Your Boat")

Brush, brush, brush your teeth,
Every night and day.
That's the way to healthy teeth.
Keep cavities away!

Pretend to brush teeth.
Head on hands to "sleep"; then "wake up."
Point to teeth.
Hand out in front to say, "Stop."

Brush, brush, brush your teeth,
Up and down each day.
See your dentist twice a year.
Keep cavities away!

Pretend to brush teeth.
Stretch up; then bend down.
Show two fingers.
Hand out in front to say, "Stop."

Linda Rice Ludlow—Preschool

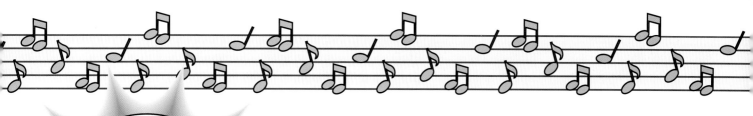

What's The Weather Like?

Each morning select a child to be the weather watcher. Sing the song below as youngsters observe the weather. When the song is over, ask the weather watcher to describe the current weather conditions.

(sung to the tune of "Where Is Thumbkin?")

Weather watcher, weather watcher,
What do you see? What do you see?
Tell us what the weather's like. Tell us what the weather's like.
Won't you please? Won't you please?

Hop Around

Hop around, twitch your nose, thump your feet, and shake your tail. Have some bunny fun!

(sung to the tune of "If You're Happy And You Know It")

If you like the Easter Bunny, [hop around].
If you like the Easter Bunny, [hop around].
If you like the Easter Bunny,
And you think he's very funny,
If you like the Easter Bunny, [hop around].

Welcome Spring!

Ask your little ones to help you brainstorm a list of springtime things such as butterflies and kites. Welcome the season with this tune, encouraging a different child each time to give a cheer.

(sung to the tune of "Ten In The Bed")

Warmer weather is here,
And [child's name] gives a cheer!
"Some [flowers]!
Some [flowers]!"
So we all clap our hands and welcome spring!

Spring Is All Around Me

Look up. Look down. Spring is all around!

(sung to the tune of "The Wheels On The Bus")

Above my head I see the sun,	*Reach up.*
See the sun, see the sun.	
Above my head I see the sun.	
Spring is all around me.	*Twirl around.*
Below my feet I see the grass...	*Reach down.*
Above my head I see a bird...	*Reach up.*
Below my feet I see a bug...	*Reach down.*
Above my head I see a cloud...	*Reach up.*
Below my feet I see a worm...	*Reach down.*

adapted from an idea by Marilyn Gold—Special Education
Public School 312
Brooklyn, NY

Where's The Bird?

Use this "tweet" activity to help little ones develop their listening skills. Using tape or a length of rope, create a circle on your floor big enough for your class to sit in. Ask your children to sit in the circle and pretend to be baby birds in a nest. Explain that baby birds listen for their mother's chirp. Ring a triangle and ask the children to imagine that it is the sound of the mother bird. Then ask the children to close their eyes and listen as you ring the triangle from a location in the room. With their eyes closed, have the children point to the area of the room from which the sound came. Continue in this manner, playing the triangle from a different location each time. If desired, ask a different child to ring the triangle with each round of the game.

Up Pop The Flowers!

Have your group form a circle—then get growing!

(sung to the tune of "Pop! Goes The Weasel")

We plant some seeds in the dirt.   *Pretend to plant seeds.*
The rain falls in a shower.   *Raise arms; then wiggle*
                                                     fingers downward.

The sun comes out, and what do you know?   *Children hold hands*
                                                     and squat.

Up pop the flowers!   *Release hands. Pop up.*

Joan Banker—Preschool, St. Mary's Child Development Center, Garner, NC

Ladybugs Fly

Youngsters will go buggy in all directions when singing this song—so make sure you provide them with plenty of room to move! To make a ladybug finger puppet for each child, collect a supply of red jug lids. Hot-glue a black pom-pom to each jug lid; then glue two wiggle eyes to the pom-pom. Using a permanent black marker, embellish the ladybug's back with dots. Insert a ball of play dough into the lid. To use his puppet, a child presses a finger into the dough. Fly, fly away!

(sung to the tune of "Three Blind Mice")

Fly, fly, fly.
Ladybugs fly.
Fly over here.
Fly over there.
They fly up high and they fly down low.
Around and around and around they go.
They fly-fly fast, and they fly-fly slow.
Oh, ladybugs fly!

craft idea by Linda Guidry—Four-Year-Olds, Butterflies Preschool, Lafayette, LA

The Days Of Spring

(sung to the tune of "The Farmer In The Dell")

The days of spring are here.
Warm, sunny days are near.
Birds in trees, flowers and bees,
The days of spring are here.

Lorraine Stolarz—Pre-K, Handicapped Class, Maywood Avenue School, Maywood, NJ

SONGS & SUCH

Happy, Happy Father's Day!

Teach youngsters the following song. Then provide each child with a copy of the song to decorate and deliver to his dad.

(sung to the tune of "Twinkle, Twinkle, Little Star")

Here's a little song to say,
"Happy, happy Father's Day!"
No one's father is so sweet.
Your kind ways just can't be beat.
Happy, happy Father's Day;
I love you in a big way!

Count To Ten!

Counting to ten is lots of fun when rhythm instruments are used! Distribute a variety of instruments and ask youngsters to play as they count.

If you're happy and you know it, count to ten.
1-2-3-4-5-6-7-8-9-10!   *Count aloud and play instruments.*

If you're happy and you know it, count again.
1-2-3-4-5-6-7-8-9-10!   *Count aloud and play instruments.*

If you're happy and you know it, and you really want to show it;
If you're happy and you know it, count to ten.
1-2-3-4-5-6-7-8-9-10!   *Count aloud and play instruments.*

Beth Jones
Niagara Falls, Ontario, Canada

Summertime Song

Summertime is a fun time! Ask youngsters to name things they like to do in the summer, such as swim, run, and ride. Then include their ideas in this summertime song.

(sung to the tune of "Mary Had A Little Lamb")

Summer is the time to [play],
Time to [play], time to [play].
Summer is the time to [play].
Enjoy those sunny days!

Lucia Kemp Henry

Splashing's So Much Fun!

Heading to the pool, lake, or ocean for a swim? Have a splashing good time!

(sung to the tune of "Ten Little Indians")

One big, two big, three big splashes,   *Sing loudly.*
Soaking even my eyelashes!
I like making water smashes;
Splashing's so much fun!

One little, two little, three little splashes,   *Sing softly.*
Soaking even my eyelashes!
I like making water smashes;
Splashing's so much fun!

Betty Silkunas, Lansdale, PA

Did You Ever See A Fishy?

Did you ever see a fishy move left and right? How about front and back, or up and down? Designate a pair of movements each time you sing this song. Then encourage your school of fish to swim this way and that.

(sung to the tune of "Did You Ever See A Lassie?")

Did you ever see a fishy, a fishy, a fishy,
Did you ever see a fishy swim this way and that?
Swim this way and that way, and that way and this way?
Did you ever see a fishy, swim this way and that?

FINGERPLAYS, POEMS, & RHYMES

Five Little Apples

 Five little apples lying on the floor.

 One rolls away, and that leaves four.

 Four little apples hanging on a tree.

 I'll pick one, and that leaves three.

 Three little apples, I know what to do!

 I'll put one in my pocket, and that leaves two.

 Two little apples sitting in the sun.

 I'll pick one up, and that leaves one.

 One little apple waiting in my lunch.

 I'll eat it up with a crunch, crunch, crunch!

—*Lucia Kemp Henry*

Poems, & Rhymes

Little Bear And The Bee

Bears love honey...but so do bees!

 Little bear, little bear up in the tree.

 Little bear, little bear looking down at me.

 Little bear, little bear, can't you see?

 Little bear, little bear, here comes a bee!

—Linda Ludlow, Pittsboro, IN

Leaves Are Falling All Around!

Take youngsters on an outdoor leaf hunt. Or have them hunt for construction-paper leaves hidden around your classroom. Follow up your leaf hunt with this fingerplay that teaches the sign-language symbols for *red, yellow, orange,* and *brown.*

 Leaves are falling all around—

 Red,

 Yellow,

 Orange,

 And brown.

 Twirling, swirling to the ground—

 Look how many leaves I've found!

—*Jan Trautman*

Poems, & Rhymes

Ten Little Firefighters

Top your little firefighters with fire hats (cut from construction paper as shown); then teach them this fiery hot fingerplay.

 Ten little firefighters,

 Sleeping in their beds.

 "Ding!" went the bell,

 And down the pole they slid.

 They raced to the fire

 And put out all the flames.

 Then the ten little firefighters

 Went back to bed again.

—Deborah Garmon—Three- And Four-Year-Olds
Pooh Corner Preschool and Daycare, Old Mystic, CT

Five Little Reindeer

Rudolph and his reindeer friends will love this flannelboard rhyme and fingerplay! For use with a flannelboard, cut five reindeer shapes from brown felt. Glue wiggle eyes and a pom-pom nose to each shape.

 Five little reindeer playing in the snow.

The first one said,

"Let's go, go, go!"

The second one said,

 "I see snowflakes in the air."

The third one said,

 "Santa won't care."

The fourth one said,

 "Isn't Christmastime fun?"

The fifth one said,

 "Let's run, and run, and run."

Then, "Ooooh," went the wind and out went the lights.

 So Santa and his reindeer flew out of sight.

Betty Rector—Preschool
Alaiedon Elementary School, Mason, MI

176

Poems, & Rhymes

Snowing All Around

Have children drizzle glue over large paper doilies, then cover the doilies with glitter. Hang the doily snowflakes in pairs from your ceiling. It *is* snowing all around!

 Way up high

In the winter sky,

 Two little snowflakes

Caught my eye.

 Down to the ground

They fell without a sound.

 And before very long,

It was snowing all around!

Ellen Boulay—Preschool
Small World Nursery School, Ansonia, CT

Fingerplays,

What's The Weather?

Today we can go outside
And have a lot of fun,
Because today's weather
Calls for **sun.**

Today we'll put on hats and coats
To make sure we don't sneeze,
Because today's weather
Calls for a **windy breeze.**

Today we'll look up in the sky
To see white puffs in crowds,
Because today's weather
Calls for **clouds.**

Today we'll watch the water
Splash on the windowpane,
Because today's weather
Calls for **rain.**

Today we'll dress up warmly
To watch the white flakes blow,
Because today's weather
Calls for **snow.**

—Lucia Kemp Henry

Poems, & Rhymes

I Feel...

A lion is big
And very strong.
It has a tail
That's very long.
A lion can roar
In a great big way.
I feel like a lion today!

A lamb is small
And soft and sweet.
It has a tail
That's short and neat.
A lamb can bleat
In a quiet way.
I feel like a lamb today!

—*Lucia Kemp Henry*

Fingerplays,

At The Beach

At the beach,
The sun shines down.

I see smiles,
On kids all around.

Smiling kids in the sand,

Smiling kids in the sea,

But the happiest kid
At the beach is me!

—*Patricia A. McMillan, Longwood, FL*

Holiday Parade

It's the Fourth of July!
A parade is today.
Put on your hat,
And march this way.

March through the town.
March down the street.
Play on your drum,
With a rat-a-tat beat.

March through the town.
March all around.
Play on your flute,
With a root-a-toot sound.

March through the town.
March with a smile.
Play on your horn,
With a tah-rah-rah style!

—Lucia Kemp Henry

181

CRAFTS FOR LITTLE HANDS

Crafts For Little Hands

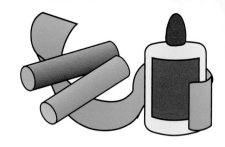

Apple Surprise

Leave youngsters starry-eyed when you cut several apples in half horizontally. Surprise! There are seedy stars inside! For a related art activity, pour green, red, yellow, and black tempera paint into separate pie tins. Cover a work area with newspaper. Personalize a white sheet of construction paper for each child. Provide each child an opportunity to dip an apple half into the red, yellow, or green paint, then press it onto his paper. After he has made several prints, instruct him to dip a finger in the black paint and then press it several times in the center of each apple print. When the paint is dry, display each set of prints or assist youngsters in cutting around the shape of each apple print. Laminate the cutouts if desired; then display them around a bulletin board for a delicious fall border.

Tammy Bruhn—Pre-K
Temperance, MI

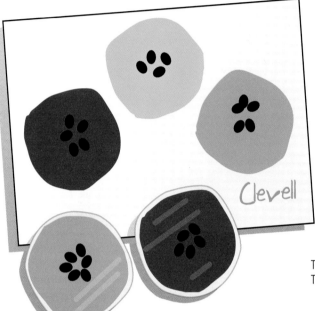

Hand-Picked Apples

Fill separate pie pans with red and green washable tempera paint. Spread brown washable tempera paint in a shallow baking sheet. To create a design that resembles a tree trunk and limbs, ask a child to press his forearm and hand in the brown paint, then onto a personalized 12" x 18" sheet of blue construction paper. Assist the child in cleaning his arm. Next direct him to dip his thumb into the green paint and then press it onto the paper to resemble leaves on the tree. Direct him to dip a finger in the red paint, then onto the tree to resemble apples. When each child has printed a tree and the paint is dry, display the trees together in a row. That's quite an orchard you have there. It must be time to gather the harvest!

Sedona O'Hara—Preschool
University Children's School
California, PA

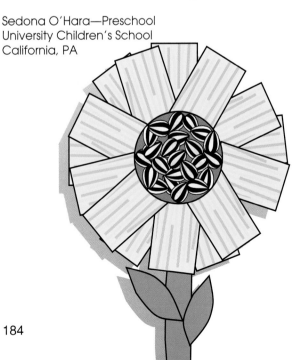

September Sunflowers

Perk up your classroom this September with the last sign of summer—sunflowers! To make a sunflower, cut a length of yellow crepe-paper streamer into one-inch-wide strips. Glue a set of strips along the edge of a two-inch brown construction-paper circle. Glue sunflower seeds to the opposite side of the brown circle. Cut out a green construction-paper stem and leaves. Glue the leaves to the stem and the stem to the base of the back of the flower. This crop of sunflowers is sure to make you smile.

adapted from an idea by Jan Hatch—Preschool
Jan's Preschool
Pleasant View, UT

Hooray For Party Hats...

There's sure to be a party atmosphere in your classroom when youngsters create these zany party hats! Prepare several different colors of glue by adding tempera paint to bottles of white glue. To make a hat, embellish the underside of a paper bowl using the glue and a variety of art supplies such as glitter, feathers, and pom-poms. When the glue is dry, punch two holes on opposite sides of the bowl's rim. Tie a length of curling ribbon through both holes. There you have it. A ready-to-wear happy birthday hat!

Carrie Lacher
Friday Harbor, WA

...And Horns!

Have more party fun with these festive noisemakers. Using markers and stickers, decorate a cardboard tube. Punch a hole about one inch from the bottom of the tube. Wrap a five-inch square of waxed paper around the tube's opposite end. Secure the paper with a rubber band. When everyone has made a party horn, put on some irresistible music. Then invite youngsters to march and toot to a birthday beat.

Carrie Lacher

I Love Your Funny Face

Everyone has eyes, a nose, and a mouth. But my—how different we all look! Be prepared for giggles when youngsters create these funny faces. In advance cut out magazine pictures of facial features. Label each of three containers with the name and a picture of a feature. Sort the pictures into the containers. Cut face shapes from various colors of skin-toned construction paper. To make a funny face, have each child select a face shape and two eyes, a nose, and a mouth from the magazine cutouts. Have him glue the face shape on a piece of paper and then glue the features on the face shape. Direct him to add hair to the face using markers or crayons. Let's face it—everybody's craft will be one-of-a-kind!

Doris Porter—Preschool
Headstart
Anamosa, IA

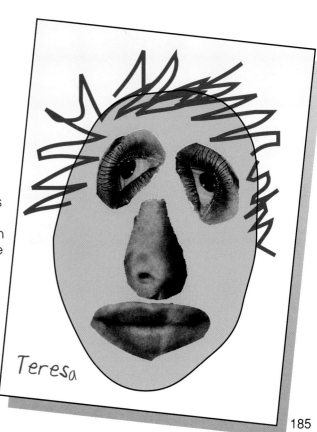

185

Crafts For Little Hands

It Feels Like Fall

Give youngsters a feel for fall by encouraging them to feel and describe a real tree's trunk and freshly fallen leaves. As a follow-up, have little ones make artistic fall trees. Glue torn, brown construction-paper strips onto a large sheet of finger-painting paper to resemble the rough trunk and branches of a tree. Randomly drop spoonfuls of different colors of liquid tempera paint onto the paper. Cover the paper with a large sheet of waxed paper; then press and rub the paint. Allow the paint to dry completely; then peel away the waxed paper. Cut around the shape of the tree and its brightly colored, leaf-filled branches. Now it feels *and* looks like fall!

Bernadette Hoyer—Pre-K
Coles and McGinn Schools
Scotch Plains, NJ

Splat! It's A Spider!

Paint a child's palm and four fingers with black paint. Have her press her hand onto a sheet of construction paper twice so that the palm prints overlap and the finger prints extend in opposite directions. When the paint is dry, glue on colorful wiggle eyes. Even Miss Muffet would invite this spider to sit down beside her!

Kathy Folz
South Elementary
Franklin Park, IL

Feeling Spacey?

If you're feeling spacey, give this project a spin! Prepare a glittery mixture by combining one part glitter with two parts liquid starch. Paint the mixture onto celestial-shaped, construction-paper cutouts. When the shapes are dry, punch a hole in the top of each and thread with lengths of glittery yarn or thread. Tie the shapes onto a plastic hanger; then suspend the project from the ceiling. My stars! What a sight!

Lynne Bordeaux—Preschool
Miss Tanya's Nursery School
Westboro, MA

Plenty Of Pumpkin, Plenty Of Seeds!

That's what youngsters will find when you give them the opportunity to dig into a topless pumpkin. It's also what they'll find when they peek into this crafty pumpkin! From construction paper, cut a stem, a leaf, and two identically shaped pumpkins. Title one of the pumpkin cutouts "What's Inside A Pumpkin?"; then glue on the stem and leaf. To one side of the other pumpkin cutout, glue short pieces of orange yarn and real pumpkin seeds that have been washed and dried. Assemble the shapes with a brad as shown; then take a pumpkin peek!

Sonja M. Harrington—Pre-K
Tiny Tears Day Care
Albemarle, NC

Turkey On A Platter

This turkey is already on a paper-plate platter and ready to serve as a Thanksgiving delight! Using different colors of tempera paint, sponge-paint a paper plate; then set the plate aside to dry. Using markers or crayons, decorate a pear-shaped, brown cutout to resemble a turkey's body. Glue the cutout to the plate. Better watch out! This turkey's so stunning he'll strut right off the table!

Gail Moody—Preschool
Atascadero Parent Education Preschool
Atascadero, CA

I am thankful for my new baby sister.

John

Wreath Of Thanks

Parents will be thankful for these decorative harvest wreaths and the sentiments written on them. To make a wreath, glue a construction-paper circle to the center of a paper plate. Glue crumpled squares of tissue paper around the rim of the plate; then glue a bow-shaped cutout to the bottom of the wreath. If desired, attach a small photo of each child to the bow on his wreath. In the center of the wreath, write the child's dictated sentence of thankfulness. To prepare the wreath for hanging, tape a length of ribbon to the back of the plate.

Debi Luke—Three- And Four-Year-Olds
Fairmount Nursery School
Syracuse, NY

Crafts For Little Hands

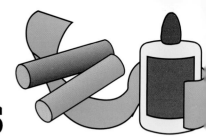

A Forest Of Decorated Firs

When these projects are displayed together, you'll have a fantastic forest of firs. To make a miniature fir tree, paint a pinecone with green tempera paint. Set the cone aside to dry. Following the package directions, mix a thick batch of plaster of paris. Drop a large spoonful of the mixture onto a piece of aluminum foil; then press the bottom of the pinecone into the plaster. When the plaster has set, embellish the fir tree by gluing on colorful beads.

Deborah Pruett, Woods Preschool, St. Mary Of The Woods College
St. Mary Of The Woods, IN

Cut It Out!

Your little ones will be crazy about these cut-up Christmas trees! Visually divide the bottom of a green or holiday-designed paper plate into four different-sized triangles. Cut along the lines; then sequence the triangles by size from largest to smallest. Glue the largest triangle—right side up—to a piece of construction paper. Above the triangle, glue the remaining pieces to the paper to form a tree. Top the tree with a paper star shape. If desired, trim the tree with glitter, sequins, or holiday-shaped confetti pieces. Each triangular tree will be in tip-top shape!

Faith Heaviside—Nursery School
Fairmount Nursery School
Syracuse, NY

A Tree With A Twist

Here's a tree with a twist. To trim a tagboard tree shape, twist pieces of green tissue paper. Glue the twisted paper to the tree; then top it with glitter-glue garland, paper ornaments, or shiny sequins. What a fantastic, fine-motor fir!

Betsy Ruggiano, Featherbed Lane School, Clark, NJ

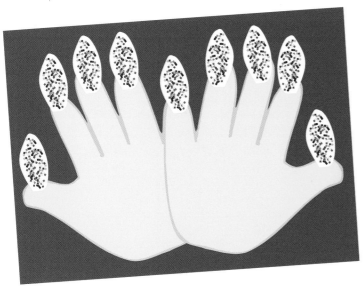

Handy Menorah

Students' eyes will light up with excitement when they make these handsome menorahs. To make one, trace both hands onto a piece of yellow construction paper. Cut out the hand shapes; then glue them on a piece of blue construction paper so that the shapes of the pinkies overlap. Cut white paper flames; then glue a flame atop each of the candles. If desired, add glitter to the flames so they shine brightly throughout the season. Happy Hanukkah!

Lori J. Kracoff—Preschool
The Curious George Cottage Learning Center
Waterville Valley, NH

What An Angel!

Have each of your little angels make a look-alike cherub to give to her mom or dad. Cut an oval from the appropriate color of skin-toned construction paper. Glue the oval atop a gold or silver doily. Use markers to add facial features. Glue a handful of decorative moss to the top of the angel's head. Attach a metallic pipe-cleaner halo to the angel with a paper clip. Heavenly!

Sandra W. Scott—Pre-K
Asheville High Child Care
Asheville, NC

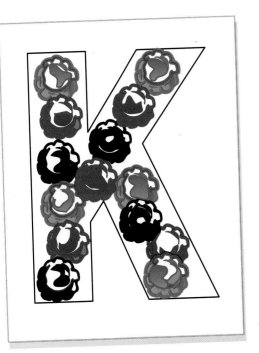

Corny Kwanzaa Craft

Here's a craft to help add meaning to your celebration of Kwanzaa. Break or cut an ear of corn into thirds. Prepare trays of red, black, and green tempera paint. Use the corn and paint to make creative prints on white construction paper. If desired, write a large *K* on a piece of paper. Print inside the outline of the letter with the corn. *K* is for Kwanzaa!

Dayle Timmons—Special Education Pre-K
Alimacani Elementary School
Jacksonville, FL

Waiting For Snow?

Wait no more! Create a blizzard of snowflakes in your classroom with this unique printing idea. Cut an orange in half horizontally; then blot the halves dry with a paper towel. Pour light blue tempera paint into trays. To make a snowflake, dip an orange half into the paint. Press the orange onto the center of a sheet of white construction paper to create a unique print. Sprinkle the wet print with clear glitter, if desired. When the paint is dry, cut a simple snowflake shape around the print. Punch a hole in the shape; then tie on a length of yarn. Hang the flurry of flakes from your ceiling. It's snowing!

Anne Oeth—Preschool, Rockwell Preschool, Omaha, NE

Showy Snowflake Ornaments

The snow must go on! So gather up some fake, dry snow from a craft store and get ready to make these showy ornaments. Glue three miniature pretzels together to resemble the shape of a snowflake. When the glue has dried completely, place the pretzel ornament on a piece of waxed paper and paint both sides white. Once again, let the ornament dry completely. Later dip the painted ornament into glue, then into a shallow container of decorative snow. To complete the ornament, tie a satin ribbon around it for hanging.

Pam H. Tribble—Four-Year-Olds
First Baptist Church
Calhoun, GA

Marvelous Matching Mittens

Match this art project with a winter unit and you'll have an activity that is sure to be a winner! Trace a mitten pattern onto a folded sheet of construction paper. Cut out the mitten shape through both thicknesses. Using eyedroppers, drop several different colors of liquid tempera paint onto one of the mitten cutouts. Place the matching mitten atop the painted mitten and press. Pull the mittens apart and set them aside to dry. Laminate, then place each child's mittens in a center for use as a matching activity. Or attach string to each child's mittens. Tie each pair of mittens to a longer length of string to drape across a door or bulletin board.

Cheryl Cicioni—Preschool, Kindernook Preschool, Lancaster, PA

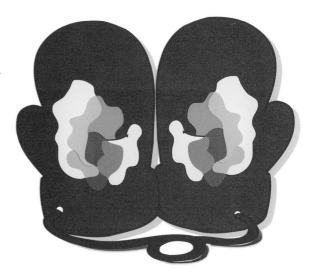

Crafts For Little Hands

"Thumb-ody" Loves You!

Loved ones will be touched by the message on these valentine gifts. To make a thumbprint hearts arrangement, cut various sizes of heart shapes from white or pink construction paper. Using red tempera paint, decorate the heart shapes with thumbprints. Set the hearts aside to dry. Personalize and write "Thumb-ody Loves You!" on a 4 1/2" x 8 1/2" piece of white paper. Tape the paper around a clean 12-ounce juice can. Glue a painted heart to the can; then glue the remaining hearts to craft sticks. Press a small amount of clay into the bottom of the decorated can; then tuck a section of red tissue paper into the can. Insert the sticks through the paper and into the clay. Isn't it nice to be reminded that "thumb-ody" loves you?

Martha Berry—Two-Year-Olds
Main Street Methodist Preschool
Kernersville, NC

Thumb-ody Loves You!

Joseph

Samuel

Valentine Pockets

Looking for a creative way for youngsters to make their own valentine holders? Pick this pocket idea! Using pinking shears, cut off a third of a paper plate. Staple the larger cut plate to a full plate to make a pocket. Beginning at the top of the pocket, use a hole puncher to punch an even number of holes along the rims of the plates. Lace the plates together with a yard of red yarn. When you've finished lacing, tie the yarn into a loop at the top of the pocket. Decorate the pocket using paper heart cutouts and heart-shaped doilies. As a final touch, personalize the pocket and glue on a photo.

Elaine Dittman—Preschool
Holy Trinity Lutheran Preschool
Chicora, PA

Still Snowing?

If you love winter, you'll be delighted with these lovely snowflake wreaths. Prepare several snowflake templates to be used as stencils. (Or purchase decorative snowflakes from a party-suppy store.) To make a wreath, cut a large hexagon from white tagboard. Place a template on the tagboard; then sponge-paint the hexagon using pastel-colored paints. Arrange and press paper heart cutouts onto the wet paint. When the paint is dry, punch a hole through the top of the wreath; then tie on a length of yarn to make a loop. Invite parents to hang the wreaths on their doors as a winter welcome.

Brenda vonSeldeneck and Donna Selling—Four-Year-Olds
First Presbyterian Preschool
Waynesboro, VA

Let's Go Paint A Kite!

Bright-and-shiny colors make these kites really soar! To prepare colorful fingerpaint that glides on smooth and dries shiny, mix one part washable liquid paint with three parts light corn syrup. Use a spoon to drizzle a small amount of the paint onto a white, construction-paper kite shape. Use your fingers to spread the paint over the kite, adding additional colors of paint if desired. When the paint is dry, attach a crepe-paper tail to the kite. Punch a hole near the top of the kite; then suspend it from your ceiling with clear fishing line. These kites in flight are quite a sight!

Amy Jenkins—Preschool
Childrens Country Day School
Mendota Heights, MN

ROAR!

Make these "fur-ocious" fine-motor lions just in time for March. On the back of a yellow paper plate, draw lines from the edge of the rim to the edge of the circle as shown. On the front of the plate, use permanent markers to draw a lion's face. Cut along the lines on the rim; then fold forward some of the sections to create the lion's mane. When these lions are displayed together, your students are sure to take pride in their work!

Gail Moody—Preschool
Atascadero Parent Education Preschool
Atascadero, CA

Fabulous Frames

These easy-to-make frames are sure to please! For each child, purchase or cut from tagboard a 5" x 7" mat that has a 3 1/2" x 5" opening for a photo. To decorate a frame, squeeze colored glue around the edge of the mat. When the glue is dry, tape a photo to the back of the frame. Send these unique frames home as gifts any time of the year.

Mary E. Maurer
Caddo, OK

Barefoot Chicks

If you're having to scratch around for new craft ideas, you're going to get a big cluck out of these spring chicks! Ask a child to remove a shoe and sock; then paint the bottom of his foot with yellow washable liquid paint (giggling allowed!). Have him press his foot onto a sheet of construction paper. When the child's foot is clean and the paint is dry, have him use crayons to add an eye, beak, and legs to his chick. Finally have him spread glue along the bottom of the paper, then sprinkle the glue with cornmeal. Expect youngsters to chirp with delight when making these barefoot chicks!

Cindy Lawson—Three-Year-Olds
Educare Center
Fort Wayne, IN

Peekaboo!

Peck, peck, peck. Cheerful chicks peek out of these decorated eggs. To make a peekaboo chick, cut two identically sized egg shapes from white construction paper. Decorate one egg shape with crayons or markers. Color the second egg shape yellow. Cut two white circles, two slightly smaller black circles, and an orange triangle from construction paper. Glue the shapes to the yellow shape as shown to create a chick. Cut the decorated egg in half to resemble a cracked egg. Tape both halves of the egg to the sides of the chick. If desired, add a holiday message. Peekaboo! Here's an Easter card for you!

Betsy Ruggiano—Three-Year-Olds
Featherbed Lane School
Clark, NJ

Crafts For Little Hands

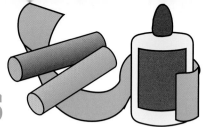

April Showers...

These radiant raindrops are sure to help bring about beautiful spring blossoms. To make one, cut a raindrop shape from blue construction paper; then trim away the center of the shape, leaving only a border. Press this border onto the adhesive side of a slightly larger piece of clear Con-Tact® covering. Press various shades of blue tissue-paper pieces on the covering. Trim around the edge of the raindrop. If desired, punch a hole near the center top of the drop and attach a length of clear thread for hanging. To create a downpour of compliments, hang the drops near a classroom window.

Amy Jenkins—Preschool
Children's Country Day School
Mendota Heights, MN

...Bring May Flowers!

Just as we promised, springtime showers will inspire a classroom full of these showy flowers. Using a wide-tip, permanent marker, trace a large flower shape onto a piece of waxed paper. Paint a layer of watered-down glue inside the entire shape. Sprinkle colorful paper or foil confetti over the shape; then drizzle another layer of glue over the confetti. Press a second sheet of waxed paper onto the glue-covered confetti. When the glue is dry, cut along the outline through all of the thicknesses. Punch a hole near the edge of the flower and attach a length of thread for hanging. Or add a paper stem to each flower and display them above windowsills to create the effect of a springtime flower garden.

adapted from an idea by Pamela Vance—Preschool
Lake Geneva Cooperative Preschool
Lake Geneva, WI

Spring Bouquets

Your little ones will learn new art techniques with this creative project. To begin, tear a page from a book of wallpaper samples; then fold it in half either vertically or horizontally. Cutting away from the fold, cut out half of a vase shape freehand. Open the paper and glue the vase cutout to a larger sheet of fingerpaint paper. Using a green marker, draw stems above the vase. Drop spoonfuls of different colors of paint onto the paper on and above the stems. Lay a piece of waxed paper atop the paint; then press, pat, and roll the colors together. When the paint dries, remove the waxed paper. Trim the paper around the vase and bouquet of flowers. Now that's creativity in bloom!

Bernadette Hoyer—Title I Pre-K
Brunner School
Scotch Plains, NJ

Home Tweet Home

Any bird would love to claim this nest—complete with eggs—as its home! Mold egg shapes from Crayola® Model Magic™ modeling compound; then set the eggs aside for a day to dry. When the eggs have dried, sponge-paint each one for a speckled effect. To make a nest, paint glue on the inside of a small paper bowl. Press short lengths of brown yarn onto the bowl. Repeat the painting and pressing process on the outside of the bowl. When the nest and painted eggs are dry, place the eggs in their new home. Tweet! Tweet!

Linda Hilliard—Preschool
Child Care Centers
Arlington, VA

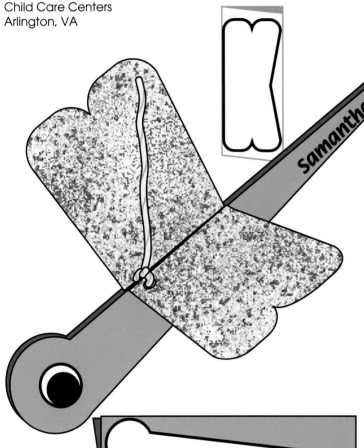

Dazzling Dragonfly

Your little darlings will "ooh" and "ahh" over these winged wonders. Prepare dragonfly body and wings templates similar to the shapes shown. Trace and cut out the body from green construction paper and the wings from waxed paper. Sprinkle assorted colors of crayon shavings onto half of the wings shape. Fold over the other half; then press the wings with an iron set on low heat to melt the shavings. Add facial features to both sides of the dragonfly body; then fold it in half. Fold the wings in half again and insert them into the fold of the body. Staple all of the thicknesses together; then press the wings down onto the body. Punch a hole through the body and wings, insert yarn for hanging, and tie the ends. Bend the wings upward before hanging this dazzling dragonfly.

Jennifer Cresina—Preschool
Trinity Center For Children
Pottsville, PA

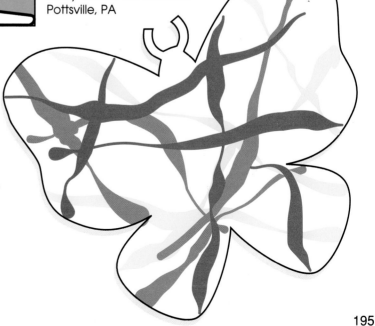

Spread Your Wings!

Youngsters will be all aflutter over these beautiful butterflies. To prepare for this painting project, pour several different colors of tempera paint into individual Styrofoam® trays. Attach a clothespin to one end of each of three one-foot lengths of yarn. Holding a piece of yarn by the clothespin, dip it into a tray of paint; then drag it over a construction-paper butterfly shape. Repeat the process as desired with the same or different colors of paint. What a beautiful effect!

Louise Anderson—Four-Year-Olds
Community Cooperative Nursery School
Norwalk, CT

195

Mommy's Little Angel

Moms will be so appreciative of this gift that you and your little ones will end up wearing halos! Purchase a white, adult-sized T-shirt for each child's mother. Using fabric paint, generously paint a child's hand yellow. Have him press his hand onto the shirt to form the wings. After the child's hand has been washed and dried, paint it once more with a different color of his choice. Have him press his hand on the shirt again to form the body. Using the appropriate colors of fabric paint for each child, add a head, hair, eyes, and a mouth. Personalize the shirt and add the phrase "Mommy's Little Angel." If necessary, follow the manufacturer's instructions to permanently set the paint. When each shirt is complete, wrap it in paper that has been embellished with youngsters' handprints.

Lisa Bayer—Preschool
The Pre-Kindergarten Center of Woodhome, Inc.
Baltimore, MD

A Corsage For Mom

Moms will be delighted to wear these corsages on Mother's Day. To make one for a special lady, scrunch squares of tissue paper to resemble colorful blooms. Glue them onto the center of a small paper doily. Tape a safety pin to the back of the corsage. For you, Mom—here's a corsage as pretty as you are!

Kathi Michaud—Preschool
Little People Nursery School
Winslow, ME

Her Favorite Cookbook

This collection of student-illustrated recipes is sure to become Mom's favorite cookbook! To make one for each child's mom, type or write on separate sheets of paper each recipe used in your class so far this year. Include snack recipes and recipes for dough, bubbles, or fingerpaint. Ask several children to illustrate each recipe. Program a title page with, "Preschool Chefs"; then have each child print a thumbprint on the page. Write the child's name and add facial features to her thumbprint. Duplicate a title page and a set of recipes for each mother. To make each book, place a set of pages between construction-paper covers; then bind them. To decorate the cover of the book, have a child use yellow paint to put several thumbprints as shown on the sheet of paper. Then have him add white thumbprint petals around each yellow print to create daisies. When the paint is dry, use markers to add stems and a bow. Now that's a gift that's as useful as it is special!

Claudia Pinkston—Four-Year-Olds
Lexington United Methodist Preschool, Lexington, SC

Crafts For Little Hands

Thanks For Helping Me Grow

These floral favors make great thank-yous to adult volunteers who have helped your class throughout the year. Trace a flower pattern onto white poster board and cut it out. Ask a child to decorate the flower with markers, crayons, or paint; then attach her photo to the blossom's center. Program each flower with the phrase "Thank you for helping me grow!" and include the date. Then give each one to a special helper.

To present a bouquet, tape a straw to the back of each of several flowers. Press a ball of clay into a plastic cup; then press the straws in the clay around the sides of the cup. Place the cup in the center of a tissue-paper square. Wrap the paper upwards around the cup, and tie it at the base of the flowers with ribbon. Attach a tag with a message of appreciation.

Kitty Moufarrege—Three-Year-Olds
Foothill Progressive Montessori Preschool
La Canada, CA

Thank you for helping me grow!

June 1997

Out On A Limb

These one-of-a-kind fliers will bring your preschoolers to their feet! To make a footprint fowl, ask a child to remove a shoe and sock. Paint the bottom of his foot with washable liquid paint; then direct him to press his foot onto a sheet of construction paper. (Have a bucket of warm, soapy water and towels nearby for easy cleanup.) When the paint is dry, cut out the footprint. The child completes his project by gluing on real feather wings, a paper beak, and wiggle eyes. Display the projects among a tangle of paper vines and leaves.

Becky Brantley—Pre-K
Patterson Elementary School
Panama City, FL

Snow Cones! Cotton Candy!

Come and get your summer treats right here, folks! To make a snow cone that will hold up in the hottest of weather, use tempera paint to paint half of a Styrofoam® ball. While the paint is wet, sprinkle the half-ball with clear glitter. Later press and glue it into a paper snow-cone holder.

For a cotton candy treat, paint a sheet of white construction paper with thinned glue; then stretch cotton balls and press them onto the paper. When the glue is dry, cut around the shape of the cotton. Spray-paint the cotton with thinned tempera paint. When the paint is dry, glue the cotton candy to a paper cone shape. The summer sun won't melt the fun of these terrific treats!

Charlet Keller—Preschool
ICC Preschool
Violet Hill, AR

Creative Castles

Here's a castle craft that encourages creativity. Cut a quantity of cardboard tubes into various lengths, cutting the tops of some to resemble a castle's towers. Encourage each child to manipulate and build with the tubes. Then provide him with a sheet of sturdy paper and a small tray of glue. To make a castle, a child dips a side of each of the tubes of his choice into the glue and arranges them on his paper. When the glue is dry, he then paints the castle gray. Or, to duplicate the look of a sand castle, have him paint the tubes yellow, then sprinkle the wet paint with a mixture of sand and glitter. Complete the castle with paper flags. To develop cooperation as well as creativity, try this craft idea as a small-group project. What stunning structures!

Kathleen Soman—Preschool
Wee Wisdom Preschool
New Port Richey, FL

Star-Spangled Fun

Oh, my stars! These projects will decorate your room with patriotic pizzazz! Using graduated sizes of star-shaped cookie cutters or different sizes of star templates, trace and cut out a supply of stars from foil; tagboard; and red, white, and blue construction paper. Select a variety of cutouts and sequence them by size; then arrange and glue them onto a flattened white paper plate. Glue layers of foil and construction-paper stars onto some of the tagboard stars; then punch a hole in each set. Punch one hole on one side of the plate and as many holes as there are tagboard stars on the opposite side of the plate. Tie the stars to the plate with lengths of curling ribbon; then thread the last hole with ribbon for hanging. Hang these projects in your room, and everyone is sure to be starstruck!

Lorrie Hartnett—Pre-K
Canyon Lake, TX

Blast Off!

Assist your aspiring astronauts as they make these rockets. To make one, paint a small cardboard tube. When the paint is dry, cut four slits equal distances apart on one end of the tube. Decorate the tube with patriotic and star-shaped stickers. Cut two equilateral triangles from construction paper. Cut a slit in one triangle from its base to its center and a slit in the other triangle from its tip to its center. Fit the triangles together; then slide the triangles into the slits of the cardboard tube. Cut away one-third of a paper circle as shown; then reshape the paper into a cone and tape the ends together. Glue the cone to the top of the rocket. 10, 9, 8,...we have liftoff!

Cheryl Cicioni—Preschool
Kindernook Preschool
Lancaster, PA

THE ART CART

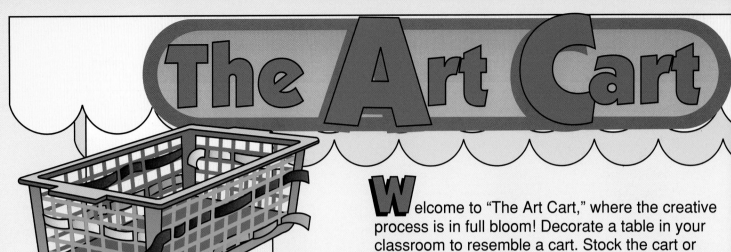

The Art Cart

Several children enjoyed the over-and-under process of weaving fabric strips into this plastic laundry basket.

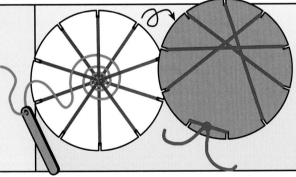

Fine-motor skills were strengthened as crepe-paper streamers were woven into a loom made by cutting slits into a placemat.

This circular loom was made by using a cardboard pizza base and ribbon. A craft-stick needle was used to weave yarn into the loom.

Welcome to "The Art Cart," where the creative process is in full bloom! Decorate a table in your classroom to resemble a cart. Stock the cart or adjacent shelving with the types of materials mentioned (at the right). Then invite your youngsters to visit the art cart to create, using any variety of the available materials. While students are at the art cart, be supportive and encourage them to enjoy the creative process. Though guidance on how to use the materials may be necessary, make a concerted effort not to advise students toward the achievement of a certain end product. Amazing things will soon be happening at your art cart!

Let the creativity begin!

Keep a Polaroid® camera nearby to capture each child's favorite creation or to capture a group's cooperative efforts. Encourage children to dismantle their work—when they are ready to—and to return the weaving materials to their storage containers for repeated uses.

To encourage weaving, stock your art cart with these types of things:

Weaving Materials—Materials suitable for weaving include yarn, ribbon, strips of fabric, crepe-paper streamers, shoelaces, construction-paper strips, cord, gift-wrapping ribbon, and plastic lacing.

Simple Looms—Young children can use a variety of items as simple looms:

- Plastic laundry baskets, plastic berry baskets, and plastic milk crates are ready for weaving without further preparation.

- Simple looms can be made by cutting same-sized slits in vinyl placemats, laminated sheets of heavy paper, box lids, or Styrofoam® meat trays.

- To make more advanced looms for individual use, cut an equal number of notches along the tops and bottoms of shoebox lids and cardboard pieces. Cut an even number of notches around the edge of a round, plastic lid or a round, cardboard pizza or cake base. Anchor yarn or ribbon in the notches, and tie the loose ends together in the back to make a loom.

- To make looms large enough for children to work on co-operatively over time, cut one side from a large appliance box. Secure lengths of cord over the open portion of the box. Or tie lengths of heavy yarn to a large, empty picture frame.

Weaving Needles—Needles aren't necessary with many weaving projects. If desired, supply large, plastic safety needles to assist children who wish to weave thinner fibers into smaller looms. Larger needles are easily made by drilling holes into the ends of craft sticks.

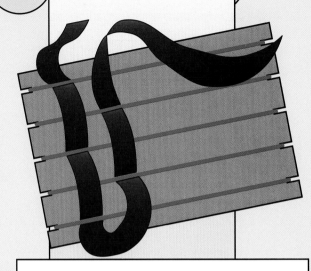

Wide ribbon was woven between the yarn on this cardboard loom.

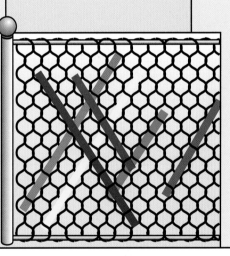

The supply of weaving materials was carted outdoors to encourage youngsters to weave materials into a chain-link fence.

The Art Cart

Welcome to "The Art Cart," where the creative process is in full bloom! Decorate a table in your classroom to resemble a cart. Stock the cart or adjacent shelving with the types of materials mentioned (at the right). Then invite your youngsters to visit the art cart to create, using any variety of the available materials. While students are at the art cart, be supportive and encourage them to enjoy the creative process. Though guidance on how to use the materials may be necessary, make a concerted effort not to advise students toward the achievement of a certain end product. Amazing things will soon be happening at your art cart!

Let the creativity begin!

Hand-eye coordination was developed as a youngster painted around geometric and unusual shapes of fingerpainting paper.

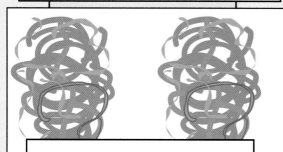

In order to take home a memory of his creative experience, a child pressed paper onto this design that he painted onto a sheet of waxed paper. His design indicates an awareness of balance and symmetry.

Fingerpainting Tips
- Provide smocks or aprons.
- Ask youngsters to use spoons to dip small amounts of fingerpaint onto their painting surfaces.
- Provide plenty of room in your painting area so that children can stand and move freely while fingerpainting.
- If your art cart is not near a sink, keep a tub of soapy water and towels nearby.
- As children paint, play instrumental music.
- If a child is hesitant to fingerpaint, encourage him to observe his peers and to start with a small amount of paint. If he is concerned about getting dirty, letting him know that the homemade fingerpaint is made with soap may be helpful.

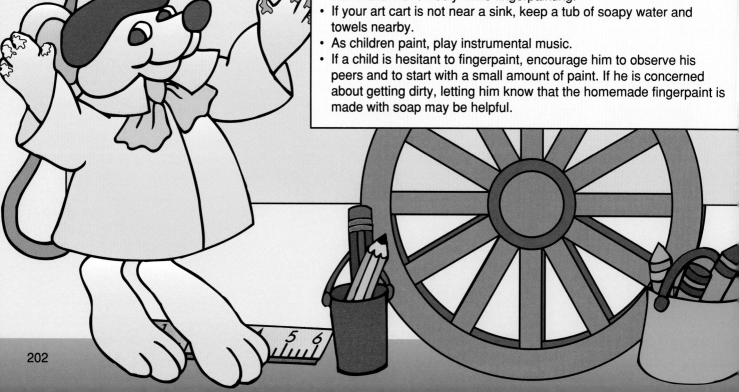

Stock your art cart with these types of things:

Fingerpaint—Provide commercial fingerpaint or use the recipe below to make your own inexpensive fingerpaint. So that students will explore the fingerpainting possibilities, put only one color of paint in the area. Later stock the cart with additional colors.

Fingerpainting Papers And Surfaces—There are many smooth surfaces that work well with fingerpainting. Consider some of these possibilities: fingerpainting paper, placemats, meat trays, waterproof wallpaper samples, waxed paper, aluminum foil, tabletops, baking sheets, a shower curtain, smooth cardboard.

Fingerpaint

1 cup flour
1/2 cup water
2 tablespoons dishwashing liquid
1 tablespoon powdered or liquid tempera paint

Stir the flour, water, and liquid detergent into a mixing bowl. Mix until it forms a smooth paste. If different colors of fingerpaint are desired, divide the mixture into equal parts. Add powdered or liquid tempera paint to the mixture.

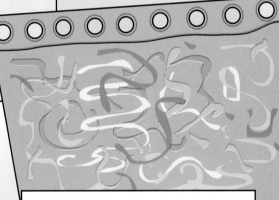

Because of the paint's transparency, a child became aware of his ability to create and change the designs made when moving his fingers through the fingerpaint. By asking questions about his work, the teacher helped the child develop an awareness of cause and effect.

Music played as several students helped to paint this shower curtain. The students had a positive social experience and responded to the music and rhythm while painting.

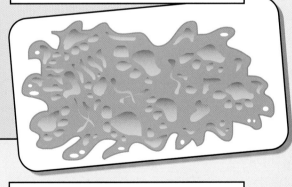

Who says fingerpainting is just for fingers? A child painted this design on a placemat with his bare toes!

The Art Cart

Coordination and muscle control were exercised as a child learned to use chalk instead of crayons. After completing his drawing, he enjoyed using his fingers to blend the colors together.

A group of children enjoyed using chalks on a sidewalk on a warm day. Lying on the ground to draw increased their upper-body strength. Each child was provided with a spray bottle of water to explore the effect of spraying water on his drawings.

Welcome to "The Art Cart," where the creative process is in full bloom! Decorate a table in your classroom to resemble a cart. Stock the cart or adjacent shelving with the types of materials mentioned (at the right). Then invite your youngsters to visit the art cart to create, using any variety of the available materials. While students are at the art cart, be supportive and encourage them to enjoy the creative process. Though guidance on how to use the materials may be necessary, make a concerted effort not to advise students toward the achievement of a certain end product. Amazing things will soon be happening at your art cart!

Let the creativity begin!

Tips For Creating With Chalk
- Spread newspapers or a plastic tablecloth over the work surface.
- Provide children with aprons or oversized shirts to protect clothing.
- Keep wet paper towels or wipes handy for easy cleanup.
- Spray hairspray on chalk drawings to seal the chalk.

Stock your art cart with these types of things:

Chalk—Sidewalk chalks and soft art chalks made for use on paper (not chalkboards) come in a variety of bright and pastel colors. Use the recipe below to create your own inexpensive supply of sidewalk chalks.

Paper—Provide drawing paper that has a good texture so that it will grip the chalk. Construction paper and good-quality drawing or watercolor papers work well.

Liquids—Chalk can be dipped into a variety of liquids—including water, white tempera paint, liquid starch, and milk—before being used on paper. The liquids can also be spread onto the paper before or after drawing with the chalk. These techniques intensify the colors of the chalk and seal the colors so they do not dust or rub off the paper.

Sidewalk Chalk

1 cup plaster of paris
1/2 cup water
2 tablespoons powdered tempera paint
four 5-oz. waxed paper cups or one ice-cube tray

In a plastic bowl, mix together the plaster of paris and the powdered tempera paint. Using a plastic spoon, slowly stir in the water until the mixture is smooth. Half-fill each of the paper cups or the ice-cube tray sections. Allow the mixture to harden for one hour. Peel away the cups or pop the chalks out of the ice-cube tray. Then allow the chalks to harden overnight. Voila! Colored chalk!

Tamie Congdon—Preschool • Lourdes Preschool • Bettendorf, IA

A child discovered that fingerpainting over his project with liquid starch made the colors shiny and bright.

Bright colors of chalk used on a mounted length of black bulletin-board paper created a fun effect on this group mural.

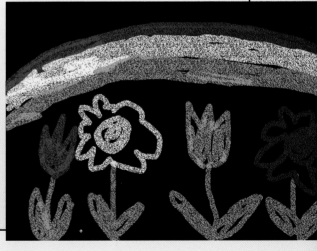

SHAPE UNITS

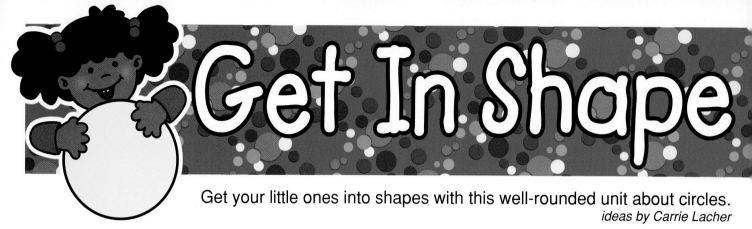

Get In Shape

Get your little ones into shapes with this well-rounded unit about circles.

ideas by Carrie Lacher

Buried Treasure

Set sail for an adventure on the high seas of learning with this discovery lesson about circles. To prepare for a class treasure hunt, gather a collection of round objects such as container lids, toy rings and bracelets, large buttons, juice-can lids, and poker chips. On the day of the hunt, hide the objects in your sand table. Place a supply of pails and scoopers nearby. Collect magazine pictures in which circular objects can be seen. Mount the pictures on construction paper and laminate the papers or place them in plastic page protectors. Display the pictures near the sand table. Or locate a copy of *Round & Round & Round* by Tana Hoban (Greenwillow Books). On or near your sand table, place a sign that reads "Discover a treasure of circles!"

Gather your crew together and weave a tale of shipwrecked pirates. Describe to them a treasure that was buried on a forgotten island. Lead youngsters on a voyage through your classroom; then "land" at the sand table. Read aloud the sign that challenges them to discover circles. Carefully examine and discuss the displayed pictures or the pictures in *Round & Round & Round.* Then encourage them to dig into the sand to get a real feel for circles.

Circles All Around

Seat youngsters in a circle and ask them to brainstorm a list of items that are round. Write their suggestions on a large, bulletin-board-paper circle. As youngsters brainstorm, lead them to name food items that can be circular in shape such as snack crackers, LifeSavers®, CheeriOs®, pancakes, and orange or banana slices. Designate a day to be "Circle Day." Send a note home with each child asking him to bring a requested food item to school on that day. When the items arrive at school, arrange them on a round table that is covered with a round tablecloth. Provide each child with a paper plate; then encourage him to select the round items of his choice for snacking. The good-health reminder of the day? Don't forget to eat your circles!

Snacktime Shape-Up

Use these placemats at snacktime to help little ones define their space and to build shape-recognition skills. Personalize a large, white, construction-paper circle for each child. Provide youngsters with a supply of dot stickers and sponge-tipped dot markers for decorating the circles. Or make your own circular stamps by cutting circles from foam insoles. Mount the fabric side of each foam circle onto a sanded wood scrap. Encourage each child to press the stamps onto inkpads, then onto her paper circle.

When each child has decorated her placemat, ask her to describe her work. Write her comments on her mat; then laminate it or cover it with Con-Tact® covering to protect it from spills and crumbs. Read aloud the comments on a different placemat each day during snacktime.

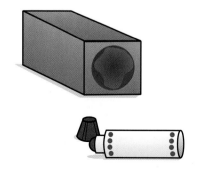

With Circles

It's Circle Time!

Here's a riddle for your little ones. What do circles like best about preschool? Circle time—of course! Incorporate this movement activity into your group time and youngsters will soon be going around in circles. Using chalk draw a large circle on the floor of your group area; then cover the chalk outline with colorful tape. Invite the children to stand on the tape. Get those math muscles moving with this shapely song sung to the tune of "If You're Happy And You Know It." Create new verses by changing the movement from *tiptoe slowly* to *stomp your feet, slide sideways, hippity hop,* and more! Go ahead...act silly on the circle and go round!

A circle is a shape that goes round.
A circle is a shape that goes round.
A circle is a shape that goes round and
    round and round.
A circle is a shape that goes round.

[Tiptoe slowly] on the circle and go round.
[Tiptoe slowly] on the circle and go round.
[Tiptoe slowly] on the circle and go round
    and round and round.
[Tiptoe slowly] on the circle and go round.

Circle Prints

Get ready for squeals of delight when youngsters make this hands-on art project. Tape a large piece of bubble wrap (bubble side up) onto a flat surface. Invite a child to spread washable paint over the slippery, bumpy wrap. (Provide foam brushes for the sensorially squeamish.) Then have him quickly wash and dry his hands before pressing a large, construction-paper circle onto the wrap. Have him peel off the paper to reveal a collection of printed circles. When the prints are dry, provide magnifiers and display the prints where your circle explorers can examine up close the variations in the multitude of circles.

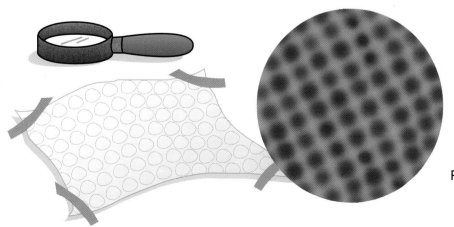

Going In Search Of Circles

Now that youngsters have experienced circles in a variety of ways indoors, it's time to take your circle search to the streets. Lead youngsters on a circle walk around your school, keeping a list as the students observe circles along the way.

Include families in on the fun by sending home a circular note suggesting that they conduct their own circle hunt.

Dear Parent, Go on a circle hunt! Help your child learn about circles by looking for circles at home.

Well-Rounded Reading

Circles, Triangles, And Squares
Written & Photographed by
Tana Hoban
Published by Simon & Schuster Children's Books

Ten Black Dots
Written & Illustrated by
Donald Crews
Published by Greenwillow Books

Wheel Away!
Written by Dayle Ann Dodds
Illustrated by Thacher Hurd
Published by HarperCollins Children's Books

Get In Shape

Teach youngsters about triangles with these fun activities that get right to the point.

ideas by Pamela Kay Priest

Triangle Town

Where's the best place to learn about triangles? Triangle Town, of course! In an open area of your room, establish the boundaries of Triangle Town by using colored tape to tape the outline of a large triangle onto the floor. Randomly tape smaller triangles inside the large triangle to create a maze of roads. Provide youngsters with various colors of construction-paper triangles, markers, glue, and cardboard tubes. Encourage them to create triangle trees and signs for Triangle Town. Supply triangular-shaped blocks and small cars for youngsters to play with while visiting the town.

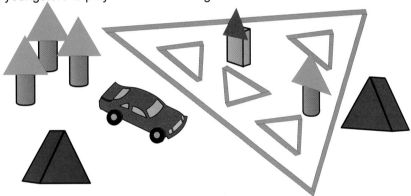

Let's Bowl!

Youngsters will shape up their triceps as they set up triangles in this easy-to-make game of bowling. Locate an area suitable for bowling, such as a sidewalk, a hall, or an open area of your classroom. Set up ten cardboard tubes to form a triangle. Mark around the triangular tube arrangement with chalk. If the bowling lane will be indoors, tape over the chalk to indicate the area for the arrangement of the bowling tubes. If desired, also mark the spot where each tube should be placed to form the bowling arrangement. To play, a child rolls a soft ball toward the set-up tubes as if bowling. Encourage each child to count the tubes in the triangle arrangement when preparing for the next set. Thanksgiving is coming soon, so let's go for a *turkey*—three strikes in a row!

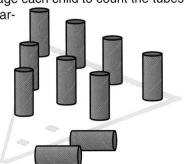

Musical Triangles

Accompany your triangle activities with the instrument of the day—the triangle. To make a triangle for each child, bend the hook of a hanger into a loop; then thread a four-inch length of yarn through the loop and tie it. Demonstrate how to hold the triangle by the yarn while tapping it lightly with a spoon. Give each child a triangle and spoon to play as children sing this triangle tune. Model how to keep a steady beat by tapping on the instrument. At the end of the song, tap each corner or side of the triangle as you sing, "One, two, three!"

This Is A Triangle

(sung to the tune of "Row, Row, Row Your Boat")

This is a triangle.
Look and you will see.
It has three corners and three sides.
Count them. One, two, three!

With Triangles

Talking Turkey

This crafty turkey is a totally triangular dude! To make a turkey, each child will need a large, brown construction-paper triangle; a small, brown triangle; a supply of colorful construction-paper squares (including orange and red); glue; markers; and scissors. Glue the small, brown triangle to the larger triangle to represent the turkey's head and body. Cut the various colors of squares in half diagonally; then glue the resulting triangles to the back of the turkey's body in order to feather him. Cut an orange square in half diagonally; then glue each triangle to the base of the turkey to resemble legs. Color eyes; then glue small orange and red triangles to the tip of the turkey's head to create a beak and a wattle. So that the turkeys will be unique, provide each child with colored glue for embellishing the feathers of his turkey.

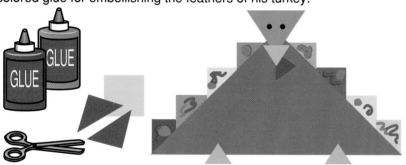

Two's Company, Three's A...Triangle!

Capture memories of your little ones getting into shape by creating this unique photo album. Place a large sheet of bulletin-board paper on the floor. Invite groups of three children at a time to lie on the paper and together form a triangle with their whole bodies, legs, arms, or fingers. Encourage each team to be creative. Take a picture of each group's pose. Glue each developed picture to a triangular-shaped piece of construction paper; then write the pictured students' names on the page. To make a photo album, title a cover "Triangles Of Friends"; then bind the pages together. Or display four, nine, or sixteen of the triangular-shaped pages together to form a giant triangle.

Triangle Problem Solving

The point of this center is to get youngsters' hands on triangles while developing their problem-solving skills as well. Store about 40 craft sticks in a container. As a group of children visits the center, demonstrate how to make a triangle using three sticks. Ask the children to help you count the sides and the corners of the triangle. Challenge the group to make as many triangles as they can or to make one giant triangle with the craft sticks. Encourage partners to make triangles with common sides. Before you know it, your little ones will have turned a corner on creative thinking.

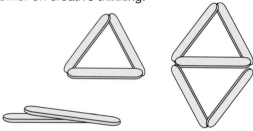

Eating To Stay In Shape

Eating to stay in shape is easy when the treats are triangles as well! Cut slices of bread, square sandwich meat, and cheese slices into triangles. If desired also provide condiments such as mayonnaise and mustard. Allow each child to make his own sandwich. On the side serve triangular-shaped chips and triangles cut from fruit rolls for dessert. Don't forget to provide square napkins folded into triangles. Why count calories when you can count corners? Shapely eating is as easy as one, two, three!

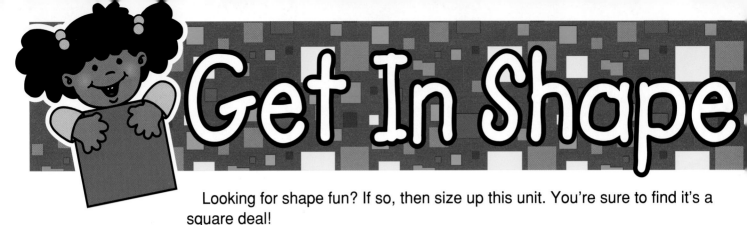

Get In Shape

Looking for shape fun? If so, then size up this unit. You're sure to find it's a square deal!

ideas contributed by Linda Rice Ludlow

Square Safari

In the jungle of your room are squares waiting to be discovered! To help your little ones spy squares, prepare "binocu-squares." To make a pair, cut off the end flaps from a margarine box. Draw a vertical line through the center of the back of the box and cut. Press the box flat so that the printed side is facing down. Fold one end of the box onto itself to meet the first crease; then fold again twice. Fold the opposite end in the same manner. Release; then refold each side to create rectangular tubes. Fold both tubes once again so that the sides touch in the center. Secure the tubes with tape. If desired, cover the completed pair of "binocu-squares" with paper.

Have each child look through a pair of the "binocu-squares" in search of unsuspecting squares around your room. At snacktime hide individual bags of square-shaped snacks such as crackers or sandwich quarters; then have youngsters search for the bags around the room. Everywhere, there's a square!

Celebrity Square

Make a square puppet to add personality to your focus on squares. Since your puppet is sure to be a celebrity, assist each child in making a square puppet of his own. To make a puppet, cut a construction-paper rectangle that measures exactly twice as long as it is wide. Fold the rectangle in half; then glue only the sides together. Encourage each child to use small paper squares and markers as desired to add facial features to his square. Teach youngsters the following song and encourage them to help their square puppets sing along!

Ode To A Square

(sung to the tune of "Clementine")

I have four sides
All the same size,
And my shape is called a square.
I can be so very useful,
And I'm seen 'most everywhere!

With Squares

The Mystery Of The Missing Square

Youngsters are sure to enjoy this shaped-up version of the game Doggy, Doggy, Who's Got Your Bone? To play, seat youngsters in a group. Ask a volunteer to sit in a chair with his back facing the group. Place a square cutout beneath the chair. Then silently motion for a child in the group to take the square, return to the group, and hide the square behind him. As a group chant, "[Child's name], [child's name], in the chair. Somebody came and took your square." The child in the chair then makes as many as four guesses (one for each side of the square) as to who took the square. Whether or not he guesses correctly, praise him for his effort and invite him to trade places with the child holding the square.

Gift-Wrapped Squares

Snacktime is all wrapped up with this special snack. Give each child a graham-cracker square to "wrap" by spreading it with frosting. If desired, have her decorate her package by adding candy sprinkles. To top the package with a bow, have her place a whole gumdrop on the center of the cracker, and then arrange four gumdrop halves around the whole gumdrop. This is one gift-wrapped package children won't have to wait to enjoy!

Squarely Centered

Get your blocks center all squared away with these suggestions. Remove all but the cube-shaped squares from your blocks center. Supplement the center with other cube-shaped items such as gift-wrapped boxes, square nesting cups, and plastic containers with lids. As each child builds, ask him to find the square sides of the blocks, boxes, containers, and lids in his structure.

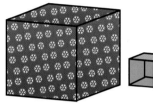
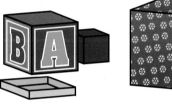
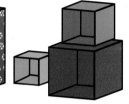

Be A Square!

You won't have to go on a square hunt to find youngsters who are willing to participate in this group activity. Divide your class into groups of four children each. Ask each child in a group to stand with her arms out; then show the children how to stand beside and in front of each other to form a group square. Then teach youngsters this shapely song.

We're A Square

(sung to the tune of "London Bridge")

Our four sides are just the same.
Just the same. Just the same.
Our four sides are just the same.
We're a square.

Get In Shape

Dazzle your youngsters as you use these sparkling activities to introduce the diamond shape.

ideas by Suzanne Moore

Presto "Change-o"

Amaze your little ones by introducing the diamond shape in this magical way. To prepare, spread glue onto the dull side of an 8" x 10" piece of foil. Press the foil onto a 9" x 12" piece of black construction paper. (Be sure the foil is completely attached to the paper so it does not separate during your magic act.) When the glue is dry, fold the paper in half so that the foil is inside. Using a pencil, lightly draw a five-inch-tall triangle on the black paper so that the base of the triangle is on the fold.

During a group time, keep the paper folded as you show your audience both sides. Review the attributes of a triangle as you dramatically cut it out of the paper. Holding the cutout at the top point, show the shape to the class. Then say the magic words, "Abracadabra, zim zam zimond. Turn this triangle into a diamond!" Flip the triangle open to reveal the diamond shape. If desired, follow up your trick by having students make their own magic diamonds in a similar manner.

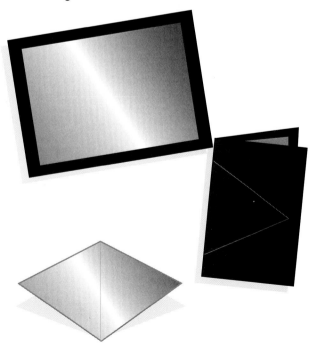

Let's Go Fly A Kite

Youngsters will be flying high—and getting a real feel for diamonds—when they make these fingerpainted kites. For each child, cut a used file folder into a diamond shape. Also cut two bow shapes from construction paper, and a length of crepe-paper streamer. Have the child place his shape on a cookie sheet or lunch tray; then provide him with various colors of fingerpaint. As he paints, help him describe the attributes of the diamond. Ask the child to set his kite aside to dry and to wash his hands. On one bow, write his description of where his kite would fly. Write his name on the second bow. Tape the bows to the streamer; then tape the streamer to the back of the kite. Suspend the kites from your ceiling. Look! Diamonds in the sky!

With Diamonds

Diamond Necklaces

These necklaces will polish off youngsters' abilities to recognize the diamond shape. For each child, cut a 5" x 3" diamond from tagboard, a 5" square from aluminum foil, and a 24" length of thick, glittery yarn. To make a necklace, wrap the foil around the shape. Punch a hole near the top of the shape; then thread the yarn through the hole. Tie the yarn at the top of the shape (so that it will lie flat when worn) and at the yarn ends. If desired, glue rhinestones to each of the four corners of the diamond. Diamond days are here again!

A Crown Of Diamonds

Your little kings and queens will feel like royalty when wearing these diamond-decorated crowns. Cut several tagboard diamond shapes and foil squares (as described in "Diamond Necklaces") for each child. Have each child cover each of her shapes with foil, then glue on craft jewels. Staple her decorated diamonds onto a sturdy sentence strip; then staple the ends of the strip so the crown fits on the child's head. Look! It's the duke and duchess of diamonds!

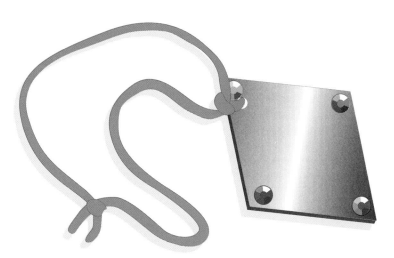

One Big Diamond

Follow up your kite craft (see "Let's Go Fly A Kite") by chanting this poem. If desired, draw a kite on a chalkboard. As you recite the poem, erase the tail of the kite to reveal a diamond.

> One big diamond high in flight.
> A diamond's shaped just like a kite.
> Take away the tail, and what do I see?
> A diamond looking back at me!

Home Run!

This movement idea is sure to be a hit! If your school has a baseball field, take youngsters out for a run around the giant diamond shape. Or arrange four game cones, game base markers, or placemats in an open area of your playground to indicate the four corners of a diamond. Have the class follow you as you run to each of the four corners of the diamond shape. Now that's a home run of an idea!

Diamond Jubilee

Diamonds are fun to wear but even more fun to eat! Invite your necklace- and crown-clad youngsters to visit a cooking center to prepare these delicious diamonds. To make one, cut a piece of bread into a diamond shape; then spread butter and jam onto the bread. Diamond desserts fit for royalty!

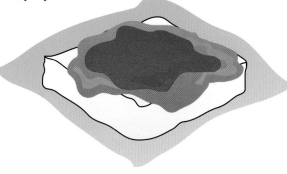

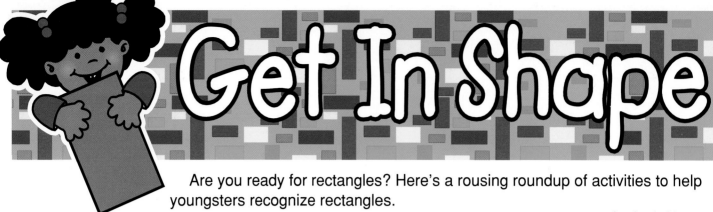

Get In Shape

Are you ready for rectangles? Here's a rousing roundup of activities to help youngsters recognize rectangles.

by Angie Kutzer

Recognizing Rectangles

Gather a collection of empty food boxes with front panels that are rectangular in shape. Cut off the front panels; then show them to students during a group time. Ask volunteers to select panels and point out the long and short sides. Then encourage children to look for rectangular-shaped food boxes at home. Send a note to parents requesting that empty food boxes be sent to class. Set aside a few different-sized boxes for "Panel Printing" (below); then cut the front panels from the remaining boxes for use with the following activities.

Tall Or Short: Challenge volunteers to arrange the collection of rectangles so that they're all "standing tall"—so that the long sides are vertical—or "lying long"—so that the long sides are horizontal.

Rectangle Reading: To help little ones begin to recognize environmental print, display labels in a collage on a bulletin board or wall. Provide a pointer and encourage little ones to read the names of the foods or brands.

Panel Printing: Put your collection of uncut, empty food boxes in the art center. Pour several different colors of paint into separate shallow trays. Have a child dip the panel of a box into a tray. Then have him press the box onto a large sheet of construction paper. Encourage him to use different sizes of boxes and different colors to make his rectangular relic.

"Panel Printing" by Diana Byrne—Pre-K Harleysville, PA

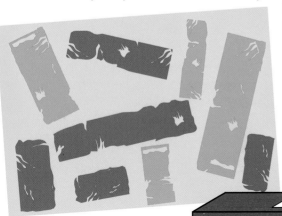

Romp And Rollick Round The Rectangle

Add a little rhythm and rhyme to your rectangle study. Using colored tape, make a large rectangle outline on your classroom floor. If desired, use one color of tape for the long sides and a different color for the short sides. Give each child a pair of building blocks or a set of sand blocks. Play excerpts from various slow and fast recordings. Encourage students to keep the beat with the blocks and their feet as they travel around the tape shape. For added fun, have them "freeze" every time the music stops. Look, we're doing the "rec-tango"!

Diana Byrne—Pre-K

Postcard Puzzlers

Get children's visual-discrimination and critical-thinking skills in shape with these rectangular puzzles. Gather an assortment of postcards. Cut each card into two or three pieces to make a postcard puzzle. Store each puzzle in a rectangular envelope. Or, for an added challenge, store the pieces to several cards in one envelope. Rectangles and postcards are a perfect fit!

With Rectangles

Rectangle Rodeo

Head out to the Rectangle Ranch to let your little broncobusters showcase their talents. Students will exercise their fine-motor skills and hand/eye coordination when making these rectangular horses *and* when bringing them back into the corral.

To make a horse, cut two 3" x 1 1/2" and one 6" x 3" white, black, brown, or tan rectangles from construction paper. Glue the rectangles together as shown. Cut lengths of yarn; then glue them to the horse to create a mane and tail. Glue one wiggle eye to each side of the horse's head. When the glue is dry, attach clothespins to the bottom of the rectangular body to represent the horse's legs. Personalize the horse; then slide a paper clip onto the horse's back.

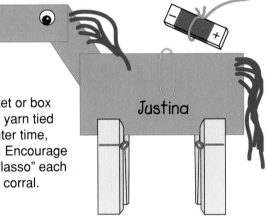

Place the horses in a basket or box (corral) along with a length of yarn tied around a magnet. During center time, stand the horses on the floor. Encourage a child to use the magnet to "lasso" each horse and put it back into the corral. Yippee-ki-yay!

Riddles On Rectangles

Collect a variety of objects that have a rectangular shape. (Refer to the following riddles for suggestions.) For each item, tell a riddle to help youngsters guess the identity of the object. Display the whole collection of items at all times. Once children are familiar with the objects, hide them in a box or bag. Pull out one at a time as guessed. What has two long and two short sides? A rectangle!

What Am I?

1. I am a rectangle. I can stand up or be hung on a wall. I decorate the edges of photographs. What am I? *(picture frame)*

2. I am a rectangle. I have lots of illustrations and words. I tell a story. What am I? *(book)*

3. I am a rectangle. I am sturdy and strong. The third little pig used me to build his house. What am I? *(brick)*

4. I am a rectangle—that is, until you chew me. I come in lots of different flavors. You can buy me in a little or big package. What am I? *(stick of gum)*

The Long And Short Of It

Help little ones differentiate between *squares* and *rectangles* with this catchy song. Hold up a rectangle and a square while singing the first verse, then just the rectangle during the second verse. Encourage the children to clap while singing the phrase "It's a rectangle," each time.

It's A Rectangle
(sung to the tune of "B-I-N-G-O")

There is a shape that has four sides,
But it is not a square….No!
It's a rectangle;
It's a rectangle;
It's a rectangle;
It is not like a square….No!

Two sides are long; two sides are short.
They all are not the same….No!
It's a rectangle;
It's a rectangle;
It's a rectangle;
The sides are not the same….No!

Get In Shape

Here it is! Our last set of exercises created to get your preschoolers into great shape! Use these activities to round out youngsters' knowledge of that oh-so-original oval.

ideas contributed by Barbara Meyers and Angie Kutzer

Looking For Ovals

Enlist the help of Little Oval to search for ovals in the classroom. To make the costume, cut a slit three-fourths of the way down both narrow sides of a paper grocery bag. Cut out an oval shape from tagboard, large enough to cover one of the wider sides of the bag; then glue it to the bag. Ask a child to put on the costume so that you can mark where to cut a smaller oval about the size of a child's face. Then cut the oval through both the bag and the larger oval. Label the costume "Little Oval."

Begin your oval unit by reading aloud *The Shape Of Things* by Dayle Ann Dodds (Candlewick Press). After reading, turn back to the page that focuses on ovals. Introduce the shape's name again and have youngsters trace imaginary ovals in the air. Invite a volunteer to put on the costume and become Little Oval. While the group quietly sings the following song, send him on a search to find an oval-shaped object in the classroom. Once the song ends, have Little Oval share his find.

Look What I Found!
(sung to the tune of "Five Little Ducks")

Oval shape went out one day
To find more oval shapes to play.
Oval shape looked all around,
Then with a smile said, "Look what I found!"

Little Oval

Optical Ovals

What can you do with potatoes, paint, and paper? Make oodles of oval prints! To get ready for the printing, slice several potatoes in half lengthwise; then fill several pie pans with different colors of tempera paint. Look again at the printed shapes in *The Shape Of Things*. Invite each student to dip a potato half into the paint and print several oval shapes onto a large sheet of art paper. When the paint is dry, encourage her to use markers and precut construction-paper shapes to turn her oval into a masterpiece. Display these creations along with the title "Can You Find The Ovals?" for others to ogle over.

Oval Munchies

Your little ones are sure to be in great shape after making and munching on these "oval-wiches" at the cooking center. To make one, use an oval-shaped cookie cutter to cut an oval from two slices of bread and one slice of processed cheese. Place one oval of bread on an oval-shaped plate or a napkin cut into an oval shape; then add the oval of cheese. Squirt an oval of mustard or mayonnaise on top of the cheese before topping the sandwich with the second oval of bread. Lean to the left; lean to the right. Pick up your "oval-wich"; then take a bite!

With Ovals

The Oval Song

Use colored tape to make a large oval shape on the floor; then invite your little ones to hop, skip, march, and otherwise move around the tape while singing this catchy oval song.

I'm An Oval

(sung to the tune of "I'm A Little Teapot")

I'm an oval made with a curved line.
I think my egg shape looks mighty fine.
Eggs, potatoes, spoons, and race-tracks, too:
All have oval shapes just for you!

Get A Feel For It

Little fingers will do the walking with this tactile activity. Insert a variety of plastic or cardboard geometric shapes into a bag or box. (Make sure that there are more ovals than other shapes.) Challenge each child to reach into the bag and pull out an oval. Feeling for ovals is fun!

Stretch And Shape, Stretch And Shape

Cooperation is the key to this shapely exercise. To prepare, sew together the ends of a four-yard length of one-inch-wide elastic. Ask each child in a small group to hold onto the loop and work together to make an elastic oval shape. As a challenge, have the group stretch the loop into previously studied shapes, then back into an oval. What a workout!

Jelly-Bean Jamboree

End your shape training session with the best oval shapes of all—Jelly Belly® jelly beans! Fill a clear container with an assortment of the gourmet jelly beans. Seat your youngsters in an oval; then pass the container around the oval for each child to observe. List volunteers' descriptions about what they see. When the container returns to you, dispense a few jelly beans to each child. Encourage the students to touch, taste, and talk about the samples as you add to the descriptive list. (Be sure to use close supervision since jelly beans may be a choking hazard.) For added fun, request that your little ones try to guess the flavors of their jelly beans. Explain to your students that the candy company would like new jelly-bean designs and flavors. Give each child an oval-shaped paper platter, and invite him to use his choice of colorful paints and painting sponges to create his own jelly bean. As each child describes his jelly bean and names its flavor, ask the group to name the jelly bean's shape. Ovals, ovals, ovals!

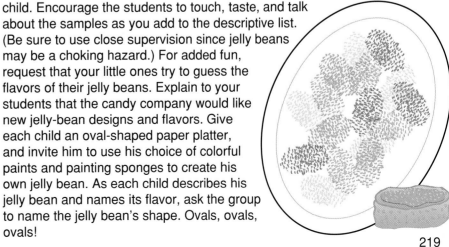

SETTING THE STAGE

Setting The Stage:

A Nature Swim

If walking through a pile of autumn leaves is not an option at your school, take little ones on a "nature swim" inside the classroom. Fill a small wading pool with dry leaves that you've collected. Then invite youngsters to walk through the leaves, listening to the crunchy sounds and smelling the aroma of autumn.

Doris Porter—Preschool
Headstart
Anamosa, IA

Science Center

Pumpkin Exploration

Encourage students to explore and record their discoveries with this seasonal science activity. Place a pumpkin in a shallow tub in your science center. Cut the top off the pumpkin or cut the pumpkin in half so that little ones can observe and feel the inside as well as the outside of the pumpkin. Provide plastic knives and spoons for the children to use when exploring the pumpkin. Near the center, post a large, pumpkin-shaped chart cut from orange poster board. As children visit the center, record their discoveries on the chart. Be sure to have disposable wipes available for a quick cleanup after students' sticky studies!

Ann Endorf—Preschool
Open Arms Christian Preschool
Bloomington, MN

"Pumpkin feels squishy." John

"There are a zillion seeds inside." Tika

Dramatic Play Area

A Creative Campsite

Ahh...that crisp, cool air is calling! It's time for a camping trip—right in your classroom! Set up camp in your dramatic play area with a small tent, a sleeping bag, a lawn chair, a cooler, and some flashlights. Tuck a few books with camping themes into the cooler. Add a box full of appropriate dress-up clothing such as boots, flannel shirts, baseball caps, and gloves. Keep toasty warm with an imaginary campfire made from a circle of rocks and some crumpled red and orange cellophane. Add a frying pan and a spatula so the children can "cook" a fireside meal. And don't forget some sticks and marshmallows for toasting!

Amy MacKay—Four-Year-Olds
Westwoods School/Head Start Program
Bristol, CT

Interest Areas And Centers

Art Center

Mr. Pumpkinhead

Place a pumpkin in your art center and your little ones will soon become quick-change artists! Cover a table with orange or green felt; then place a large pumpkin in a shallow tray on the table. Add some washable markers, a damp sponge, and some paper towels. Invite children who visit the center to use the markers to draw a face on Mr. Pumpkinhead, then use the sponge to erase their handiwork and start again! Add hats, scarves, wigs, and glasses for extra fun and creativity.

Darla Dee Burris—Four- And Five-Year-Olds
Play-N-Learn Playschool
Louisville, OH

Block Center

Build An Observatory

Are your youngsters involved in a nighttime theme? If so, then transform your block area into an observatory so little ones can do a little stargazing. Have youngsters use wooden blocks to form a circle with a wall three or four blocks tall and large enough for at least one child to sit inside. Then create a telescope by covering a paper-towel tube with yellow construction paper. Decorate it with star and moon stickers. Place the imaginary telescope inside your observatory. To provide students with some stars to gaze at, cut star shapes from sheets of foil wrapping paper glued to sheets of tagboard. Suspend the stars from your classroom ceiling using yarn or fishing line. Invite students to visit the center and take turns with the telescope. Twinkle, twinkle!

Charlet Keller
ICC Preschool
Violet Hill, AR

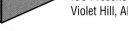

Games Area

Placemat Partners

There's no match for this easy-to-make activity that helps students practice visual-discrimination skills. Simply purchase two identical vinyl placemats that display letters, numerals, characters, or seasonal designs. Cut apart one placemat to create individual pieces. Store the pieces in a zippered plastic bag; then clip the bag to the uncut placemat. To use the activity, a child simply matches the pieces to the identical figures on the placemat.

Betsy Duplechain—Four-Year-Olds
St. Martha Catholic School
Kingwood, TX

Setting The Stage:

Housekeeping Area

Christmas-Tree Decorating

Your little ones will improve their matching skills each time they decorate this tree. Cut a three-foot-tall Christmas-tree shape from bulletin-board paper. To make ornaments for the tree, cut seasonal shapes from colorful tagboard. Lay the tree flat; then arrange all of the ornaments on the tree before tracing their outlines with a marker. Laminate the tree. Attach the hook side of a piece of self-adhesive Velcro® to the back of each ornament. Attach the loop side of a Velcro® piece inside each outline on the tree. Mount the tree in your housekeeping center, store the ornaments nearby, and encourage tree trimming during center time. Oh, Christmas tree! Oh, Christmas tree!

Jackie Wright—Preschool And Gr. K
Summerhill Children's House
Enid, OK

Block Area

Homemade Blocks

Detergent boxes of all sizes make lightweight but sturdy blocks for your little ones. Simply gather the empty boxes, tape them closed, and wrap them with colorful Con-Tact® covering. Let the building begin!

Sue Brewer—Pre-K
First Stages Daycare
Sharon, TN

Dramatic Play Area

Hibernation Station

Help your little ones experience life underground by creating a burrow in your classroom. Set up rows of chairs to create an aisle similar to an underground tunnel. Add a table at one end of the aisle to make a burrow. Drape sheets across the chairs and table. Scatter acorns and other nuts around the room for the children to gather and take to the burrow. Be sure to include books about hibernation for children to browse through while inside the underground animal hole. Now you see me, now you don't!

Kristen Sharpe—Preschool
Kristen's Corner
Mansfield, MA

Interest Areas And Centers

Water Table

Gone Four-Wheelin'

To create perfect conditions for winter driving, squirt mounds of shaving cream into an empty water table. Your little ones will love plowing through the snow with toy vehicles to get to their imagined destinations. There's "snow" telling what will occur in this blizzard of activity.

Joan Banker—Three- And Four-Year-Olds
St. Mary's Child Development Center
Garner, NC

Manipulatives Center

Tabletop Menorah

Sharpen your children's patterning skills with this enlightening suggestion! Use masking tape or colored tape to make a menorah design on a tabletop. Have your children create their own unique patterns along the design using a variety of math counters. As you admire a student's work, ask her to describe the attribute she used for patterning. Your little ones will light up when it's their turn at this festive center!

Nancy Barad—Four-Year-Olds
Bet Yeladim Preschool And Kindergarten
Columbia, MD

Reading Area

A Good Book And A Warm Fire

There's nothing better than curling up with a good book on a cold winter's day. To create this mood in your reading area, cut corrugated board that has a brick design (found at craft stores) to resemble a fireplace. Mount it on a wall. Stack cardboard blocks that look like bricks at the bottom of the fireplace to make a hearth. Add stockings, a rug, a teddy bear, and a rocking chair to your scene along with seasonal reading selections. Little ones will want to warm up to reading! This scenery also makes a terrific backdrop for holiday pictures to give as gifts to parents.

Joan Banker—Three- And Four-Year-Olds

Season's Greetings

Setting The Stage:

Block Center

Tending The Garden

Cultivate the roots of your little ones' imaginations with this fun garden idea. Encourage students to make garden rows with blocks. Provide an assortment of plastic vegetables for the children to "plant" around, on top of, and under the blocks. Have children's garden tools and baskets nearby for the harvest. There is sure to be lots of class-grown fun in this bountiful block garden. Don't be surprised if a produce stand is the next thing in demand!

Linda Blassingame—Pre-K And Gr. K
JUST 4 & 5 Developmental Laboratory
Mobile, AL

Art Center

Suddenly Salad

Give youngsters an opportunity to create an enticing salad while developing fine-motor skills. Stock the center with scalloped sheets of green paper in various shades to represent lettuce. Add an assortment of construction-paper, vegetable-shaped cutouts; play dough; scissors; and plastic bowls.

To make a salad, a student tears the green paper into "bite-size" pieces and puts them in a bowl. She then uses scissors to cut up her choice of vegetable cutouts to add to her salad. If any other vegetables or toppings are desired, encourage her to mold these from play dough, then use them to garnish her salad.

If desired, invite the child to carry her salad over to the housekeeping center. Provide empty salad-dressing bottles, tongs, and plastic forks for a pretend feast. These salads are scrumptious skill builders, any way you toss them!

Linda Blassingame—Pre-K And Gr. K

Dramatic Play Area

Visiting The Vet

Celebrate National Pet Week (the first full week in May) by converting your dramatic play area into a veterinarian clinic. Bring in pet carriers or cut boxes to resemble animal cages. Put a toy doctor's kit in the area as well as other props—such as masks, rubber gloves, paper, pencils, and a clipboard. Also include a roll of gauze and an elastic bandage wrap for treating the "injured." Invite youngsters to bring stuffed animals from home to fill the clinic with patients. (Be sure to tag each toy pet with its owner's name.) Is there a doctor in the house?

Colleen Keller—Preschool And Prep-K
Clarion-Goldfield Elementary, Clarion, IA

Interest Areas And Centers

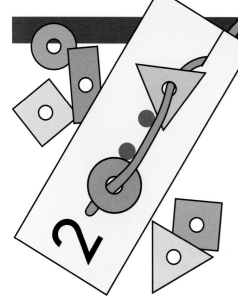

Math Area

Counting Strips

String up some counting fun with these counting strips! To make one, cut sturdy cardboard into a 3" x 8" strip. Write a numeral on the left side of the strip. To the right of the numeral, punch a hole; then draw a row of the corresponding number of dots. Cut a one-inch slit in the center of the right edge of the strip. Cut a 12-inch length of heavy string; then wrap a small piece of tape around one end and knot the other end. Thread the knotted end of the string through the hole; then tape it to the back of the strip. Finally cut out a variety of geometric shapes from meat trays. Punch a hole in the middle of each shape.

For independent counting practice, a child chooses a strip, reads the numeral on the strip, and threads the same amount of shapes onto the string. To secure the shapes, he pulls the end of the string through the slit. One, two, three, a good counter he will be!

Carol Pochert—Four- And Five-Year-Olds, ABC Kids Care, Grafton, WI

Discovery Area

Start Your Engines

Your children will zoom over to this magnetic raceway to practice hand/eye coordination. Draw and color a racetrack on a large piece of tagboard. Then draw, color, and cut out several car outlines from tagboard. Laminate the track and the cars. Slide a large paper clip onto each car. Tape the ends of the tagboard raceway to the edges of two tables so that the track is suspended in air. Place the cars on the track. Invite a child to use the raceway by moving a magnet underneath the tagboard. On your mark, get set, go!

Kim Richman—Preschool
The Learning Zone, Des Moines, IA

Water Table

Rain, Rain, Go Away

If you teach in a church-affiliated day care or preschool, use April's rainy weather as an inspiration to recall the story of Noah. Then add a toy ark (or boat) and lots of toy animals to the water table so children can reenact the miraculous event. For added effect, provide little ones with a prism to use with the water and sunlight to create a rainbow for the promise of a better day.

Setting The Stage:

Housekeeping Area

What Should I Pack?

It's time for summer vacation! Help your little ones pack for imaginary excursions with this handy luggage. To make suitcases, cover handled detergent boxes with colorful Con-Tact® covering. Place the boxes in your housekeeping area along with small clothing articles and various travel items—such as sunglasses, empty film canisters, and empty trial-sized containers. For added fun, include items for cold-weather lovers, too, so that youngsters will get some critical-thinking practice while packing up for their getaways. Bon voyage!

Crystal Sirmans—Preschool
Child Care Contacts R & R
Milledgeville, GA

Art Center

Seashell Sensation

Bring the seashore to the art center by making each of your youngsters a shell to paint. Obtain a collection of clamshells and a package of Crayola® Model Magic® modeling compound. (Or mix a batch of your favorite clay.) To make a shell for each child, press the clay onto the outside of a shell. Peel it off, reshape it, and then trim around the edges of the resulting shape. Once the shell replicas have hardened, hide them in a tub of sand located near the art center. Invite each student to use a shovel and a paintbrush to find and clean one shell. Encourage him to paint his shell, then set it aside to dry. Display this one-of-a-kind seashell collection on a sandy tabletop for all to admire!

Bonnie McKenzie—Pre-K And Gr. K, Cheshire Country Day School, Cheshire, CT

Play Dough Center

Hamburger Helpers

'Tis the season for yummy cookouts, fa-la-la-la-la....Celebrate summer with this sizzlin' center. Provide a wire baking rack to represent a grill. Then add other props—such as an apron, a checkered tablecloth, paper plates, waxed paper, a hamburger press, a spatula, and empty condiment squeeze bottles—to create an atmosphere of short-order fun. Be sure to include several colors of play dough for children to use when making charbroiled burgers with all the toppings, such as green lettuce, red tomatoes, and yellow cheese.

Interest Areas And Centers

Science Center

Just Buggy

Youngsters will swarm over to the science center for a closer look at this enticing insect display. Collect dead, intact insects from a nearby swimming pool. Allow the insects to dry; then pin them to a Styrofoam® tray. Store the tray in a freezer until you're ready to take the specimens to the classroom. When displaying your collection in the science center, provide magnifying glasses so that children can get a closer look. Challenge youngsters to find the six legs and three body parts of each insect. This center is sure to be buzzing with buggy conversation!

Karen Bryant—Pre-K
Miller Elementary
Warner Robins, GA

Dramatic Play Area

Look At Those Fish!

When visiting this aquarium, students will have the opportunity to act a little fishy! Arrange four chairs so that their positions create the four corners of a rectangle—with the chair backs facing out. Wrap tinted plastic wrap around one chair's back; then stretch more of the wrap to the next chair's back. Continue extending the wrap from chair to chair until you have made four sides. Place some small shells and plants in the aquarium for added effect. Children who crawl into the aquarium can pretend to swim around like the fish do. Splish, splash!

Elisa Futia—Three-, Four-, And Five-Year-Olds
Circle Of Friends
Ravena, NY

Sand Table

Down And Dirty

Get the dirt on a unique sensory experience for the sand table—plastic creepy crawlers buried in soil! Partially fill your sand table with loose soil. Collect a supply of plastic critters—such as worms, spiders, and insects—and add them to the dirt. Add shovels and suggest that little ones get down and dirty! Be sure to have some disposable wipes available for temporary cleanup until students can get to the sink for a thorough handwashing.

KinderCare® Region Trainer Jane Brom-Pierzina and KinderCare® District 1 And 2 Center Trainers
Minnetonka, MN

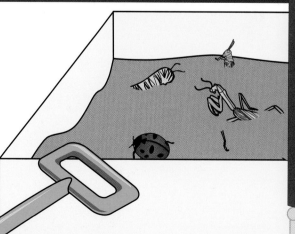

MATH MATTERS

MATH MATTERS

Math On The Playground

Ready? Get set. Go out on the playground! Take advantage of the outdoor opportunities for teaching math skills as your little ones run, jump, swing, and play.

A Spatial Snake

Using a permanent marker, draw facial features on one of a jump-rope's handles. Next time this jump-rope snake just happens to be lying on the ground, you'll have the perfect opportunity to reinforce youngsters' understanding of spatial terms. Call several nearby students' attention to the jump-rope snake. Direct them to stand beside, on, under, in front of, or behind the snake. Or encourage a child to place a ball in similar positions.

Keep a supply of colored manipulatives handy and you'll have yet another way to slip in math skills. For example, you might suggest that a youngster place a blue counting bear in front of the snake and a yellow bear behind the snake or that he place three red bears beside the snake. Sneaky and fun!

Running To Circles

This following-directions game will have your little ones running *to* circles—and squares and triangles! Cut large geometric shapes from different colors of vinyl, placemats, or tagboard. (The vinyl or placemat shapes can be washed after playground fun.) Randomly place the shapes on the ground in an open area or around the playground so that there is plenty of room to move between the shapes. As children express an interest in interacting with you on the playground, challenge them to follow directions such as "Skip to the blue circle," "Hop to the red triangle," and "Run to the yellow square." To increase the difficulty, try announcing two or more directions at a time. For example, "Touch the blue square; then run to the orange oval." Soon youngsters will be giving directions and playing on their own! (For added fun, try this game inside a gym on a rainy day.)

Tonie Liddle—Pre-K
Central Baptist Christian Academy
Binghamton, NY

Number Catch

Here's a catchy idea for numeral recognition and counting. Write a different numeral on each section of an inflated beach ball. Gather a group of interested students together. Announce the name of a child in the group; then throw or roll the ball to that child. When the child has the ball in her possession, have her point to one of the numerals. If necessary assist her in naming the numeral. Then announce an action—such as clapping, jumping, or touching toes—for the rest of the group to complete the identified number of times. Have the child then throw or roll the ball back to you. Continue the game until each child has caught the ball or as long as interest dictates.

More Or Less?

Are hoops a hot item on your playground? If so then place one on the ground and invite a small group of students to jump inside. Have a child help you decide if there should be more or fewer (less) children in the hoop. If you announce more, have one or two children join the children already in the hoop. If you announce less, have one or two children hop out of the hoop. Continue in this manner as children hop in and out to create sets of more and less. Be sure to have the group help you decide which request, more or less, is appropriate with each round. Get hoppin'!

Patterns Please

Opportunities to reinforce patterns are sure to pop up all over your playground. While encouraging several children to take turns, for example, have youngsters chant the order of the children. ("John, Shaun, Cam. John, Shaun, Cam.") As children play on a seesaw, alternate the names of the children on the ground. ("Sheila, Pam. Sheila, Pam.") A "Hello, good-bye" chant as you push a child on a swing will also reinforce patterning. On a playground, patterns are everywhere!

Match Me

Don't put those hoops away yet! Keep a supply of manipulatives, such as beanbags or small balls, handy and you'll have a way to reinforce one-to-one correspondence. Working with a pair of students, provide each child with a hoop. Direct the children to sit on the ground; then supply both students with the same number of manipulatives. Ask one student to place as many items as he would like into his hoop. Encourage his partner to match the same number of items in his own hoop. Then have them place their items side by side to see if they have the same number in each set. Alternate play so that each child has several turns as the leader.

Keep Your Eyes Open!

There will be plenty more teachable moments on the playground. Here are just a few!

- To reinforce classification skills, describe the play ground items during cleanup time. For example, you might say, "Bring all of the blue balls to the bucket."
- Count aloud as you push a child on a swing.
- Identify ordinal positions as you assist a child in climbing a ladder.
- To facilitate measurement discoveries, encourage a child to describe his work as he scoops and pours the sand in a sandbox.
- Ask a child to compare the lengths of several jump ropes or the sizes of different balls.

233

Math In The Housekeeping Area

Use these ideas for teaching math concepts as students play in your classroom housekeeping area. Pretty soon your little ones will be right at home with math!

Margarine Tubs And Manipulatives—
What's The Math Matchup?

Invite several youngsters to join you around the table in your housekeeping area for this game that reinforces counting and one-to-one correspondence. Hide a different number of small manipulatives under each of four margarine tubs. Announce a number that matches the amount of manipulatives in one of the sets. Ask the students to peek under each tub and count the hidden manipulatives until they find the set that corresponds with the number you requested.

For a variation, hide the same number of manipulatives in two of the four sets. Again ask that the youngsters peek under each tub and count the manipulatives until they find the matching sets. Have them compare the matching sets to the remaining two sets. Which set(s) has (have) more? Which has (have) less?

Fine China

You can count on this collection of dinnerware to provide many fine opportunities for reinforcing math skills. Number each of five sturdy, plastic cups with a different numeral from one to five. Draw a different dot set from one to five on each of five sturdy, plastic plates. As students set the table, encourage them to match each plate to the cup with the corresponding numeral.

Challenge youngsters to put the number of plastic food items on each plate that corresponds with the dot set on the plate and the numeral on the matching cup.

What's Your Number?

Say hello to number fun when students use this phone book and a toy phone. To make a phone book for your housekeeping center, glue a duplicated school picture of each child to a large index card or similarly sized piece of tagboard. Personalize the card and write a three-digit number on each child's card next to his picture. Laminate the cards for durability, if desired. Punch two holes near the top of each card; then bind the cards with metal rings. Place the phone book near a toy phone. Encourage and assist youngsters as they look for friends' pretend phone numbers and as they "give them a ring"!

Divided House

There's always plenty of room for classifying in this house. If you have a spacious housekeeping area, divide it into rooms by placing masking tape on the floor to indicate the imaginary boundaries of the rooms. Provide several youngsters with a box full of various household items. Encourage them to sort the items by putting them in the appropriate rooms. Be sure to ask youngsters to explain their classifications.

Sort Of Hungry? Eat Your Shapes!

You'll be delighted to watch students sort, count, and make patterns with these "math-licious" crackers! Collect boxes of different-shaped crackers. Empty the boxes and store the different types of crackers separately in plastic bags or storage containers. For each cracker box, cut tagboard crackers that correspond to the shape of the removed crackers. Color the tagboard crackers so that they match the real crackers in color as well as shape. Refill the empty boxes with the tagboard crackers. To use, encourage youngsters to empty the tagboard crackers into a bowl. Have them sort the crackers by shape. Assist them in making simple patterns with the crackers. Count the crackers as they are dropped back into the appropriate boxes. Be sure to keep the real crackers on hand for shapely snacking!

Counting On Cookies

One-to-one correspondence is made easy with this no-bake cookie idea. To prepare, use colored tape to divide a metal cookie sheet into 12 sections. Roll up a batch of 12 cookie shapes using an air-drying modeling compound, such as Crayola® Model Magic™, or collect 12 cookie-shaped magnets. Provide a child with a large foam die. Have him roll the die and count the number of dots on the side facing up. Have him place the same number of cookies on his cookie sheet. Have him continue to roll the die and count cookies until the sheet is full. For a variation, place all of the cookies on the tray and ask the child to remove cookies from the sheet with each roll of the die.

Kathy Rywolt—Four- And Five-Year-Olds, Redeemer Nursery School, Cincinnati, OH

Keep Your Eyes Open!

There will be many more teachable moments in the housekeeping area. Here are just a few!

- Stock your dress-up area with plenty of shoes. Encourage youngsters to pair the shoes, compare their lengths, and seriate the shoes by size.
- Keep a container of play dough available so that students can shape pretend foods. Discuss *whole* as students mold the shapes and *part* as they cut the shapes into parts with plastic knives.
- Challenge a child to make a pattern using plastic cutlery.
- Ask students to help you weigh plastic food using a balance scale.
- Cut pairs of squares from wallpaper samples. Encourage your homemakers to find the matching pairs.

235

MATH MATTERS

Math In The Art Center

Take a good look at your art center. There's a whole lot of math going on! Use these ideas to facilitate your little ones' discovery of math concepts as they smoosh, paint, cut, and paste!

Popsicle® Math

Popsicle® sticks make great, inexpensive manipulatives to help reinforce a variety of math skills. Have youngsters paint a supply of sticks using a mixture of tempera paint and glue. When the sticks are dry, store them in the art center for the group's use or prepare personalized resealable bags so that each student has his own set. Provide sheets of black construction paper to serve as work mats. As the youngsters use the sticks to form creative images, use the opportunity to reinforce counting, sorting, and patterning.

Karen Jones—Director, Preschool Arts Center
Charlotte, NC

Painting Takes Shape

Little ones love to paint, and paint, and paint! With this idea, their creative efforts will really take shape. Using masking tape, tape the outlines of geometric shapes to large pieces of fingerpainting paper. Encourage a young artist to select a piece of paper and to use brushes and paints to paint the entire sheet with the colors of her choice. When the paint is dry, assist the child as she carefully removes the tape. Surprise! What shapes did you paint?

Pat Johnson—Three-Year-Olds
Church of the Redeemer United Methodist Preschool
Columbus, OH

Stamp Of Math Approval

Keep a wide variety of stamps and colorful stamp pads in your center and your efforts to teach number concepts and patterning are sure to get a stamp of approval. Ask a youngster to help you count the stamps on her own creation. Challenge a child to create sets of prints that have the same number of stamps but in different arrangements. To develop one-to-one correspondence, provide sheets of paper that have sets of open circles. Encourage youngsters to stamp in each circle on a page. Use the pages to make individual counting books. For big-number fun, provide strips of paper for printing large sets of prints or patterns.

What Beautiful Necklaces!

Prepare these materials in advance, and youngsters who visit your art center will make mathematically marvelous necklaces. Cut a supply of geometric shapes from various colors of meat trays. Punch a hole in each shape. Cut a supply of straws in various lengths. Stock your art center with the shapes, straw pieces, and yarn. Encourage each child to make a necklace to wear. Challenge her to find a pattern in her necklace. Ask her to describe the colors in her necklace. What shapes did she use? Count the shapes. What shape did she use the most? The math fun goes on and on!

Bernie Bussacco—Preschool, R. D. Wilson Elementary
Waymart, PA

Measure Me From Head To Toe!

Using heavy yarn, tie a roll of adding-machine tape to the ceiling near your art area so that the tape is within reach. When a child visits the center, pull the tape down until it reaches the child's feet. Then cut the paper so that it matches the child's height. Ask youngsters to use markers, crayons, and other supplies from your art center to decorate their own personal measuring tapes. Encourage youngsters to measure other items at school and at home to compare lengths.

Karen Jones

Measure Me Around My Middle!

Introduce your little ones to measurement with this nifty idea. Using clear packing tape, measure a child around her waist. Cut the tape to the appropriate length; then have the child put her tape in a bag full of art materials such as paper and foil confetti, popcorn, and packing pieces. Have the child shake the bag, then remove her tape to discover a stylish belt! Compare the lengths of the belts. Then tape the ends of a child's belt together around her waist and encourage her to wear it home!

Karen Jones

Keep Your Eyes Open!

There will be many teachable moments in your art center. Here are just a few!

- Ask a child to sort the crayons or markers by color or size.
- Use the markers and crayons to create patterns.
- Model how to use markers as nonstandard units of measurement.
- Ask, "Does your project need *more* glue? *Less* glitter? Do you want the paper to be *smaller? Bigger?*"
- Stock your art center with die-cut numerals. Encourage youngsters to paint, draw, or make creative collages on the cutouts.

MATH MATTERS

Math In The Block Area

Build an understanding of math concepts with these constructive ideas to use in your block area.

ideas by Lori Kent

"Toot-ally" Terrific Trains

Toot! Toot! Youngsters who visit your block area are sure to get on board with this measurement activity. In advance, cut a large train-engine shape from bulletin-board paper; then mount it on a wall in your block area. Tape various lengths of colored tape to the floor of the area. Encourage youngsters to build trains by placing blocks end-to-end along the tape lines. As each child completes a train, ask him to count the number of blocks he used. Then assist him in measuring the train with yarn. Ask the child to hold one end of a ball of yarn at one end of the train as you roll the ball to the other end. Cut the yarn. Attach a piece of masking tape to one end of the yarn and label it with that child's name. Tape the yarn to the train shape.

Twin Towers

Invite a few children to join you in your block area for this game that reinforces spatial awareness and shape recognition. Using a large piece of cardboard to hide your work, build a simple tower using different-shaped blocks. Remove the cardboard and challenge the children to make a twin tower. After the children have duplicated your structure, invite each student to make a tower behind the cardboard for the remainder of his group to copy.

Pleasing Patterns

This patterning activity is sure to be a crowd pleaser. To make a set of pattern cards, trace each different-shaped block in your collection onto a tagboard card. Laminate these cards for durability, if desired. Invite a child to work with you in the center; then create a pattern by displaying several of the cards in a row. Ask the child to use the appropriate blocks to copy and extend your pattern. You'll be as pleased as punch with your students' patterning perfection.

Body Builders

Help youngsters reach new heights with this counting idea. Challenge little ones to build structures that reach from the floor to various parts of their bodies. For example, you might ask a child to build a tower that reaches her knees, her belly button, or even her shoulders. Once she has built the structure, encourage her to count the number of blocks used. For added fun, compare and contrast different structures built to the same body part—but using different-sized blocks. Soon your little ones will be body building on their own!

Block Baskets

A tisket, a tasket; let's count with blocks and baskets! Collect five plastic baskets; then label one side of each basket with a card displaying a different numeral or dot set from one to five. Encourage youngsters to put the correct number of blocks in each basket. To reinforce classification skills, label the opposite sides of the baskets with cards displaying different block shapes or colors. Encourage children to sort the blocks and fill the baskets for a bushel of fun.

Mr. Blockhead

Sorting and classifying will be cinches with Mr. Blockhead. In preparation, collect a box (such as a paper box) and several matching lids. Cover the box and lids with solid-colored Con-Tact® covering. On one side of the box, draw a simple face. On the top of each of the lids, trace the shapes of different shapes and sizes of blocks. Cut out these shapes using a utility knife. Place the box and the lids in your block area. To use them, a child puts a lid on the box and selects the blocks that correspond to the cut-out shapes. He then drops those blocks through the holes in the lid into the box. When the box is full, he removes the lid and dumps the blocks out to be sorted again.

Keep Your Eyes Open!

Be on the lookout for more teachable moments in the block area. Here are a few blockbuster ideas:

- Ask a child to lie down on the floor. Ask another child to help you as you use blocks to measure the child.
- To help develop matching skills, trace blocks onto pieces of tagboard. Ask a child to place the corresponding blocks on the outlined shapes.
- Encourage a child to seriate blocks of different sizes from largest to smallest.
- Challenge a child to balance three blocks of the same shape, but different sizes, on top of each other.

239

Math At The Sand Table

Reinforce math concepts with this treasure chest of ideas for use at your sand table.

ideas by Lori Kent

Buried Treasures

Your little royals will be rich with matching skills when they play this treasure-hunt game. In advance hide pairs of identical, small objects—such as shells, keys, and manipulatives—in your sensory table sand. Challenge a child to use both hands to search for buried treasures. When he thinks he has found a matching pair, have him pull out the objects to see if they match. Then have him hide the objects in the sand before beginning his search for another matching pair.

From Cottage To Castle

Build up seriation skills with this quick and easy activity. Assist a pair of youngsters in arranging a set of nesting cups from smallest to largest. Make sure that the sand is damp; then challenge the children to use the cups to make a kingdom of sand cottages and castles. For additional opportunities to reinforce size comparisons, provide props such as toy cars and wooden figures in graduated sizes.

The Royal Crowns

Your little ones will feel like math kings and queens when playing this jewel of a game that reinforces one-to-one correspondence. To prepare, collect 55 jug lids to represent jewels. Make gameboards by cutting ten crown shapes from poster board. Using a jug lid, trace a different number of circles from one to ten on each crown. Color the circles; then label each crown with the numeral that corresponds to the dot set. To use the crowns and jewels, a child first hides the jug lids in the sand. A different child then selects a gameboard and begins to search for the buried jewels. When he finds a jewel, he places it on a dot, continuing in this manner until his crown is completely adorned with jewels.

Birthday Cakes

A celebration will be in order as youngsters cook up counting skills at your sand table. Stock your sand area with a supply of birthday candles and sand molds. Keep a water spritzer nearby so that youngsters can moisten the sand. Encourage a child to mold birthday cakes from the sand and to top the cakes with the candles. Model one-to-one correspondence by touching each candle as you count aloud each one on a cake. Then challenge the child to continue counting the candles on each of her cakes.

Copycat

To reinforce shape recognition, play a game of Copycat with a youngster at your sand table. Make sure that the sand is damp; then use an unsharpened pencil to draw a geometric shape in the sand. Provide the child with a pencil and encourage him to copy the shape in the sand. As a challenge, have the child carefully observe as you draw a shape; then wipe the shape away. Encourage him to draw the same shape in the sand.

Balancing Buckets

Youngsters will have buckets of math fun with this measurement idea that's sure to be a sandy success. Provide a variety of small containers and scoops in your sand table, and place a balance scale on a nearby table. Encourage students to experiment with balancing weight by filling the containers with varying amounts of sand and then weighing them on the balance scale.

Keep It Going

Keep the learning possibilities piled high in your sand kingdom with these quick and easy ideas.

- To your sand table, add various lengths of cardboard tubes for scooping and pouring.
- Reinforce shape recognition with geometric cookie cutters, and develop numeral recognition with numeral-shaped cutters.
- Encourage a child to create a pattern using sand molds. Or have one partner in a pair start a pattern for the other partner to finish.

Math At The Water Table

Your little ones will dive into math with these wet and wild activities.

ideas contributed by Lori Kent

Five Little Ducks

Extend the fun of the favorite song "Five Little Ducks" with this small-group activity. Invite five children to the water table. Give each child a plastic duck, and keep one to represent the mother duck. Encourage the children to manipulate their ducks in the water as you sing the song together. Quack, quack, quack, quack! All of your little ducks will want to come back!

Treasure Hunt

Assorted types of treasures in your water table will entice your little ones to dive into sorting and patterning skills. Add small, sinkable items—such as manipulatives, marbles, and fake jewels—to your water table. Place several pairs of ice tongs and foam trays nearby. Challenge a child to use the tongs to retrieve the items of his choice and place them on the trays. When he has accumulated the desired amount of treasure, encourage him to sort and pattern the items by attributes such as size and color.

"Size-able" Laundry

Size up youngsters' seriation skills with this fun water-table idea. Create a miniature clothesline near your water table by tying heavy yarn onto two chairs or two wall hooks. (As a precaution, make sure that the clothesline is not in a path of travel.) Cut terry cloth into various sizes of squares. Place the squares in the water table. Store a bucket of clothespins nearby. When visiting the center, a child wrings each square dry and then arranges them on the clothesline in order by size.

Moving Water

Your youngsters will be shipshape with this activity that reinforces spatial awareness and counting skills. Place two plastic tubs side by side. Fill one with water and leave the other empty. Provide large, plastic containers or measuring cups. Encourage visitors to this center to transfer the water in the filled tub to the empty tub. Be sure to count aloud as each container is filled and emptied. Now that's a moving experience!

Star Fishing

Youngsters will feel like superstars when they are successful at catching these matching starfish. From different colors of construction paper, cut pairs of starfish. If desired, label each pair with matching shapes or corresponding numeral and dot sets. Laminate the shapes; then attach a metal paper clip to each one. Prepare a fishing rod by attaching a string and magnet to a dowel or curtain rod. Place the starfish in your water table, and locate the rod, a pail, and a towel nearby. When visiting the center, a child uses the rod to catch a starfish and then fishes again until he catches its match. He continues until he has caught and put all of the starfish pairs in the pail. For a variation, add an extra rod and encourage two children to work together to catch matching pairs of starfish.

Number Float

Here's a way for little ones to soak up numeral-recognition skills. Using a die-cutter, cut one set of numerals from flat sponges and another set from construction paper. Glue each paper numeral to a separate sheet of construction paper; then use a marker to add a corresponding set of dots to each sheet. Laminate the sheets. Place the sponge numerals in the water table along with various types of plastic manipulatives. To use the center, a child squeezes the water out of a numeral-shaped sponge and places it atop the matching numeral on a laminated sheet. He then collects the correct number of manipulatives from the water and places each one on a dot.

Ping-Pong® Scoop

Encourage your little ones to roll up their sleeves and have a ball at this "scooper-duper" center. In advance collect a supply of plastic berry baskets and a quantity of colorful Ping-Pong® balls. Float the balls in your water table. To enjoy this fun center, a child uses a berry basket to scoop up a number of balls. He then counts the balls in the basket. Can he scoop just one ball? How many balls can he scoop at one time?

For a challenging variation, label each of ten plastic key rings with a different numeral from one to ten. Attach one of these key rings to each of ten baskets. To use the center, a child selects a basket, reads the number, and scoops that number of balls into the basket.

Betty Silkunas
Lansdale, PA

Keep It Going

Use these simple ideas to keep your little ones' understanding of math concepts afloat!

- Cut sponges into geometric shapes; then put them in the water table.
- Encourage pouring and filling by adding muffin tins, measuring cups and spoons, and graduated nesting tubs to your water table.

THE MAGIC OF MANIPULATIVES

The Magic Of Manipulatives

Buttons

Invite youngsters into a world of "fasten-ating" learning opportunities with these button-filled activities. To prepare, gather a large assortment of buttons in a variety of colors, shapes, sizes, designs, and numbers of buttonholes. Then button up and let the fun begin!

by Mackie Rhodes

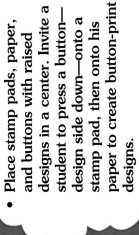

Tim

- Have a child glue buttons on a strip of tagboard to create a pattern according to the color, size, shape, or design of the buttons.

- Place stamp pads, paper, and buttons with raised designs in a center. Invite a student to press a button—design side down—onto a stamp pad, then onto his paper to create button-print designs.

- Place a variety of buttons in the sand table. Challenge students to scoop, dig, and sift to find as many buttons as possible in the sand.

- Obtain a lidded plastic container. Cut a slot in the lid and place it on the container. Encourage a youngster to count aloud as he places a designated number of buttons, one at a time, through the slotted lid. When he is finished, have him remove the lid, pour the buttons from the container, and count them again to check for correctness.

- Encourage youngsters to sort buttons by color, size, shape, or the number of holes in each button.

- Have students create shapes, designs, and letters by gluing buttons to a fabric square.

246

- Use a button to play a memory game. As a student watches, place the button in the palm of one of your hands; then close both hands into fists. Spin yourself or the child around three times. Hold both fists out toward the child and challenge him to select the hand holding the button.

- Spread a handful of buttons out on a table. Encourage a child to scan the button selection as you describe one of the buttons to him. Ask him to find the button described. Invite students to describe buttons in the same manner for each other to find.

Margie Dunlevy—Rocky River, OH

Buttons are marvelous manipulatives, but can be a choking hazard to very young children. Provide adequate supervision during these activities.

- Challenge a youngster to sequence a variety of buttons by size from smallest to largest.

- Have your little ones lace buttons onto pipe cleaners. Twist the ends of each pipe cleaner together to create a bracelet.

- Place some buttons in a resealable plastic bag. Ask a student to estimate the number of buttons in the bag. Then have him pour the buttons out of the bag and count them.

- Partially fill several resealable plastic sandwich bags with buttons. Seal each bag; then tape the top edges of the bag together. In turn invite little ones to toss the bags of buttons to a target from a given distance.

The Magic Of Manipulatives

Keys

Your little ones hold the keys to learning with these fun and interesting activities. Collect an assortment of old, miscellaneous keys; then get ready for youngsters to unlock the doors to unlimited learning opportunities!

ideas by Mackie Rhodes and Betty Silkunas

• Have students sort keys by color, size, the shape of the head (the large end), the number of cutouts in the head, and the number of carved edges.

• Use these Pog® key chains with an assortment of 55 keys to give youngsters practice with counting and number-recognition skills. Label each of 11 Pogs® with a different numeral from 0–10. Punch a hole in each Pog®; then thread one end of a pipe cleaner through each hole and twist it securely onto itself. Have a child thread the appropriate number of keys onto the pipe-cleaner portion of each key chain.

• Have your little ones toss keys into a box, basket, or Hula-Hoop® from specified distances.

• Invite each child to remove one key from a basket of assorted keys. Ask him to imagine that his key will unlock a chest full of precious treasures. Then give him a construction-paper chest shape. Have him fill his chest with glued-on magazine cutouts or personalized illustrations of a variety of treasures. Remind him to also glue his key onto his treasure chest.

• Challenge students to place keys end-to-end to make different shapes, designs, and letters.

• Play a modified matching game with a set of 24 keys. To prepare, attach a foil star sticker to each of 12 keys. Randomly turn these keys facedown on a table, along with the 12 additional keys. To play, a child turns over two keys at a time to search for a match—either two keys with stars or two without.

248

- Hot-glue a wooden clothespin handle onto each of several keys. Prepare a tray of tempera paint. Encourage a child to draw the head and body of a person on a sheet of construction paper; then invite him to create arms and legs for his person using key prints.

- Strike up the band with these key instruments! Invite each student to create one of the following to play during a musical activity:

  —Place several keys in a lidded coffee can to make a shaker.

  —String several keys onto a length of yarn; then tie the ends together to make some jingle keys.

  —Punch holes along the edge of a foil pie plate; then lace a string through each hole. Tie one key onto each string to make a tambourine.

Lilli

- Invite youngsters to play a seriation game using keys of various sizes. Encourage each child to sequence the keys from smallest to largest.

- Trace a number of different keys on a sheet of tagboard. Place the keys in a container. Have a student match each key to its corresponding outline.

- Have little ones lace keys onto yarn lengths for use as necklaces or wind chimes.

- Invite youngsters to use keys as markers in a game of tic-tac-toe. In advance spray-paint ten keys: five red and five blue. To make the gameboard, draw a tic-tac-toe grid on a 12-inch-square sheet of poster board. Laminate the gameboard for durability. To play, each of two players in turn puts a key on the gameboard, attempting to place three of his keys in a row.

The Magic Of Manipulatives

Bows

Wrap up learning and top it with a bow—rather, a bunch of bows! Request bags of gift bows to use with these manipulative ideas that your little elves are sure to enjoy.

ideas contributed by Betty Silkunas

Guess How Many

Play Put The Bow On The Present! Gift wrap a piece of poster board; then laminate it. Mount it at students' eye level. In turn, give each child a self-adhesive gift bow. Gently turn the child around once or twice; then direct him to put the bow on the present. Everybody wins!

Have your little ones toss bows into boxes or baskets from specified distances.

Fill a gift-wrapped box with bows. Challenge children to estimate the number of bows in the box. Empty the box; then ask the group to count aloud as each bow is dropped back into the box.

Using a fine-lined marker, write a different child's name on each of a classroom supply of bows. Ask a volunteer to hide (or place) the bows around the room; then have each child find his personalized bow. Hide and *bow* seek!

Place a supply of two or three different colors of bows in a basket along with lengths of ribbon. To practice fine-motor skills, have a child thread bows onto a ribbon length to create a simple pattern.

For gross-motor fun, scatter bows on the floor around an open area. Encourage youngsters to walk, hop, run, etc. around the bows.

250

Program sheets of construction paper with dot sets from one to five. Ask a child to count each dot in a set and to place a bow on each dot.

Cut various lengths of package ribbon. Assist youngsters as they use a supply of bows to measure the length of each piece of ribbon.

Have each child close his eyes and select a bow from a bag. Direct him to open his eyes and find a student or students with the same color of bow.

Stock an art center with a supply of bows, pipe cleaners, glue, and a variety of art supplies such as buttons, sequins, stickers, etc. Encourage youngsters to create bow sculptures by twisting the bows together, then decorating them.

Insert a straw into each of several pieces of Styrofoam®. Challenge youngsters to sort the bows by color or size and stack them accordingly onto different straws. Or have them create equal sets of bows on the straws.

The Magic Of Manipulatives

Pom-Poms

You'll need a pom-pom assortment of different sizes and colors for this hodgepodge of hands-on learning. Set up the skill-building opportunities listed below; then watch as the pom-poms steal the show!

by Angie Kutzer

Make tactile number cards by hot-gluing pom-poms onto tagboard squares in set formations.

Use four pom-poms of different colors to practice ordinal numbers. Align the pom-poms in a row and ask a child which color is *first, second, third,* or *fourth.* Or have him order the pom-poms according to your oral directions. For example, "Put the yellow pom-pom first."

Andy

Squirt different colors of paint into separate plates. Place a pom-pom that matches each color in its corresponding plate. Encourage each child to repeatedly press the pom-poms in the paint, then onto paper to fill a simple pattern with lots of paint dots!

Invite each youngster to glue two wiggle eyes onto a large pom-pom to make a fluffy critter. Ask volunteers to tell stories about their imaginary pom-pom pets.

Provide tagboard strips, pom-poms, and glue so that little ones can make puffy patterns.

Use three paper cups and one pom-pom to play this guessing game. Turn the cups upside down and arrange them in a row on a tabletop, placing one of the cups over the pom-pom. Without lifting the cups, slide them on the table to change their positions. Invite children to use words such as *first, middle, last, second,* and *third* to guess which cup the pom-pom is under.

Attach a small piece of Double-Coated Scotch™ Tape to each fingertip of a child's hand. Direct the child to attach a small pom-pom to each piece of tape. Recite a counting rhyme or song, such as "Five Little Monkeys" or "Five Little Speckled Frogs." Invite each child to manipulate the pom-poms as each verse is completed.

Fill a plastic bag with pom-poms. Invite a child to take as much as one handful of pom-poms out of the bag. For each pom-pom that she took, ask her to tell you one thing she likes to eat, one thing she likes at preschool, and so forth.

Challenge a pair of youngsters to work together to sort a variety of pom-poms by size and color.

Insert a collection of round items (including a pom-pom) in a paper lunch bag. Have each child reach inside the bag, feel the items, and pull out the object that she thinks is the pom-pom.

Draw a gumball machine on each of ten sheets of construction paper; then label each machine with a different numeral or dot set from one to ten. Have each child place the corresponding number of pom-poms on each sheet.

Invite each child to place a pom-pom at the end of a table. Count aloud the number of breaths it takes him to blow the pom-pom off the other end of the table.

EXPLORATIONS

Explorations

C-C-Cold?
Put On A Jacket!

It's autumn and cooler temperatures are here. To demonstrate how jackets keep body heat in and cool air out, just try these activities on for size!

STEP 1

To prepare to demonstrate how jackets keep us warm, make a hand jacket by inserting the batting pieces into one of the plastic bags.

STEP 2

Just prior to your group time, half-fill the bowls with water and ice.

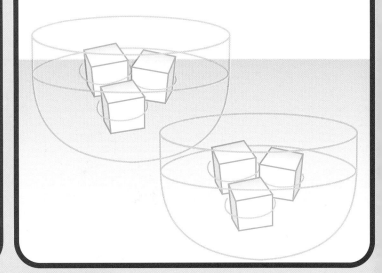

STEP 5

Have the children take off their jackets and examine them carefully. How do jackets help us to stay warm?

STEP 6

Give each child an opportunity to participate in this demonstration. Have a child put one hand in the empty plastic bag and the other hand between the layers of batting in the hand jacket. Next have him immerse each hand into one of the bowls of water.

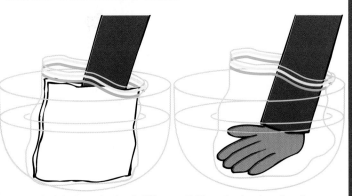

How do his hands feel different? How is the batting in the bag like a jacket?

Science You Can Do by Ann Flagg

To learn how jackets keep us warm, you will need:
—a cool or cold day
—children's coats
—two quart-size (7" x 8") resealable plastic bags
—two 6" x 7" pieces of polyester bonded batting
—two deep bowls
—ice
—water

STEP 3

Ask a small group of children to gather their coats and join you in your group area. Have the children put on their coats.

Ask some questions to get youngsters warmed up for your demonstration.
- Why don't we wear jackets in the summer?
- Why do we wear jackets in the fall?
- Are you comfortable wearing your coat inside the classroom? Why not?

STEP 4

Next direct each child to feel his face with one hand and a window with the other hand. How do they feel different? Lead children to conclude that their bodies are warm and the outside air is cool.

Did You Know?

- Heat is a form of energy.
- Our bodies use the food we eat to produce the heat we need to keep our bodies at about 98.6 degrees.
- Heat flows from a warm object or area to a cooler object or area.
- Insulation stops the movement of heat.
- In cold weather we wear insulated clothing to keep body heat from escaping.
- In warm weather we wear light clothing to let heat escape from the body.
- In addition to jackets, thermos bottles and coolers are examples of insulated items that keep heat from escaping an area.

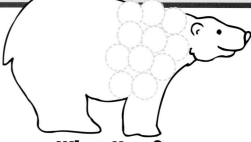

What Now?

- Animals wear coats, too! Provide children with precut animal shapes, cotton balls, felt scraps, scissors, and glue. As the children glue "coats" onto the animals, help them understand that an animal's fur is similar to a person's coat.
- Gather clothing of varying thicknesses such as a T-shirt, a thinly lined coat, and a heavy winter coat. Have children compare the different thicknesses of the fabrics and the insulating liners.

Explorations

Windy Days

Science is a breeze with these activities about the wind. Get ready to be blown away!

STEP 1

During a group time, record youngsters' ideas about the wind. Ask some questions:
• What is the wind?
• Can you see the wind?
• How do you know when the wind is near?

To encourage discussion, read aloud a book about the wind.

> The wind is very busy today!
>
> Preston
>
> The wind picks the leaves up and makes them move everywhere else.
>
> Andrew

STEP 2

On a cloudy, breezy day, go outside for a "wind watch." Look for signs that the wind is moving, such as a flapping flag or blowing leaves. Focus youngsters' attention on the clouds in the sky. Ask, "What makes the clouds move?"

STEP 5

Challenge youngsters to move the cotton-ball clouds without touching them. When the children discover that they can blow on the clouds to make them move, provide straws to extend the experience.

STEP 6

Encourage each child to find other items (such as pieces of paper, fabric scraps, bottles that pump air, etc.) in your room that can be used to move air. Have them use their items at the sky table to make the clouds move. Which items work best?

Science You Can Do *by Ann Flagg*

To learn about the wind, you will need:
— chart paper
— a marker
— a book about the wind (see "What Now?")
— a cloudy, breezy day
— a large, clear plastic bag (as used by dry cleaners)
— a small table

— blue bulletin-board paper
— bulletin-board border
— tape
— large cotton balls
— straws

STEP 3

Hold the plastic bag over your head. "Capture" the wind in the bag; then twist closed the opening. Ask the children to describe the wind in the bag. How do they know air is in the bag? Will the wind "escape" if you open the bag?

STEP 4

Make a sky table for your science center by covering a table with blue bulletin-board paper. Tape strips of bulletin-board border around the edge of the table to create a barrier. Have the children stretch cotton balls to resemble clouds. Put the clouds on the sky table.

What Now?

Check out these books about wind and air.

Air Is All Around You
Written by Franklyn M. Branley
Illustrated by Holly Keller
Published by HarperCollins Children's Books

Feel The Wind
Written & Illustrated by Arthur Dorros
Published by HarperCollins Children's Books

How Does The Wind Walk?
Written by Nancy White Carlstrom
Illustrated by Deborah Kogan Ray
Published by Simon & Schuster Children's Books

Did You Know?

• Wind is air moving across the surface of the earth.
• Wind may move so slowly and gently that it can hardly be felt. Wind that blows fast and hard can damage trees and buildings.
• The sun makes the wind blow. When air is warmed by the sun, it expands and rises. Cooler air moves into the empty spaces.
• Changes in the weather are caused by moving air.

Explorations

Fruity Floaters And Sinkers

Surprise your students with this tutti-frutti floating and sinking activity.

STEP 1

Gather a group of children around your water table. To introduce the word *sink,* drop a rock into the water; then display the sign labeled "sink." Ask the children to show thumbs-down gestures. To introduce the word *float,* drop a pencil into the water; then show the sign labeled "float." Ask the children to show thumbs-up gestures.

STEP 2

Place the signs on a nearby table. Show the children a basket of fruit. Explain that the group will discover which fruits float and which sink.

STEP 5

Encourage the children to look carefully at the two groups of fruit. What similarities can they find? What differences? Next provide time for the children to pick up the fruit in each of the two groups. Which fruits are heavy? Which are light?

STEP 6

When each child has had an opportunity to participate in Steps 1 through 5, slice the fruits open; then compare and contrast the insides. Ask volunteers to give reasons why some of the fruits sink and others float. Record the comments. If desired paraphrase the information given in "This Is Why."

The cantaloupe is empty.
Courtney

The grape is full of grape stuff inside. It's like a rock.
Nichole

Science You Can Do *by Ann Flagg*

To learn about floating and sinking, you will need:
— a water table or large container filled with water
— a rock
— a pencil
— one sign labeled "sink" with a thumbs-down illustration; — a marker
   one sign labeled "float" with a thumbs-up illustration
   (see Step 1)
— a basketful of fruits that vary in size and density
— a dish towel or paper towels

— a table
— a knife
— chart paper
— a marker

STEP 3

Hold up a piece of fruit. Ask each child to show a thumbs-up gesture if he predicts that it will float, or a thumbs-down gesture if he predicts that it will sink. (Remind the children that a prediction is a guess, and that they can change their minds and gestures when they see the results.) Have a volunteer drop the piece of fruit into the water. Ask the group to observe the fruit, then show the appropriate gestures to indicate if the fruit floats or sinks.

STEP 4

Remove the fruit from the water and wipe it dry. Place it near the appropriate sign. Continue until the group has made a prediction and an observation about each piece of fruit.

This Is Why

Buoyancy, displacement, and *density* determine whether an object floats or sinks. When an object is put in water, the water pushes up on it. This buoyancy makes an object float. At the same time, when an object is placed in water, it pushes some of the water away. The displacement of the water causes an object to sink. Density has to do with the amount of matter in an object. If an object is denser than water, it will sink. If an object is less dense than water, it will float.

What Now?

• After you have completed Step 6, make fruit salad or have a fruit-tasting party. Do more children like the fruits that float or the fruits that sink?

• Place a variety of vegetables near your water table. Encourage children to independently find out which vegetables float and which sink.

SPECIAL TOUCHES

My Texture Book

For the student who avoids touching different textures, this personalized book may provide the bridging necessary to help him build tolerance for environmental textures. To make the book, gather a variety of textured materials such as thin pieces of wood, foil, packing bubbles, cotton balls, and different types of fabrics. Help the child glue each item onto a separate square of tagboard. When the glue dries, write the child's dictated description of each item's texture on the appropriate page. On a separate square of tagboard, write the title "My Texture Book" and the child's name. Using a hole puncher, punch two holes through the tops of all the pages; then bind them together with metal rings. Encourage the child to share his book with his classmates.

Louise Anderson—Four-Year-Olds
Community Cooperative Nursery School
Norwalk, CT

I was mad because I thought it was my turn.

Angry Red Crayon

Give youngsters with special behavioral or emotional needs an appropriate outlet for expressing their anger. Place some paper and a basket of red crayons (and a variety of other colors, if desired) in a designated area. During times when a child becomes *very* angry, he may take a crayon from the basket and draw his anger on a sheet of paper. While an angry child is using a crayon from the basket, permit him to color as hard as he desires, even though his crayon may break. As his anger diminishes, invite the child to share his drawing with you, encouraging him to express the reasons for his anger. Discuss with the child appropriate ways to express and deal with his feelings.

Andria Donnelly—Four- And Five-
    Year-Olds
Head Start/Sugarland Elementary
Sterling, VA

Dancing In The Dark

Do you have a student who is so shy that she seems to slip into the shadows of other students or into the dark corners of your classroom? If so, help draw her out by having a dance in the dark. Simply dim or turn off the lights; then play some lively dancing music. Invite all the students to move and groove in their own creative ways. The comfortable atmosphere created by the low lights and rhythmic music will surely help your shy student lighten up and become less timid.

Susie Kruger—Pre-K
Marquette School
Champaign, IL

My Texture Book

Louise

This feels slick.

Special Touches

Ideas For Use With Students Who Have *Special* Needs

A Trip Down Texture Trail

Take special needs children on a trip down texture lane with this creative idea. To make a texture trail, laminate ten 12" x 18" sheets of construction paper. Tape the sheets together end-to-end so that when spread on the floor, a 12" x 180" trail is created. On each sheet of paper, adhere a section of a uniquely textured material such as bubble wrap, sandpaper, fake fur, vinyl, or felt. Attempt to include on the trail materials with as great a variety of color and density as possible.

Encourage children to explore the texture trail by feeling each texture with their hands, crawling along the trail, or walking barefoot down the trail. As a language extension, ask children to help you describe the attributes of each section of the trail. To store the trail, simply fold it accordion-style. Happy trails to you!

Linda Becker—Pre-K
Parents Are Important In Rochester
Rochester, MN

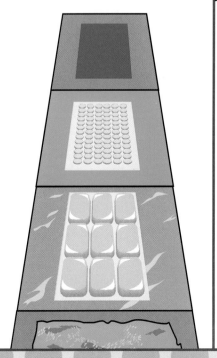

Powerful Picture Books

Use simple picture books designed for infants and photo-illustrated books by authors such as Tana Hoban with language-delayed children. As you share a book experience with a child who has this special need, encourage her to identify the pictured object, or use the picture to engage her in a conversation about the object. Not only will you be helping her increase her language abilities; you'll also be spending quality time together. Now *that's* special!

Pam D'Esopo
North Easton, MA

Letters With Ridges

Here's a tactile idea that uses a surprising material—lightbulb cartons! Using a die-cutter or letter templates, cut letters from ridged lightbulb cartons. Glue the letters onto sheets of construction paper for youngsters to feel, or to make crayon rubbings. Or cut strips from the material and encourage youngsters to glue the strips onto a sheet of paper to create letters without curves such as *E, F,* and *T.* What a bright idea for recycling!

Mary E. Maurer
Caddo, OK

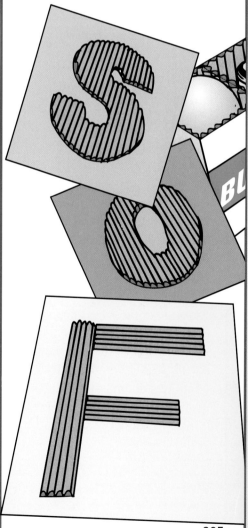

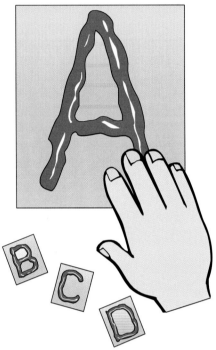

A Touchable Alphabet

Use these textured alphabet cards to help youngsters with special needs get a feel for letter formations. To make the alphabet set, cut thirteen 4" x 6" index cards in half. (These smaller-sized cards allow little hands to feel entire letters.) Using different colors of Slick® fabric paint, label each card half with a different letter of the alphabet. When the paint dries, post the sequenced cards in a row on a wall within children's reach. Or place them in a center for students to manipulate. Encourage students to feel their way through the alphabet as they sing a favorite alphabet song.

Laleña Williams—Four- And Five-
    Year-Olds With Special Needs
St. Francis Preschool
LaGrangeville, NY

266

No-Mess Fingerpainting

Here's a way to include children who are tactile sensitive or who are squeamish about messy hands during fingerpainting activities. Simply put a blob of fingerpaint between two sheets of waxed paper. As the child "fingerpaints" on the waxed paper, a picture appears but the mess doesn't. Now you can provide fingerpainting fun for everyone!

Doris Porter
HACAP Head Start
Anamosa, IA

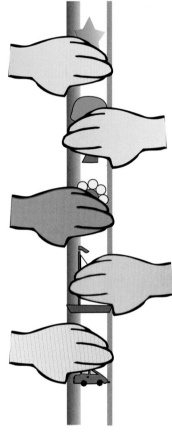

Line 'em Up!

Help your small group of special needs children travel in a line by having them hold onto this simple walking stick. Obtain a length of PVC pipe that is narrow enough for young hands to grasp. At even intervals, attach different stickers to the stick to designate each child's place in the line. Because it stays straight and firm, this walking stick makes it easier for children to stay in a uniform line. So line 'em up and get going!

Melissa Hill—Preschool Special
    Education
S.T.E.P.S. Program, Muscogee County
    School District
Columbus, GA

BUILDING CHARACTER

Building CHARACTER

Ideas For Teaching Virtues In The Preschool Classroom

by Lisa Cowman

Helpfulness

Help Wanted

Introduce youngsters to the virtue of helpfulness with the helping hand of a favorite class puppet. Carry on a dialogue with the puppet about the satisfied feeling that comes from helping others. Explain that to help a friend or family member, one must be on the lookout for what others need instead of thinking only about personal needs. To help your little ones begin to recognize opportunities for helping, encourage volunteers to share with you and your puppet friend ways that they have been or could be helpful at home, school, and play.

Helping Hands

Give your eager beavers an opportunity to be helpful each day during snacktime. Just prior to snacktime, pair youngsters. Then encourage one partner in the pair to serve his mate a snack. The remaining partner can then serve the drink. As the children put the virtue of helpfulness into practice, provide praise by describing their gestures and letting them know you are proud of their behavior. Be sure to deliberately model helpfulness during this time by emphasizing your own wording, facial gestures, and positive body language. That's service with a smile!

Help, I Need Somebody!

Your little ones will enjoy this not-so-typical relay race. Divide the class into two teams standing in two parallel lines. Provide the leader of each line with a large spoon and a Ping-Pong® ball; then instruct the two children to walk to a finish line and then back to their teams. If one child drops his ball, the other child should stop to help him pick it up and wait until he is holding it to start walking again. This game just gets sillier and sillier, but all the giggles will teach youngsters that helping really is fun!

Help Yourself

Help yourself to a collection of stories that provide the perfect opportunity to discuss helpfulness. As you read aloud *A Pocket For Corduroy* by Don Freeman (Puffin Books) encourage your young listeners to identify the helpful people in the story and their actions. Follow up a reading of *Just For You* by Mercer Mayer (Western Publishing Company, Inc.) by asking youngsters to describe the ways they help at home. *Farmer Duck* by Martin Waddell (Candlewick Press) and *Anansi And The Moss-Covered Rock* retold by Eric A. Kimmel (Holiday House, Inc.) both provide humorous illustrations of animal friends helping each other.

Building CHARACTER

Ideas For Teaching Virtues In The Preschool Classroom
Peacemaking

What Is Peacemaking?

Peacemaking involves listening to another person's side of a conflict. Peacemaking requires recognizing anger and managing it. No doubt, peacemaking can be a difficult virtue for young children to understand and put into action! To help your little ones begin to understand anger, conflicts, and peaceful resolutions, read aloud the following book suggestions. Ask youngsters questions like, "Can you think of a situation that would cause an argument? How do you feel when you are having an argument? What can happen when people argue? How can you solve the problems in an argument?"

I Was So Mad!
Written by Norma Simon
Illustrated by Dora Leder
Published by Albert Whitman & Company

The Quarreling Book
Written by Charlotte Zolotow
Illustrated by Arnold Lobel
Published by HarperCollins Children's Books

What Makes A Peaceful Classroom?

Gather your group together to discuss ways that each child can make your classroom a friendly and peaceful place. Write each child's suggestion on a large piece of bulletin-board paper. Make sure that each child has contributed something to your conversation—even if he simply repeats the thought of another child. Ask each child if he agrees with the suggestions written on the paper; then ask him to choose a color of paint and to make a handprint on the paper. Explain that by putting his handprint on the poster, he is agreeing to help make your classroom a peaceful place. Display the poster in an area of your room previously designated as a cool-down or time-out area.

A Man Of Peace

Happy Birthday, Martin Luther King by Jean Marzollo (Scholastic Inc.) is an appropriate way to introduce older preschoolers to a famous American who had a dream of peace. If possible locate sources that have photographs of Dr. King to help your little ones realize that he was a real person and not a fictional character. Then read aloud and discuss the book.

Pass The Peace

Promote Martin Luther King, Jr.'s dream of peace with this feel-good idea. Seat the class in a circle on the floor. Have youngsters pass a peaceful gesture—such as a handshake, hug, smile, tickle, or wink—from one child to another until it completes the circle. Positive words and phrases can also accompany the gesture. What a pleasant and gentle way to begin or end the day!

Donna Henry • Portsmouth Catholic School • Portsmouth, VA

Building CHARACTER

Ideas For Teaching Virtues In The Preschool Classroom
Honesty

The Best Policy

How does a three- or four-year-old understand honesty? Ask your youngsters to explain what they think it means to be *honest*. Then follow up your discussion by reading aloud one of the following preschool-appropriate titles. Help the children see cause and effect by discussing how the character in the selected story felt before and after being honest. What are other reasons that honesty is really the best policy? After your discussion, continue to build youngsters' desires to be honest by encouraging them to be careful of parents' and friends' feelings by telling the truth.

Franklin Fibs
Written by Paulette Bourgeois
Illustrated by Brenda Clark
Published by Scholastic Inc.

Harriet And The Garden
Written & Illustrated by Nancy Carlson
Published by Carolrhoda Books, Inc.

What's So Terrible About Swallowing An Apple Seed?
Written by Harriet Lerner and Susan Goldhor
Illustrated by Catharine O'Neill
Published by HarperCollins Publishers, Inc.

Tell The Reason Why!

Here's a fun little rhyme to reinforce the meaning of honesty. Clap, slap, or stomp a steady beat as you chant.

> I will not tell a lie.
> I'll tell the reason why.
> The truth is best.
> I must confess.
> I will not tell a lie.

I Cannot Tell A Lie

Inspire your little ones by telling them the legendary story of George Washington and the cherry tree. Familiarize yourself with the story as found in *The Children's Book Of Virtues* edited by William J. Bennett (Simon & Schuster, Inc.). Then retell the story in appropriate language for your little ones. Though your children may be too young to understand whom George Washington was, they'll remember the lesson of the virtue of honesty taught by this simple tale.

Have children make these cherry necklaces to wear home so that parents will be aware of your efforts to emphasize honesty. Instruct each child to trace a circle shape onto a piece of red construction paper, then cut out the circle. Have her poke half of a brown pipe cleaner through the paper, then twist as shown to resemble the cherry's stem. Thread a length of green yarn through the pipe-cleaner loop; then tie the ends of the yarn to complete the necklace. On one side of each child's cherry, write "I'm learning about honesty." Have the child write her name on the opposite side, then wear the necklace as a reminder to tell the truth.

I'm learning about honesty.

OUT & ABOUT

Big Book Of Playground Rules

Involve youngsters in this whole-language activity that emphasizes playground safety. Take your class to the playground along with markers, crayons, large sheets of construction paper, drawing paper, and a class supply of clipboards. Ask youngsters to brainstorm rules for playground safety. Write each rule on a separate sheet of large construction paper. Then supply each child with crayons, a sheet of drawing paper, and a clipboard. Have each student choose a rule and illustrate it. Later glue each child's illustration to the corresponding large sheet of paper. Bind the pages together to make a big book. Read and review the rules each day before your youngsters head out to the playground or whenever a reminder of the rules is needed.

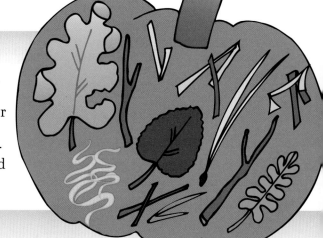

Walk around the swings, NOT in front of the swings.

Janet Ann Collins—Pre-K And Gr. K, Alameda, CA

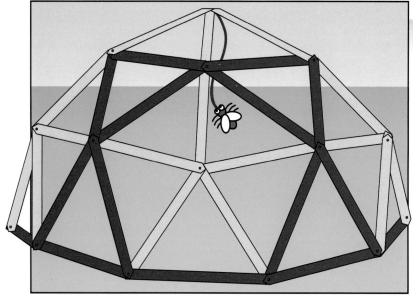

Spider Climbing

Have your itsy-bitsy spiders try this fun gross-motor activity. In advance cut a large insect pattern from tagboard. Punch a hole in the pattern and use a piece of yarn to tie it to the top of a playground play dome or net climber. Then have your little ones pretend that the dome or net climber is a spiderweb and that they are spiders. In turn, have each child climb the dome or net—imagining that it is a sticky web—to reach the insect.

adapted from an idea by Lori Kracoff, Thornton, NH

Signs Of Autumn

What better way to gather up signs of autumn than to head outdoors for an autumn hunt? Provide each child with a resealable plastic bag. Have each of your little ones search for and collect signs of autumn such as pinecones, leaves, nuts, twigs, and acorns. When the hunt is over, return to the classroom. Supply each child with a tagboard pumpkin shape and glue. Have him glue the items from his bag onto his cutout.

W. L. Harris, Columbia, MD

Out & About
Things To Do Outdoors

by Angie Kutzer

Snowball Fun

Your little ones will love this outdoor game—with or without snow on the ground! Take two long jump ropes, a bell or whistle, and your children outdoors. Extend the ropes on the ground so they are end-to-end in a straight line. Divide your class into two groups; then ask the groups to stand on opposite sides of the ropes. Distribute one white piece of paper to each student and have him crumple it up to resemble a snowball. On your signal, instruct the children to throw their paper snowballs to the opposite side of the ropes. Have them pick up and throw any snowballs that land near their feet. After a minute or two of throwing, signal your children to freeze. Count the snowballs on each side of the rope as a group. Then redistribute the snowballs. On your mark, get set, throw!

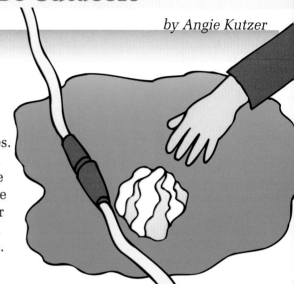

Whose Tracks?

To teach your little ones that some animals are still out and about even though it's winter, lure animals to a snack. Spoon some peanut butter onto a plate. Add bread crumbs if desired. Before your children leave for the day, take them out to watch as you place the plate on the snow-covered ground in a place that will remain undisturbed through the night. Or, if there is no snow, smooth out the sand in a sandbox and put the plate in the middle. Explain that hopefully some animal visitors will nibble on the snack during the night. The next morning, take your group out and check the area for tracks. Compare the tracks with a reference book such as *Whose Tracks Are These? A Clue Book Of Familiar Forest Animals* by Jim Nail (Roberts Rinehart Publishers). Your children might be surprised when they discover the tracks of the animals that came for this snack!

What Makes A Flake?

Take advantage of youngsters' excitement during a snowfall with this science activity. Have your little ones bundle up, hand each one a dark-colored piece of construction paper, and take them outside. Instruct the children to catch snowflakes on their papers and observe them. Have hand lenses available for close-up observation. Direct your little ones back inside and have them watch to see what happens to the flakes on their papers. Discuss that snowflakes are made of frozen water and no two flakes are alike. Distribute chalk and dry paper to your children and have them draw snowflakes. No two will be alike!

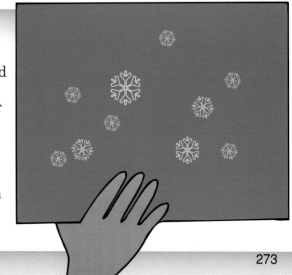

Doris Porter—Preschool, Headstart, Anamosa, IA

Out & About
Things To Do Outdoors

Pull!

Going *up* the slide will be as much fun as going down it with this strengthening activity. Knot a thick rope at short intervals along its entire length. Then tie one end of the rope to the top step or to the overhead bar of a short slide. Encourage each child to travel up the slide by using the rope to pull himself up as he climbs. Make sure that participants are wearing rubber-soled shoes (for traction), that children are asked not to slide down while the rope is on the slide, and that this activity is closely supervised. In no time at all, your little ones will be boasting of big biceps!

Mary Johnson—Preschool
Indian Hills Preschool, Gallap, NM

Paint!

Take advantage of sunny, hot days to encourage a little touch-up "painting" outdoors. Fill several buckets with water. Take the buckets—along with several wide, household paintbrushes—outside during play periods. Invite your little ones to use the buckets and brushes to give the playground equipment, fence, and other items in sight a coat of this invisible, quick-drying paint. Your school or center will be spruced up in no time at all!

Jenny Swanson—Pre-K, Early Childhood Learning Center
Scotts Valley, CA

Hop!

Help youngsters differentiate between left and right as they hop down this curvy caterpillar. On a sidewalk or section of pavement, use chalk to draw a caterpillar with ten connected circular segments. Then alternately draw either a left or right foot shape on the left or right of each circular segment. To do the caterpillar hop, a child hops from the end of the caterpillar to the head by matching her hopping foot to the foot shape on each segment. To modify this activity for younger preschoolers, use two different colors of chalk to draw the left and right feet, or shorten the length of the caterpillar. Hop 'til you drop!

Amy Provencio—Four-Year-Olds
Merry Moppet Preschool, Belmont, CA

GETTING YOUR
DUCKLINGS IN A ROW

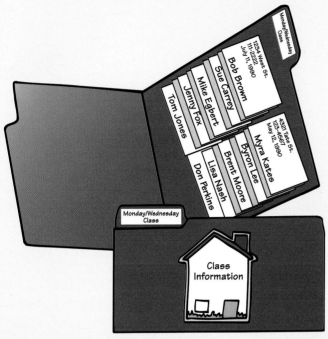

Hanging Art

Need a helpful hint for moving students' wet paintings from one place to another? If so, then try this neat idea. Clip a sheet of art paper to each of several clip-style hangers. Place the hangers in your painting center on a tension rod or clothes-drying rack. Encourage each youngster who visits the center to place the hook of a hanger over the top of the paint easel. After he paints on the paper, have him hang the picture up to dry. Using this technique is a great way to display artwork while keeping little fingers clean.

Michelle Miget—Four-Year-Olds
Humboldt Elementary Preschool
St. Joseph, MO

Class Information Folder

Have students' personal information right at your fingertips when you organize it in a folder. For each child program the front of an index card with his name, address, phone number, and birthday. Program the back of each child's card with other important information such as the names of the adults who are permitted to pick him up from school. Alphabetize the cards. Then tape them to the inside of the folder, staggering them as shown. If desired tape additional index cards under each child's information card to use for anecdotal records. This system is a great way to keep all of your important student information in one place.

Penni Wells—Pre-K
Park Village Elementary
San Antonio, TX

Classroom Mailbox

Store your correspondence in a classroom mailbox. Use paint or permanent markers to program the side of a mailbox with your name; then decorate the mailbox as desired. Set the mailbox on your desk or on a counter near your classroom door. Place your mail, parent correspondence, and professional catalogs in the mailbox for easy storage. What a festive and homey way to dress up your room and end clutter!

Joan Banker—Three- And Four-Year-Olds
St. Mary's Child Development Center
Garner, NC

IN A ROW

Crayon Cartons

Storing individual students' crayons will be easy with this nifty idea. Collect a classroom supply of half-pint milk cartons. Cut the top portion from each carton. Cover each carton with Con-Tact® covering. For each child personalize a seasonal cutout or shaped notepad sheet; then mount the cutout on the carton. Place each child's crayon carton on his table, or store it on a shelf and have him locate it as needed.

Jackie Wright—Preschool And Kindergarten
Summerhill Children's House
Enid, OK

Sand Area

Weekly Organization

Organize the teaching materials that you'll need for the week with this idea. Label each of five large wicker baskets with a different day of the week. Sort your teaching materials—such as books, poems, flannelboard pieces, cassette tapes, puppets, and games—for each day into the appropriate basket. With this system, daily planning will be simplified and materials will be easy to locate.

B. Childery—Three-, Four-, And Five-Year-Olds
Walnut Creek Elementary
Azle, TX

Quick Identification

Use small wooden cutouts from craft stores to help your little ones identify their cubbies, coat hooks, and learning centers. For each child, purchase multiple copies of a different wooden cutout. If the cutouts are unpainted, identically paint each set of matching cutouts. Have each child select a cutout design; then hot-glue the matching cutouts onto his cubby and coat hook.

Use the remaining cutouts to manage the flow of students in learning centers. To the back of each of the cutouts, attach the loop side of a Velcro® circle. Attach the hook sides of the Velcro® circles to learning-center signs. When a student selects a center to visit, he attaches his cutout to the corresponding sign.

Amy Aloi—Three- And Four-Year-Olds
Prince Georges County Head Start
Bladensburg, MD

Alphabetical Order

Try this handy organizational method for quick access to your precut bulletin-board letters. Insert a set of alphabet-tabbed index cards into a 4" x 6" index-card or recipe-card storage box. Then sort and file the letters into their correct divisions. No more wasted time going through mounds of mixed-up letters. Captions are ready in a flash!

Janice Lagard—Three- And Four-Year-Olds
Discovery Years
Hamburg, NJ

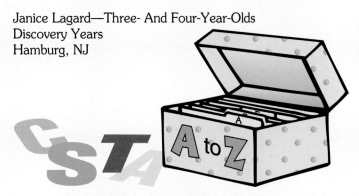

Tickets, Please!

Use this idea to promote your children's responsibility in keeping the classroom clean and orderly. After a creative art session, ask each child to pick up a piece of paper from the floor. Explain that each piece is a ticket, and that each child will need a ticket in order to join the group's next activity. When scraps are at their worst, request two or more tickets. Tidy up in no time!

Jennifer Barton
Elizabeth Green School
Newington, CT

Pizza Plus!

What's better than a hot, fresh-from-the-oven pizza? The *box* it comes in! Pizza boxes hold lots of materials, are easy to label, and stack well for storage. Wipe the inside of a used box with a damp cloth. If desired, cover and line the box with Con-Tact® covering. Need extras? Here's a good excuse to order more pizza! (Or politely ask your neighborhood pizza parlor for donations.) A great idea—any way you slice it!

Doris Porter—Preschool
Headstart
Anamosa, IA

IN A ROW

Nifty, Thrifty Nametags

Here's an idea for making nametags that are inexpensive, easy to make, and durable. Cut a classroom supply of shapes from colored felt. Use a permanent marker to label each shape with a different child's name. Spread a layer of glue across the back of the shape; then lay one side of a spring-type clothespin on the shape so that the gripping end is at the top of the nametag. When the glue is dry, these clip-on nametags are ready for action. So clip this idea to your must-do list!

Becky Jones—Three- And Four-Year-Olds
Mt. Calvary Christian Preschool
Greenville, MI

Becky

Literature Index

When gathering books for teaching your next unit, grab an index card, too. Label the top of the card with your unit's theme. As you find related books, list their titles and their locations on the card. Store the cards for the units you teach together in an index-card file box. This information will be a huge time-saver the next time you prepare to teach a favorite unit.

Robin Love Bowman—Preschool
St. Joseph Preschool
Owosso, MI

Dishwasher Keepers

Here are some surprise uses for the dish racks and silverware holder from a discarded dishwasher. Stack books in dish racks with wheels for use as mobile book baskets. Mount the silverware basket to a wall (or set it in a center) for storage of crayons and markers. These handy items provide you with creative alternatives for organizing your classroom.

Deborah Kohanbash—Three-Year-Olds
Hillel School
Pittsburgh, PA

Handy Holders

Make painting easier for little ones by using an individual serving–sized applesauce container to hold each block of compressed tempera paint. You'll find that youngsters manipulate a container better than a whole tray, and you can determine how many colors are available for any given project. Use extra containers to hold small craft items and manipulatives, too. How do you get a supply of these handy holders? Have applesauce for a snack one day. Little ones will enjoy eating the contents to empty the containers for you!

Cindy S. Berry—Two-Year-Olds
Christian Kindergarten And Nursery School
Little Rock, AR

"A-peel-ing" Names

Here's a timesaving tip to help youngsters label their own work. For each child, have an adult volunteer program a sheet of computer labels. Instruct each child to keep his labeled sheet in his supply box or cubby. When the child finishes a piece of work, he peels a label from the sheet and attaches it to his work. As an incentive, have blank labels ready for children who are primed to program them with their names themselves.

Amanda
Amanda
Amanda
Amanda
Amanda

Eleanor Jean Willits—Pre-K
Allan Elementary School
Austin, TX

Glamorous Glue

Use nail-polish bottles instead of glue bottles to give little ones more success with gluing activities. Clean empty nail-polish bottles and brushes with nail-polish remover, rinse them in water, and let them dry. Then fill the bottles with glue. Fine-motor skills are exercised as a child uses the nail brush to apply glue to his projects. Rub cooking oil on the brushes periodically to keep them soft. A glamour tip from the pros—less is more!

Kitty Moufarrege—Three-Year-Olds
Foothill Progressive Montessori Preschool
La Canada, CA

Tips For Getting Organized

Portable Centers

Short on center space? Here's a practical tip. Make your writing and art centers portable by using fast-food drink carriers and 16-ounce plastic cups. Label a sentence strip with the center's name; then attach the strip to the side of the carrier. Insert a cup into each of the carrier's sections. Fill each cup with a different item—such as markers, glue, or scissors. Set the tray on a table and voila, an instant center!

adapted from an idea by
JoAnn Brukiewa—Pre-K
St. Clare School
Baltimore, MD

Display Saver

Try this idea to keep Sticky-Tac from leaving greasy spots on favorite visuals and letter cutouts that are not laminated. Put pieces of transparent tape on the back of the visuals; then attach the Sticky-Tac to the tape. The tape stops the moisture from penetrating through to the front of the visuals. It also helps keep the visuals from tearing when it's time to remove them from the wall. Now that's a mint of a hint!

Renee Culver—Pre-K
Rogys Gingerbread House
Peoria, IL

Stick It Or Stamp It

Preparing classroom newsletters and calendars will be easy with this nifty idea. Instead of clipping, saving, reducing, enlarging, gluing, and taping clip art, use rubber stamps and stickers. They fit in small spaces, copy well, and are readily available. With the tremendous selection on the market, you're sure to find just what you need. So stick it or stamp it!

Beth Lemke—Pre-K
Heights Head Start
Coon Rapids, MN

MAY

Sunday	Monday	Tuesday	Wednesday	Thursday	Friday	Saturday
				1	2 ZOO TRIP!	3
4	5 IMPORTANT Parent Conferences this week	6	7	8 Jennifer King's Birthday	9	10
11 Mother's Day	12	13	14	15	16	17 Picnic in the Park!
18	19	20	21	22 Spring Musical 7:00 PM	23	24
25	26 Memorial Day	27	28	29	30	31

THE SECOND TIME AROUND

THE SECOND TIME AROUND
Recycling In The Preschool Classroom

Take-Home Bags

Recycle department-store shopping bags to transfer students' large art projects from school to home. Provide each child with a personalized shopping bag; then have him decorate it. Provide youngsters with their bags when they need to carry their masterpieces home. Little ones and parents will be delighted with these easy-to-carry totes.

June Moss—Pre-K
Sunbeams And Rainbows Pre-School
Elmhurst, IL

Egg-Carton Storage

If you want a practical way to store students' classroom supplies, this idea may be "eggs-actly" what you need. To make a holder for each table of students, turn an empty, cardboard egg carton upside down. Through the top of each divided section of the carton, cut a hole large enough to insert supplies such as scissors, crayons, and pencils. Then use markers to draw a face on each section of the carton. Insert the supplies in the holes and place the carton on a table. Little ones will have supplies right at their fingertips.

Joan Banker—Three- And Four-Year-Olds
St. Mary's Child Development Center
Garner, NC

Money Holders

Collect a classroom supply of 35mm film containers for use as money holders. Label each container with a child's name and your name for easy return if misplaced. Have little ones use these containers to store milk or lunch money when traveling to and from school.

Pat Bollinger
Marble Hill, MO

THE SECOND TIME AROUND
Recycling In The Preschool Classroom

More Paint, Please!

If your paint containers are frequently empty and you need a way to store liquid tempera paint, give this idea a try. Remove the labels from a quantity of clean, squeeze-type ketchup bottles. Then fill each bottle with a different color of liquid tempera paint. This quick-and-easy tip can be a terrific time-saver. More paint, please!

Brenda Berger—Preschool
Ottawa-Glandorf Titan T.I.K.E.S. Preschool
Ottawa, OH

Bottle-Cap Memory

Save old plastic bottle caps and milk-jug lids for a fun game of Memory. First wash and dry a quantity of matching caps. Then pair the caps and place matching stickers on the inside of each pair. Using the caps, model how to play a game of Memory with your children. Then place the caps in a basket and set the basket in a games center. Little ones will enjoy the game, and the bottle caps will be easy for them to manipulate.

Kathie Deann Thornton—Preschool
Wake Forest, NC

The Cereal-Box Book

Recycle cereal boxes to make a class book that's just perfect for emergent readers. Collect a quantity of cereal boxes; then cut off the front from each box. Bind the front portions of the boxes together between two tagboard covers to make a book. Title the book "The Cereal-Box Book." Share the book with your class and have them "read" the different cereal names. To vary this activity, use individual-serving-sized boxes of cereal to make a smaller cereal-box book for each child.

Jennifer Barton
Elizabeth Green School
Newington, CT

THE SECOND TIME AROUND
Recycling In The Preschool Classroom

Puppets For Pennies

Discarded stuffed animals make great, inexpensive puppets. Simply open the seam at the bottom of the toy animal, empty the old stuffing, and sew a hem around the open seam. By using this suggestion and visiting a few garage sales, you can fill your classroom with puppets for just a few pennies.

Kim Richman—Two- And Three-Year-Olds
The Learning Zone
Des Moines, IA

Recycled Reptile

Use your accumulation of plastic grocery bags to "slither" this creative idea right into your classroom. To begin, tie the ends of three bags together into one knot. Then tie additional bags to the ends of each of the first three bags, making three long strands. When the strands are of a desired length, braid them together and tie a knot at the end. This plastic rope makes a "s-s-super s-s-snake" for jumping-rope and movement activities.

Kitty Moufarrege—Three-Year-Olds
Foothill Progressive Montessori Preschool, La Canada, CA

Stenciling

Vinyl samples that a local floor-covering dealer no longer needs can be converted into durable stencils that last for years. To prepare a stencil, trace a simple shape onto a piece of vinyl. Cut along the outline using an X-acto® knife. Prepare stencils that relate to your favorite teaching themes; then store each set of stencils in a labeled, resealable plastic bag. To use a stencil, a child places one on a sheet of art paper. He then traces the outline of the stencil with a crayon and colors in the shape. Or he may paint the entire opening of a stencil. Students will create savvy art with these simple stencils!

Donna Leonard—Head Start, Dyersville, IA

INSECTS

286

BUILDING BRIDGES BETWEEN HOME AND SCHOOL

Building
Between Home

Back-To-School Coffee

Invite youngsters' families, friends, and neighbors to a back-to-school coffee to celebrate the start of a new school year! Request that, along with their ideas and concerns, the participants bring classroom donations such as crayons, art paper, or boxes of tissues. Gather the donations; then take the opportunity to chat with parents and interested community members as you serve a variety of baked goods and hot coffee.

Nancy Kaczrowski
Luverne, MN

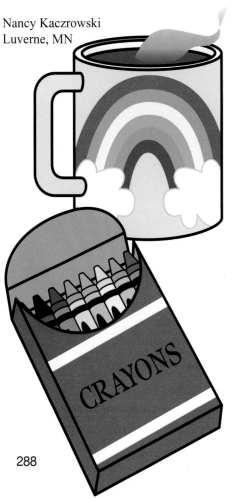

Mommy-Daddy Pictures

Comfort uneasy little ones on the first day of school—and throughout the year—with a Mommy or Daddy picture. On the first day of school, take an instant photo of each child with one or both of her parents. *After* the parent leaves, give the photo to the child to hold as a reminder that Mommy or Daddy will be returning later in the day. Keep these photos on hand throughout the year to provide comfort whenever a child needs a bit of extra attention. At the end of the year, present the pictures to Mommy or Daddy as precious keepsakes.

Kitty Moufarrege—Three- And Four-
    Year-Olds
Foothill Progressive Montessori Preschool
La Canada, CA

Potluck Preschool Picnic

Prior to the first day of school, invite students and their families to a potluck picnic to help both youngsters and parents feel more at ease on that potentially scary first day of school. A few weeks before your picnic, send a letter to each new student's family. Relate the picnic's date and time, and ask youngsters to bring along a photo of themselves and any requested school supplies. During the picnic, get to know the children and parents and talk informally about the upcoming year. Then invite everyone into your classroom to find individual cubbies and put away school supplies. Mount each child's photo around the outside of your doorway.

When the first day of school arrives, each youngster will easily find your room and recognize your face. And there will be less commotion since supplies have already been put away. No more first-day-of-school blues!

Randi Gottenborg
John F. Kennedy Elementary
Sioux Falls, SD

Bridges
And School

Class Directory

Help parents get to know their child's classmates with this informative idea. At the beginning of the school year, take a photo of each child. Attach it to a biography sheet similar to the one shown. Complete the information on each child's biography sheet with his help; then place all of the sheets in a three-ring binder. Have each child, in turn, take the finished directory home to share with his family. Oh, so *that's* Joshua!

Cheryl Cicioni—Preschool
Kindernook Preschool
Lancaster, PA

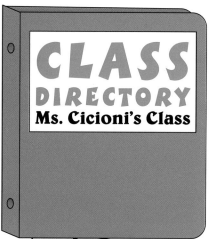

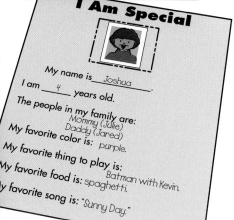

Video Lending Library

Give children an enriching experience and offer families a convenient service when you set up a video lending library. Purchase educational, high-quality videos such as those based on children's books. To each video's jacket, attach a colored dot sticker and a library pocket. Inside each library pocket, place an index card labeled with that video's title. Request that a parent sign the card when he checks out a video; then have him place the card in a designated box. When he returns the video, ask him to locate and return that video's card to the library pocket.

To recoup the cost of each video, charge parents a small fee until the video has been rented enough times to cover its cost. Then remove the colored dot sticker and place the video on a separate shelf designated for videos available for loan at no cost.

Cheryl Cicioni—Preschool

Break The Ice

If your school holds a parent orientation, try having an icebreaker near the beginning of the meeting. Ask each parent to take a few minutes to introduce herself to a parent she doesn't know. Then ask each person to introduce her new acquaintance, give the name of that person's child, and tell one thing that person wishes for his child in the coming year. This information exchange will develop a sense of community while helping parents and teachers learn more about one another.

Pamela DeSpain—Three-, Four-, And
  Five-Year-Olds
Bright Beginnings Preschool
Colville, WA

A Valentine For My Family

Give your children a peek inside the postal system by having them mail love letters to their families. Write each child's family name and address on individual envelopes. Obtain a classroom supply of postage stamps. Prior to Valentine's Day, have your little ones make their own unique valentine cards for their families. Write each child's dictated message inside his card and encourage him to sign his own name. Direct each child to fold and insert his valentine into his envelope, lick the seal, and affix the stamp. When everyone is ready, take a class trip to the nearest post office or mailbox to mail these letters of love. Special delivery!

Laura McDonough—Preschool
Integrated Special Education
Brightwood Elementary
Springfield, MA

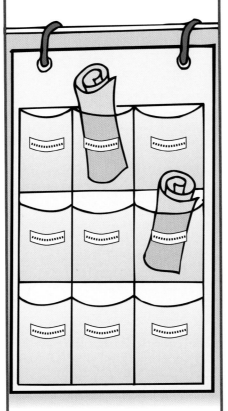

It's In The Bag

Parent communication is a "shoe-in" with this easy idea. Use an over-the-door shoe bag as a holder for important class information. Label each pocket of the bag with a different child's name; then hang the bag on or near the classroom door. To use, simply insert notes and papers into the pockets as needed. Encourage parents to check their child's pocket to collect any news at the end of each day.

Lori Kent—Preschool
Hood River Kid Company
Hood River, OR

Adopt-A-Puppet

Encourage lots of communication and social skills among your little ones by setting up an Adopt-A-Puppet program in your classroom. To make a puppet, sew two washcloths together in a basic puppet shape. Trim around the puppet shape; then have your children help you decorate the puppet using buttons, fur, bows, wiggle eyes, and other decorative materials. To make a special home for the puppet, have a group of little ones decorate a handled detergent box. Now the puppet is ready for adoption.

Invite each child to sign up to "adopt" the puppet for a weekend or weeknight. Before the puppet goes home with a child, discuss with your students how the puppet should behave while staying with guests. Also discuss how the guests should treat the puppet. Write your little ones' list of dos and don'ts on a sheet of paper along with a note to parents describing the program. Put the puppet and parent note inside the box and wave it good-bye for the weekend! Your little ones will be anxious to hear about the puppet's adventures upon its return to school.

Crystal Sirmans—Preschool
Child Care Contacts R & R
Milledgeville, GA

Bridges
And School

How Does That Song Go?

Help children's parents enjoy classroom music at home with this songbook suggestion. Write the lyrics to your students' favorite songs and compile them in a notebook. Have copies of the songs available for parents to take home. Update the notebook and make duplicates as new songs are learned. For added impact, make a tape recording of your little ones singing their favorite songs. Place the tape in the listening center with a tape recorder that has a duplicating feature. Invite parents to bring a tape and make a copy of the original. Practicing with parents at home will increase participation during music time at school. So get parents in tune and start the music!

Reneé S. Piper—Director
Tippecanoe County Child Care South
Lafayette, IN

Parent Resource Box

Help parents help themselves by creating a parent resource box. To prepare, gather articles (from journals and magazines) about topics that interest and concern parents. Make copies of the articles; then place each set of article duplicates in a folder labeled with the article's topic. Store the folders in a box near the entrance to your room or school. Invite parents to browse through and take articles that interest them. Ask parents to notify you if they have an interest that isn't represented in the box. Be sure to change the collection as newer and better articles are found. If one parent is helped or better informed, it's well worth the effort!

Reneé S. Piper—Director

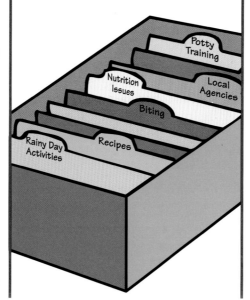

Read All About It!

Celebrate Newspaper In Education Week (the first full week in March) by creating a classroom newspaper with your youngsters. Provide each family with a sheet of paper that is blank on the left half and programmed with ruled lines on the right half. Ask each family to write and illustrate (in black crayon or pencil) a story about themselves. Use a copier to reduce each illustrated story. Show your little ones several authentic newspapers; then have them come up with the title, headlines, and sections for their own paper. Arrange and tape the students' stories on legal-sized sheets of paper. Fill in the spaces with newsworthy phrases and advertisements clipped from a real newspaper. Duplicate the pages to create a newspaper for each child to take home and share with her family. Be sure to have some extras, extras!

Jennifer Wardlow—Pre-K
Time For Tots, Inc.
Philadelphia, PA

Building
Between Home

Good News!

Announce special happenings in your classroom with this newsworthy display. Cut a newspaper page so that it is slightly larger than a piece of duplicating paper. Laminate the newspaper page for durability. When something exciting happens at school, describe the event on a piece of white paper; then tape it to the middle of the newspaper. Post the announcement on your door for parents to read when they arrive.

As a variation, send home a similar note announcing a child's accomplishment. In advance, cut newspapers so that you have a supply of sheets that are slightly larger than the size of duplicating paper. Describe a child's good news on a piece of paper; then tape it to a newspaper background. Hear ye, hear ye!

adapted from an idea by
 Kristy Curless—Infants
Chesterbrook Academy
Champaign, IL

Healthy Snack Suggestions

Breads	Fruits	Vegetables	Juices

Spreads

Healthful Snacks Are In The Bag

Use this nifty idea to ensure that parents who volunteer to provide daily snacks for your class will send healthful and suitable ones. Use a permanent marker to label a tote bag with suggestions for healthful snacks. Send the bag home with the child whose parent is in charge of sending the snack supply for the following day or week. When using this method, you'll find that parents are thankful for the suggestions, and you're assured of having appropriate snacks for growing boys and girls.

Susan Burbridge—Four-Year-Olds
Colonial Hills United Methodist School
San Antonio, TX

Parents' Corner

Make parents feel welcome in your room by setting up a special center just for them. Place a table, a small bookcase or shelving, and a few chairs in one corner of your room. Provide supplies and instructions for materials that parents can make and take home for use with their children. Also include informative handouts and reference books on popular parental issues—such as discipline, healthful living, and developmental concerns. Invite parents to take advantage of this great opportunity to become more knowledgeable about their children's growth.

Amy Aloi—Head Start
Berkshire Elementary
Forestville, MD

GLUE

Recipes For Kids

Welcome Parents!

Big News!

ews!

An airplane pilot visited our class today!

Bridges And School

Read Me A Story

Use this idea to initiate a home-reading program for your classroom. To prepare, insert each of a class supply of books into a separate, resealable plastic bag. Label each bag with a different number. Prepare a checklist including each child's name and the number assigned to each title. Duplicate a supply of verification slips for parents to complete and return after reading each book; then insert one of the slips into each bag.

Each time you send a plastic book bag home with a child, mark the book's number beside that child's name on the checklist. Encourage parents to read the book, sign the verification slip, and return the book within several days. When the book bag is returned with the signed slip, circle the number on your checklist. Then send a new book home with the child. What a great way to encourage a special family-time routine!

Janis Woods—Four-Year-Olds
Ridgeland Elementary
Ridgeland, SC

#5

Ladybug's Adventure

	1	2	3
Jamie	①	2	
Kyle	1		
Blair	①	②	3
Tommy	1	②	3
Tracie	1		③
Yvette		②	
Hunter			③
Charles	①	2	

I read the book
Ladybug's Adventure
to my child.

Letter Boxes

Get set to teach the alphabet! Ask parents to help you fill these handy letter boxes for use with various alphabet activities. In advance, collect 26 empty Huggies® Baby Wipes containers. Use a permanent marker to label each container with a different letter of the alphabet (both upper- and lowercase). Send home a different letter box with a different child each day. Request that parents contribute one or more small items that start with the letter shown on the box. When you have an assortment of items in each box, use the boxes to introduce beginning sounds to your youngsters, as well as to reinforce letter recognition.

Kim Richman—Preschool
The Learning Zone
Des Moines, IA

A Day In The Park

Celebrate spring with an afternoon in the park. Designate a weekend afternoon for students and their families to meet at a park. Reserve a shelter or several picnic tables in advance. When inviting parents to the event, ask them to bring a picnic lunch for their family and an outdoor toy. (You may want to provide the drinks and dessert.) Remind parents that they should accompany their children so that you are free to mingle. During this fun event, the children can play with their classmates outside the school or center setting. As a bonus, parents can observe their children's interactions and social skills and meet new friends of their own!

Building
Between Home

Come To School

Prepare this game in the summer, and you'll have a way in the fall for parents to have fun while helping their children learn classmates' names, take turns, count, and just get excited about preschool! In advance, obtain an individual photo of each child. To prepare a gameboard as shown, sponge-paint and/or draw one large house (start), a smaller house for each student, a large school (finish), a stop sign (wait one turn), a tree (wait one turn), and square shapes in a winding path on a piece of poster board. When the paint is dry, glue each child's picture onto a different house. Label the areas of the gameboard and label each house with the pictured child's name. Laminate for durability. Insert a die, two game markers, and simple directions into a resealable plastic bag; then clip the bag to the gameboard.

Send the game home with a different child each night or present each child with his own game during a home visit. To play the game, a child and a parent take turns rolling the die and moving their markers from the large house to the school. As each player passes a small house, she names the pictured classmate and asks him to come to school. Each player is a winner when he arrives at school.

Mileen McGee—Three-, Four-, And Five-Year-Olds
George O. Barr Elementary, Silvis, IL

You're special! So come to a special day!

Daddies' Day

Host a special time just for dads on the last school day before Father's Day in June. Send each dad (or grandfather, uncle, etc.) an invitation to bring his child to school and enjoy a light breakfast. Have your little ones assist you in making muffins and juice the day before; then encourage each child to decorate a construction-paper necktie nametag for his dad. Both the children and the daddies will be all smiles and full of pride on this special day!

Diane Beane—Director
Plymouth House Nursery School
Framingham, MA

Bridges

And School

These Families Love Books

Here's a great display that encourages reading at school *and* at home. Simply send home a disposable camera along with a note requesting that a parent take a photo of his child reading a favorite book with another family member. Have the film developed; then tape each picture behind a child-decorated construction-paper frame. Mount the framed photos along with a border of colorful book jackets on a bulletin board. Title the board "These Families Love Books!"

adapted from an idea by
    Andrea Esposito—Preschool
VA/YMCA Child Care Center
Brooklyn, NY

We smiled for the camera
The whole year through.
Now we have pictures
To share with you!
(Parents, help yourself to a photo or two to remember this special year.)

Share A Smile

If you take pictures throughout the year and get double prints made, consider sharing the smiles with parents. At the end of the year, fill a basket with the duplicate pictures and post the above poem near the basket. Parents will really appreciate your help in capturing their children's special school memories on film.

Leah Rae Harden—Preschool
Kirklin Christian Church Preschool
Kirklin, IN

Family Ties

Focus on families with this "tie-riffic" display. Cut out a class supply of necktie shapes from wallpaper samples. Ask each parent to help his child find a family photo to bring to school. Invite each child to share her photo and name the family members in the picture. Then attach each photo to a wallpaper necktie, label the tie with the child's name, and display these family ties on a door or bulletin board. We are family!

Kristy Curless—Infants
Chesterbrook Academy
Champaign, IL

295

BULLETIN BOARDS
AND DISPLAYS

BULLETIN BOARDS

THE NEW CROP IS IN!

Twist brown bulletin-board paper; then mount it on a sky blue background so that it resembles a tree and branches. Personalize an apple cutout for each child; then attach a photo of each child to his cutout. Attach the apples to the branches along with green leaf cutouts. Title the board to complete a delicious Open House display. Later remove and laminate the apple cutouts. Attach magnetic tape to the backs to create magnets well worth picking!

Lynn Cadogan, Starkey Elementary, Seminole, FL

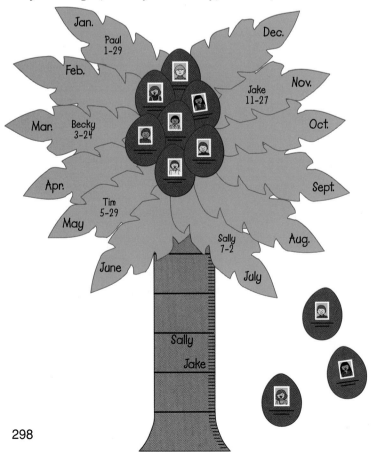

Cut a five-foot-tall tree trunk and 12 palm fronds from bulletin-board paper. Label each frond with a different month. Mark inch indications on the trunk, drawing a line across the trunk every 12 inches. Laminate the pieces; then attach them to a wall, being sure to place the trunk even with the base of the wall. For each child personalize and attach a school photo to a coconut cutout; then attach the cutouts to the center of the fronds. Using a wipe-off marker, write each child's birthday on the appropriate frond and indicate his height on the trunk.

Terri Johnson—Three- And Four-Year-Olds, Learning Tree Of America, Carrollton, GA

AND DISPLAYS

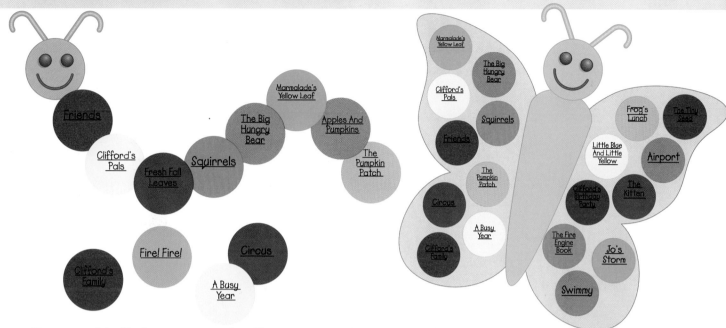

To create this display, cut a supply of large construction-paper circles. Add pom-pom eyes, a yarn mouth, and pipe-cleaner antennae to one circle to resemble a caterpillar's head. Attach the circle to a wall. Each time a book is read aloud, write the title on a new circle; then attach it to the wall to create an ever-growing caterpillar. In the spring, remove the circles from the wall and rearrange them on a large butterfly shape. A year of reading takes flight!

Kathryn D. Small—Three- And Four-Year-Olds, Parkminster Preschool, Rochester, NY

All aboard the Newsletter Express! Mount a construction-paper train. Attach one clear, plastic envelope to the train for each day of the week that your students attend preschool. Before dismissal, record students' dictation of the details of the day such as snack, crafts, and special events. Duplicate a class supply of the letter and slip the copies into the appropriate envelope. As parents pick up their precious cargo, encourage them to take a copy from the Newsletter Express.

Liz Harkness—Preschool/Special Education, Dupont Elementary, Commerce City, CO

BULLETIN BOARDS

This display will have you singing, "We've got the sun in the morning and the moon at night!" Embellish a sun cutout with paper facial features and glitter; then add bottle-cap craters to a crescent-moon shape. Add cotton balls to cloud cutouts and foil streamers to metallic-paper star cutouts. Mount all of the items on a board along with a tissue-paper rainbow. Surround the items with students' dictated statements about day and night.

Nancy Barad—Four-Year-Olds, Bet Yeladim Preschool And Kindergarten, Columbia, MD

Here's a display that will go perfectly with your unit about families. Ask each child's family to attach photos of family members to a personalized sheet of construction paper. Mount the collected sheets together on a wall to resemble a quilt; then add a border. Invite parents to take a good look at your display of classy families.

Penny Horne—Preschool
University Of Maine At Presque Isle Daycare
Presque Isle, ME

Mount a brown construction-paper tree onto a wall. Attach a titled sign to the tree. Enlarge a set of squirrel cutouts; then color and program them with the titles of your classroom jobs. Enlarge a classroom supply of acorn cutouts; then color and program each with a different student's name. (Patterns on page 308.) Mount the squirrels on and around the tree. Mount a student's acorn near each squirrel, replacing the acorns as new helpers are desired.

Wilma Droegemueller—Preschool And Gr. K
Zion Lutheran School
Mt. Pulaski, IL

Folks will really fall for this fantastic display! On a blue and green background, mount a real trash bag filled with orange and yellow crepe-paper streamers. Mount a character dressed with children's articles of clothing. Add a paper rake so that your character appears to be gathering student-made leaves decorated using a variety of art techniques. Complete the board with a border of leaf cutouts.

Nancy Barad—Four-Year-Olds, Bet Yeladim Preschool And Kindergarten, Columbia, MD

301

Filling Santa's sleigh with presents is a "ho-ho-ho" lot of fun! Enlarge a sleigh design; then have youngsters help you paint it. When the sleigh is dry, mount it on a wall along with an enlarged version of the jolly, old elf himself. Ask your own little helpers to use scraps of ribbon and paper to decorate personalized sheets of construction paper. Pile the presents high!

Tanya Bator—Preschool
Mont Marie Child Care Center
Holyoke, MA

We were tired of winter days
Being cold and wet and gray.

So we talked to winter's wizard—
He made it snow a rainbow blizzard!

This colorful display will blow away the winter blues! Mount a winter wizard on a background. Surround him with colorful construction-paper snowflakes that have been embellished using a variety of art supplies. Add the winter rhyme and get ready for a flurry of compliments.

Kimberly Caldwell—Pre-K, Smart Start Preschool, Fair Haven, NJ

AND DISPLAYS

Friends Work Together

We can share crayons.

We are building a tower.

We can help clean up.

We can do the puzzle together.

Enlarge a set of friendly characters for this bulletin board that encourages cooperation and friendship. Mount the characters on a background. Then, as you see children working together, take an instant photo. On construction paper, write the students' description of their activity. Add the picture and the statement to the display. Friends work together!

Laura McDonough—Integrated Special Education Preschool, Brightwood Elementary School, Springfield, MA

Reluctant to put away your class Christmas tree? Remove the holiday ornaments and replace them with ornaments that emphasize the letters of the alphabet. Using a die cutter and simple patterns, make an ornament for each letter. Have students help you decorate the tree, or add an ornament to the tree each time you focus your studies on a different letter. Top the tree with a paper rainbow.

Sharon Sinn—Pre-K
IACC Daycare Center
Ithaca, NY

ALPHABET TREE

Bb Ww Cc Aa Dd Hh Ii Kk Tt Gg Oo

MRS. GUFFEY'S SWEET ONES

Aaron • Ben • Rosa • Pip • Kevin • Ramona • Mary • Seth • Katie • Spencer • Jackson • Erin • Carlos • Carrie • Jessie

Have your sweet ones help you make this valentine display. Enlarge, color, and mount a cart-carrying character. To fill the wagon, have youngsters paint candy-kiss shapes brown, then wrap the candies in foil. Label each kiss with a personalized tag. Border your display with pink handprints on white paper circles that have been mounted on red and pink hearts.

Diane Guffey—Three-Year-Olds, ABC Learning Center, Rockport, TX

Need a handsome door display? Cut a large basket shape from bulletin-board paper; then have youngsters paint handprints on the basket to give it texture. Trace one of each child's hands onto construction paper. Personalize the hand shapes; then cut them out. Mount the basket on your door; then arrange the hands over it to form a handle. Secure a real bow to the door. Fill the basket with snazzy student-decorated eggs.

Carolyn M. Patterson—Preschool, Grove City Head Start, Grove City, PA

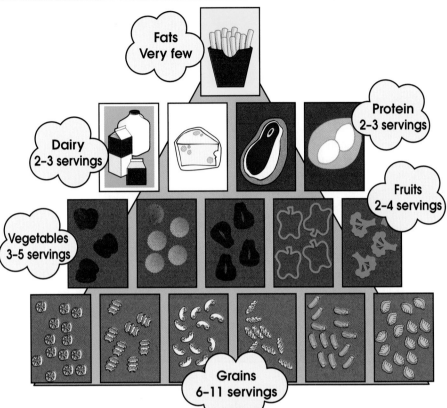

Fats
Very few

Dairy
2-3 servings

Protein
2-3 servings

Fruits
2-4 servings

Vegetables
3-5 servings

Grains
6-11 servings

Have students help you create this giant nutrition pyramid that gives parents power-packed information. Mount a bulletin-board paper triangle on a wall. Glue pasta pieces to six sheets of tan paper. Use yellow, red, and green paint to print cut fruits and vegetables onto five orange sheets. Glue magazine pictures of dairy products to two white sheets. Glue pictures of meat products to two brown sheets. To a yellow sheet, glue a french-fries package stuffed with strips of foam. Mount the sheets and nutritional information as shown.

Charlet Keller—Preschool, ICC Preschool
Violet Hill, AR

"Eggs-tra" Nice Eggs!

Hippity hoppity! Here comes the Easter Bunny with some "eggs-tra" nice eggs. Mount your favorite bunny character on a background. Have each child use watercolor paints to paint a large, construction-paper egg shape. When the paint is dry, cut a circle from the center of each child's egg; then tape a picture of the child to the back. Add the eggs, a border of fringed-paper grass, and a title to your seasonal display.

Barb Johnson and Dona Peck—Preschool, ECSE Preschool, John Cline Elementary, Decorah, IA

BULLETIN BOARDS

Our Favorite Foods

Pizza
Call the guy on the phone. Pay him when the doorbell rings. Eat your slices... pepperoni first!
Mi Lynne 3 yrs.

Soda Floats
Open the soda, but wipe the foam up. Drop the ice-cream chunk. Use your straw. Slurp if you need to.
Ryan 4 yrs.

Birthday Cake
Put 5 bags of powdery stuff in a pan. Bake the pan for 7 hours.
Mattie 4 yrs.

Lemonade
Buy a lemon. Put it in a jar, and then squeeze it for juice. Drink it but spit out the seeds.
Krista 3 yrs.

Hot Dogs
Put the hot dogs in a pan until they are hot. Then put it in a bun with lots of ketchup and eat it.
Kyle 4 yrs.

Here's the recipe for a display that's sure to become one of your favorites. Label a large recipe card–shaped piece of paper with a child's favorite food; then write as he dictates the steps for preparing his selection. Have him complete the card with an illustration of his choice food. Mount each child's card on a background along with a chef character and a title. Later, to make a giant recipe book, bind the cards together between similarly shaped covers. Delicious!

Florence Paola—Preschool, Briarfield Day School, Stratford, CT

Get ready for summer fun with this sunny display. On a separate strip of orange or yellow bulletin-board paper, write each child's dictation of an activity he will enjoy in the summer. Then have him illustrate his summer plans on the strip, before adding some glittery touches. Mount all of the strips around a labeled circular cutout. Summertime is fun time!

Sheri McGarvey—Pre-K
Garrett's Way Learning Center
Newtown Square, PA

AND DISPLAYS

Sailing Off To Kindergarten

Ahoy, teachers of four-year-olds! Here's a display just for you! Mount blue plastic wrap onto a blue background. Add a title along with sun and cloud cutouts. Take pictures of your youngsters in various poses; then cut the developed pictures around each child's body shape. Arrange the photos on construction-paper boats; then add them to your scene. Set the sails for a terrific display!

Eleanore Cirigliano—Preschool, KidsPort Learning Center, Plymouth, MA

Have your crew help you prepare this whale of an ocean mural. To create the ocean floor, paint glue onto scalloped lengths of tan paper; then sprinkle on a mixture of dried beans. Later mount the lengths onto a blue background. Cut whale shapes from papers that have been fingerpainted blue, black, and white. Add a wiggle eye to each whale; then display the whales on the background.

Nancy Perkins—Pre-K, Itty Bitty Preschool, Glendale, AZ

Patterns

Use with "We're Nuts About Helping!" on page 301.

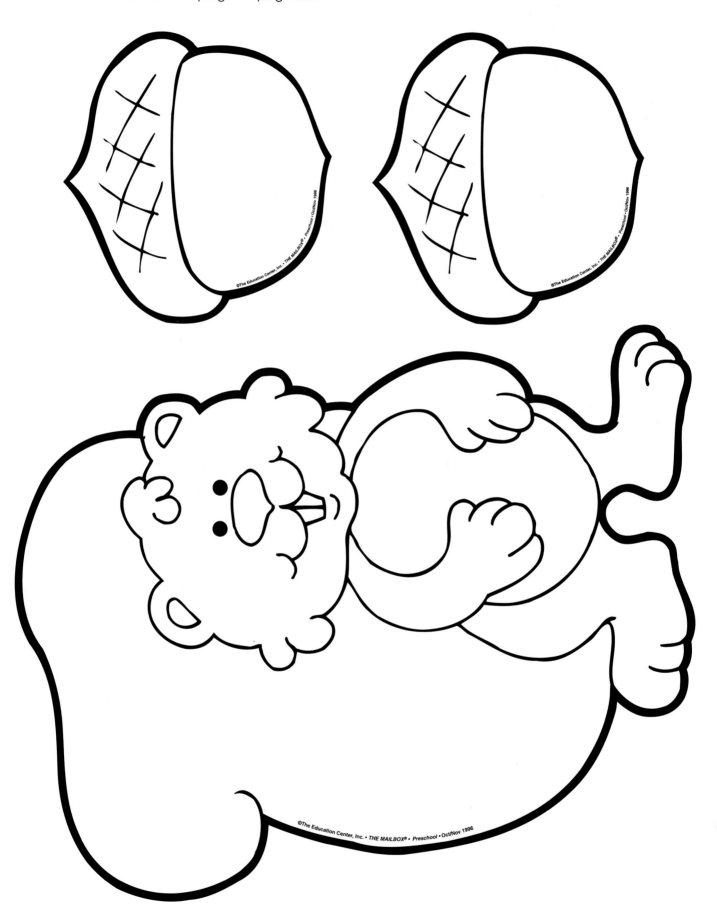

©The Education Center, Inc. • THE MAILBOX® • Preschool • Oct/Nov 1996

OUR READERS WRITE

Our Readers ▷ Write

Clown Greeter

Help youngsters find their classroom by sitting a cheerful clown greeter by the door. To make the clown's head, use fiberfill to stuff a cut-off panty-hose leg. Tie the open end of the panty-hose; then attach a colorful clown wig and construction-paper facial features to it. Attach a red foam ball or small inflated balloon to serve as the nose. To make the body, stuff a clown costume and attach the head at the neck of the costume. Attach a stuffed glove to the end of each sleeve and a glittery tennis shoe to the end of each pant leg. As a final touch, place a large, tissue-paper flower on the clown's head to serve as a hat. Position the clown in a chair outside your classroom door. Children will proudly greet the clown as they independently find their own classroom each day.

Melissa Epling—Preschool
Panther Creek Preschool
Nettie, WV

Customized Labels

Add a special touch to youngsters' school-made projects with customized labels. Have an inexpensive order of labels printed to read "I made this in [name of school and grade]," or "I made this with [name of teacher]." As each child completes a project, attach one of the special labels to it to serve as a memento.

Chava Shapiro
Beth Rochel School
Monsey, NY

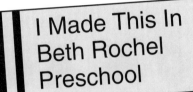

I Made This In
Beth Rochel
Preschool

Good-Morning Aprons

Greet each child personally with this neat apron idea. Purchase or make an apron for each child. Print his name on the apron using a permanent marker or fabric paint. During a morning group time, hold up one apron at a time so the children can see the name on it. As each child recognizes his own name, have him raise his hand and greet you. Return the child's greeting; then place the apron on him. With these aprons, not only does each child receive a personal greeting, but he's prepared to tackle any messy activities that await him!

Rebecca A. Rush—Special Education, Mt. Pleasant Elementary, Claymont, DE

Looking Glasses

Are you looking for a different way to help youngsters focus their attention? Well, look no more! This great glasses idea will keep your little ones' sights fixed on the task at hand. For each child, purchase a pair of inexpensive children's sunglasses. Remove the lenses from the frame. Provide each child with a pair of these looking glasses to wear as they tour the school or meet school personnel. Then use the glasses throughout the year for activities such as looking for a particular teacher on her birthday, examining items in the science center, looking for trash on the playground–or anytime as an extra incentive to maintain students' attention.

Sue Lewis Lein—Four-Year-Olds
St. Pius X
Wauwatosa, WI

Follow The Streamer

Little ones will soon be finding their own way around the classroom with this streamer idea. On the lower portion of a wall outside your classroom, post a nametag for each child. Attach the end of a streamer to each child's nametag; then attach the other end of the streamer to the child's cubby. As each child arrives on the first day, encourage him to find his nametag, then follow the attached streamer into the room to locate his cubby. Within the classroom, have students follow streamers that attach their cubbies to particular centers, or that attach one center to another. By simply following the streamers, youngsters will independently transition from one area of the room to another!

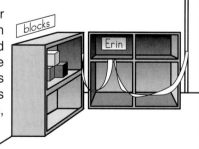

Amy Barsanti—Pre-K, St. Andrew's Preschool, Nags Head, NC

Artistic Names

Youngsters will be delighted to see their personalized name strips displayed on a class welcome board! Using block-style stencil letters, trace each child's name onto a strip of art paper. Have each child decorate the letters in his name using a variety of art mediums such as paint, crayons, and markers. Invite the children to help arrange the decorated name strips on a welcome-board display.

Melinda Davidson—Preschool/Integrated Special Needs
Brockton Early Childhood Program
Brockton, MA

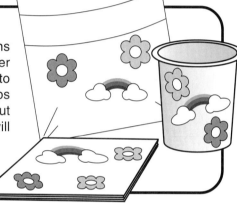

Window Murals

Do you have a large window in your classroom that needs to be livened up? If so, paint a mural on it. To make a mural, use washable markers to draw a seasonal scene or some characters on the window. Mix a small amount of dishwashing liquid with different colors of washable paint. If the students can easily reach the window, have them paint the mural. When it dries, use the mural as a topic for discussion or encourage youngsters to add their own related artwork to it. When you are ready to remove or replace the mural, simply wash the paint off the window.

Kim Richman—Two- And Three-Year-Olds
The Learning Zone
Des Moines, IA

Inexpensive Party Supplies

Invite youngsters to help you prepare some of these easy, inexpensive decorations for classroom celebrations. To make a decorative tablecloth, cut a piece of butcher paper slightly larger than a tabletop. Have students sponge-paint designs related to the celebration theme on the paper. Invite children to decorate solid-colored cups and napkins with theme-related stickers. To create treat bags, have the children put stickers on plastic sandwich bags. With these ideas, celebration preparations will be just as much fun as the celebration!

Janine Nordland—Four- And Five-Year-Olds, Kids' Korner, Owatonna, MN

Name Cards

Make these multiple-use name cards to help your students recognize their own and their classmate's names. Print each child's name on a separate index card. To provide each child with numerous exposures to her name, use the name cards for activities such as lining up, grouping students for centers, and playing games that require taking turns. When the students are familiar with their first names in print, write each student's last name on the back of her name card.

Elaine Swindell—Preschool, Providence Preschool, Swan Quarter, NC

Easy Blender Applesauce

Invite youngsters to take advantage of a harvest-time favorite when they help make this applesauce recipe.

Applesauce

6 large apples
3/4 cup water
sugar to taste
cinnamon to taste

Peel, core, and cut the apples into chunks. Put the water and a few chunks of apple in a blender. Blend the mixture, adding the remaining apple chunks a few at a time until the mixture becomes soft. Add sugar and cinnamon to taste and mix well. Serve the applesauce to each student in a small paper cup. This recipe makes approximately three cups of applesauce.

Linda Lopienski
Asheboro, NC

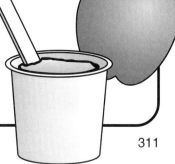

Name Match Game

Use these matching games to give students practice in sequencing the letters in their names. To make a game, write a child's name on a length of sentence strip. Write each letter in the child's name on a separate 2 1/2" length of sentence strip. Attach a piece of adhesive-backed magnetic tape to the back of each piece. To play, have a child place his name strip on a magnetic board. Encourage him to sequence the letter strips on the board to correctly spell his name, referring to the name strip as necessary. Store each child's name and letter strips in a resealable plastic storage bag.

Jane Hall—Four-Year-Olds
Trinity Church Day School
Long Green, MD

Yarn-Painted Border

Turn an age-appropriate art activity into a beautiful bulletin-board border. Provide youngsters with sheets of bulletin-board paper, shallow trays of tempera paint, and lengths of yarn. Invite each of your little ones to dip a length of yarn into the paint, then drag it across the paper to create a design. When the paint has dried, cut the paper into equal-width strips. Add an interesting scalloped or zigzag edge to each strip, if desired, before attaching the border to a bulletin board. Your preschool painters will be so proud!

Karen Bryant—Pre-K
Miller Elementary School, Warner Robins, GA

X Rays

During a unit on health or body awareness, take an imaginary X ray of each child's arm and hand. If possible, show the children a real X ray. Explain that when a real X ray is taken, the patient must wear an apron. Then ask each child, in turn, to don an apron for her imaginary X ray. Have the child press her hand and arm into a shallow tray of white tempera paint, then onto a sheet of black construction paper. Use a white crayon or colored pencil to label each child's X ray with her name and the date. Send each X ray home as a preschool memento.

Brenda vonSeldeneck and
    Donna Selling—Preschool
First Presbyterian Church
Waynesboro, VA

Nate Williams   October, 19

Mystery And Discover

Add a little excitement to your center time! Create two new centers for your youngsters to visit—Mystery and Discover. At a Mystery center, encourage youngsters to explore and create with a new, previously untried set of manipulatives. At a Discovery center, place any bright, attractive, unusual gadget you can find, along with magnifying glasses, a microscope, measuring tapes, pencils, and paper. Invite little ones to discover all they can about the object and record their findings.

Dawn Moore, Mt. View Elementary, Thorndike, ME

Halloween Costumes All Year Long

Dressing up is fun all year long—not just at Halloween! Take advantage of sales on Halloween costumes just before and just after the holiday to build a collection of costumes for your dramatic-play area. You might also send a note to each child's family prior to Halloween, requesting that used costumes be donated to the class after the holiday is over. If desired, specify the types of costumes you are interested in for the classroom.

Jill McClain—Preschool, Grand Rapids, MI

Glue Boo

There's not a ghost of a chance that your little ones will boo this Halloween handicraft! To make a ghost necklace, invite each youngster to squeeze the outline shape of a ghost onto a scrap piece of laminating film. Have her fill the outline completely with glue. Allow the glue to dry overnight; then peel it off the laminating film. Encourage each child to use a permanent marker to draw a face on her ghost. Punch a hole at the top and thread the pendant onto a length of orange or black yarn. Goodness gracious—what gorgeous ghosts!

Jeanne Puyau—Three-
    And Four-Year-Olds
Julius Rosenwald Elementary
New Orleans, LA

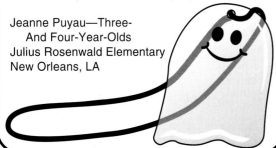

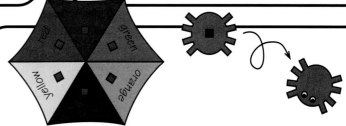

Creepy-Crawly Color Game

Use some paper spiders and their web to create a color-matching activity. First make a playing board by cutting a six-sided, spiderweb shape from white poster board. Draw lines to divide the web into six equal-sized, pie-shaped sections. Color each section a different color; then print the corresponding color word on the outer edge of each section. Cut six spiders from black construction paper; then hole-punch a pair of eyes for each spider that corresponds to a color on the playing board. Glue a pair of eyes to each spider. Finish assembling the game by affixing one piece of adhesive magnetic tape to each section of the playing board and one to the back of each spider. To play, a child matches each spider's eye color to the corresponding color on the web playing board.

Niki Huff—Pre-K, Stilwell United Methodist Preschool, Stilwell, KS

Magic Eyes Matrix

Little ones will be delighted to use their "magic eyes" to discover the hidden pictures on this matrix. To prepare the matrix, draw a three-column grid of equal-sized boxes on a sheet of poster board. Select a theme, such as a holiday, or a topic such as bears. Duplicate, color, and cut out six copies of as many different pictures as you have rows on your matrix. Across each row, glue one picture in the first box, two pictures in the second box, and three pictures in the third box as shown. Cut a piece of tagboard the size of one box on the matrix to use as a screen. Discuss the chart with the class, leading youngsters to understand the relationship between the columns and rows. Then cover a box with the screen. Ask youngsters to use their "magic eyes" to examine the matrix to "see" the hidden pictures.

Judy Aronson—Integrated Preschool
Salem Early Childhood Center, Bentley School
Salem, MA

Snowy Science

Let it snow and you'll have a super science lesson that only takes minutes to prepare. At the start of a snowy school day, fill a fishbowl with lightly packed snow. Set the bowl in your science center; then place a small toy sailboat atop the snow. Encourage youngsters to observe and comment on the changes that take place during the day as the snow melts and the boat begins to float.

Sharon Patterson—Four-Year-Olds, Littlestown Christian Academy
Littlestown, PA

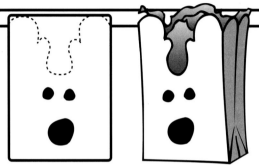

Rudolph Gift Bag

Rudolph with his nose so bright, makes a gift bag look just right! To make a reindeer gift bag, trace an antlers shape onto the top of a flattened brown paper lunch bag. Cut along the lines; then use markers to add eyes and a nose. Open the bag; then tuck a sheet of colorful tissue paper inside. Fill the bag with hot-chocolate packets, dry cookie ingredients, or a student-made gift.

Jean M. Long—Preschool, Heart Of The Lake Schools, Perham, MN

Inexpensive Holiday Puzzles

Keep an eye out for inexpensive cardboard decorations this season; then buy double! To make a magnetic puzzle set, laminate each pair of decorations. Cut one of the decorations into several pieces. Attach self-adhesive magnetic tape to the back of each piece and to the whole decoration. To use the puzzle set, a student places the whole decoration on a magnet board, then places the pieces on the board to create a matching picture. What an inexpensive way to add to your classroom puzzle collection!

Tonie Northcutt—Preschool, Mother's Morning Out, Ancient City Baptist Church
St. Augustine, FL

Write And Wipe

Give students plenty of practice writing their first and last names. For each child, program a sentence strip by writing his first name on one side and his last name on the opposite side. Laminate all of the strips. Place the strips in a writing center along with wipe-off markers and Handi Wipes. Once a student traces and writes his name, have him wipe his work away and practice again another day.

Rita Confer—Preschool
Gazebo School, Summerville, SC

Watch That Amaryllis Grow!

An amaryllis bloom is sure to brighten your winter classroom. And because the plant grows about an inch a day, it's the perfect math and science project for preschoolers! Purchase your bulb at a home-and-garden store; then follow the package directions as your little ones assist you in planting the bulb. When the bulb sprouts, measure and record its growth each day. Beautiful!

Pat Smith—Pre-K, Bells Elementary, Bells, TX

Framed!

Transform Styrofoam® meat trays into colorful frames using Elmer's® GluColors™. From the center of each tray, cut out the dimensions of a photo. Encourage each child to decorate a frame using the glue to create designs. When the glue is dry, attach a piece of magnetic tape to the back of each of the frames. Parents can tape a picture to the back of the frames, then attach them to refrigerators.

Amy Provencio—Four-Year-Olds
Merry Moppet Preschool, Belmont, CA

Four Little Doughnuts

Cut felt doughnut shapes to accompany this rhyme that teaches coin recognition. Give each of four children a different coin. Chant this rhyme as a class, including each child's name and the coin that she holds. Have her give you the coin as she removes a doughnut from the felt board.

[Four] little doughnuts in a bakery shop,
Round and fat with sugar on top.
Along came [child's name] with a [coin] one day.
[She] bought a doughnut and took it away.

Julie Sopczak—Preschool, Mystical Dreams Nursery School, Oakdale, CT

Healthy Teeth

Make these healthy teeth from linoleum floor samples and you'll be ready for Dental Health Month! Ask a local floor company for samples of white linoleum. Cut tooth shapes from the linoleum; then put them in your art center for use as templates. Or place them in an activity center along with toothbrushes. These teeth are sure to create lots of smiles!

Vicky Long—Three-Year-Olds
Del Norte Baptist Weekday School
Albuquerque, NM

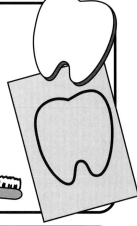

Ten-Cent Snack

This snack idea is right on the money! To prepare for this math and snack-making activity, pour several different types of snacks—such as raisins, chocolate chips, pretzels, miniature marshmallows, Chex® corn cereal, and banana chips—into separate bowls. Put a spoon in each bowl. Next give each child a personalized resealable plastic bag and ten pennies. Explain that each penny will buy one spoonful of the snack of his choice. (If desired, place limits on the number of scoops that can be "purchased" from items such as the chocolate chips.) If desired, plan this activity for the morning of a field trip and take the snacks along for the ride!

Sue Smout—Three- And Four-Year-Olds
Pearce Memorial Church Nursery School
North Chili, NY

Over Here, Sweetheart!

Cupid will know every child's mailing address when youngsters transform Huggies® Baby Wipes containers into valentine delivery boxes. Collect an empty box for each child; then personalize each box using glitter glue or paint pens. Encourage each child to embellish his box using precut Con-Tact® covering heart shapes, Con-Tact® covering scraps, and seasonal stickers.

Susan Cooperider—Four-Year-Olds
The Learning Nook
Springfield, IL

A Basket Of Hugs And Kisses

Here's a gift project that can be customized to almost any holiday or special occasion. To make a basket of hugs and kisses, tuck a four-inch square of fabric into a 2 1/2-inch chipwood basket (available from craft stores). Fill the basket with several Hershey's Kisses® and Hershey's® Hugs™. Tie two nine-inch lengths of ribbon into a bow; then hot-glue the bow to the front of the basket. To complete the gift basket, add a note that is appropriate to the special occasion.

Kathryn Logan—Preschool, Alaiedon Elementary School, Mason, MI

Flannelboard Relief

Are you frustrated with pieces constantly falling off your flannelboard? Save your sanity by converting to a magnetic board. Attach a piece of self-adhesive magnetic tape to the back of each of your flannelboard pieces. The magnetic pieces stay right where you put them—on the board, not the floor!

Susan Tenpas—Preschool, Wee Wisdom Childcare Center
Oshkosh, WI

Fresh Veggies

Invite children to harvest the garden with this interactive big book. From construction paper, cut five of each different type of vegetable you would like to include in your book. To prepare the cover and inside pages of your book, glue brown paper to the bottom half of as many large sheets of white construction paper as you have different types of vegetables, plus one more. Write the title "My Vegetable Garden" on a page; then glue on one of each different type of vegetable. On each subsequent page, glue three of only one type of vegetable. Program each page with the repetitive text "I went into my garden and picked a [vegetable name]." Laminate the pages and the remaining vegetable shapes. Use self-adhesive Velcro® to attach each remaining shape to its corresponding page; then bind the pages together. Read the book aloud during circle time. After you read the text on a page, invite a volunteer to pick the attached vegetable. Continue until the garden has been harvested; then "replant" the veggies for the next reading!

Dana Smith—Noncategorical Preschool
Donaldsonville Elementary
Donaldsonville, LA

Finger-Fitting Scissors

Keep little fingers from slipping and sliding in scissor handles with this helpful tip that's a cut above the rest. Simply pad the handle's holes with a reusable adhesive such as Sticky-Tac. This material is pliable and can be easily molded again and again to fit different sets of tiny fingers.

Pat Davidson—Pre-K And Gr. K, Special Education
Padonia International School, Kingsville, MD

An "As-sort-ment" Of Skills

Give little ones an opportunity to practice their sorting skills, color recognition, and social skills with this game idea. Tap nine nails into a 12-inch wooden square. Divide a supply of 1 1/2-inch circle tags (found at most office supply stores) into nine equal sets. Color each set of tags with a different color. Set up the game by placing one tag from each set on a different nail. Store the rest of the tags in a container. Have a pair of children take turns picking a tag, naming its color, and placing it on the correct nail.

As a variation, color one side of each tag and write the corresponding color word on the opposite side. Encourage students to select a tag, read the color word, and flip the tag over to check for correctness before placing the tag on the appropriate nail.

Nancy Pratt—Preschool
Nancy's Preschool
Scottsdale, AZ

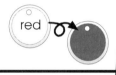

Make Note Of This

Youngsters will enjoy recording field-trip happenings on these handy clipboards. To make a clipboard for each child, simply cut off the front or back panel of a cereal box. Then staple several pieces of white paper to the top of the panel. Encourage students to record with pictures what they see during special trips.

Kimberly Rizzo—Pre-K
Together We Grow Childhood Center
Lake Havasu, AZ

A Closer Look

Give youngsters a closer look at seeds to improve their classifying and comparing abilities. Put a different type of seed into each section of an ice-cube tray. Cover the top of the tray with clear packaging tape. Label the seed names on the tape with a permanent marker. Turn the tray over so that the seeds in each section stick to the tape. Provide a magnifying glass for up close observations. Little ones will sprout with this new seed knowledge.

Susan Stevenson—Four-Year-Olds
East Woods School
Oyster Bay, NY

Index

318